THE SLAYING OF
JOSEPH BOWNE ELWELL

THE SLAYING OF JOSEPH BOWNE ELWELL

JONATHAN GOODMAN

St. Martin's Press
New York

For Richard and Molly —
a going-away present

Library of Congress Cataloging-in-Publication Data

Goodman, Jonathan.
    The slaying of Joseph Bowne Elwell / by Jonathan Goodman.
        p.   cm.
    ISBN 0-312-01513-5 : $15.95
    1. Murder—New York (N.Y.)—Case studies.   2. Elwell, J. B.
(Joseph Bowne), 1874–1920.   3. Victims of crimes—New York (N.Y.)-
-Biography.   I. Title.
HV6534.N5G66 1988
364.1'523'097471—dc19   87-27117
                                                          CIP

First published in Great Britain by HARRAP Ltd.

First U.S. Edition

10 9 8 7 6 5 4 3 2 1

CONTENTS

. . . suppose the poor murdered man to be out of his pain, and the rascal that did it off like a shot, nobody knows whither; suppose, lastly, that we have done our best, by putting out our legs, to trip up the fellow in his flight, but all to no purpose — 'abiit, evasit, excessit, erupit', etc. — why, then, I say, what's the use of any more virtue? Enough has been given to morality; now comes the turn of Taste and the Fine Arts. A sad thing it was, no doubt, very sad; but *we* can't mend it. Therefore, let us make the best of a bad matter; and, as it is impossible to hammer anything out of it for moral purposes, let us treat it aesthetically, and see if it will turn to account in that way.

Thomas De Quincey, 'On Murder
Considered as One of the Fine
Arts'; *Blackwood's Magazine*, 1827

No Gaboriau or Conan Doyle, or even an Edgar Allan Poe, could have concocted a murder mystery as clean-cut, from an artistic standpoint, as this one. None of the vulgar elements of such crimes either in reality or fiction is present. . . . The mystery is not a police puzzle, but a psychological puzzle. The ravelled ball must be unravelled by finding the thread's end in Elwell's own mysterious self.

Anon., 'The Man of Many Masks';
The New York *Times*, 1920.

THE WIZARD OF WHIST

The bald-headed man, who was wearing only a pair of red silk pajamas, nothing on his feet, was sitting in an upright armchair of the type that is sometimes provided for consorts of sovereigns of unimportant nations; the visible timber of the almost regal chair was daubed with gilt, and the swollen upholstery was of crimson plush, unevenly faded and flattened.

The man's eyes were shut, but the lids quivered, as if in response to a nightmare. He was noisily fighting for breath, his mouth gaping to reveal that he was left with just three teeth, none contiguous.

A cone-shaped hole, never less than the diameter of a .45 bullet, was burrowed through his head, starting, obscenely symmetrical, midway between the top of his eyebrows and the place where, in his younger days, there had been the apex of a widow's peak.

As a study of trial transcripts shows, the adding together and linking of facts does not invariably produce verity. But, generally speaking, that is the least inefficient way of seeking a truth.

No matter whether a man acquires celebrity or does not, the architecture of his life is limned by public facts; and by facts known only to a few people who have either pried into his unobtrusive deeds or been privy to his admissions; and by facts that he has tried to keep secret.

The inaugural public fact in the life of Joseph Bowne Elwell is that he was born before breakfast-time on Sunday, 23 February 1873. His birthplace was Cranford (a name derived from Crane's ford), which had been incorporated as a township in Union County, New Jersey, less than two years before. Remarked upon by outsiders for its pepperidge tree, round and rare, which had taken root during the Revolutionary War, and for its produce of fancy pincushions and 'Jersey lightning', a throat-searing kind of apple brandy, Cranford, which had a population of a couple of thousand, was situated 15 miles west of the island of Manhattan and rather more than twice that distance from Babylon.

In the 1860s, so many people had migrated to Cranford from Babylon and parts of Long Island to the west of that town, allured by estate agents' catchpenny phrases ('the Venice of America' and suchlike), that the long-time residents had needed to band together to stop the township's being called 'New Brooklyn'.

Joseph Sanford Elwell, who had been born in Brooklyn in April 1848, made his home in Cranford, renting a small timber-clad house on Union Avenue, not because an estate agent persuaded him to, but because Cranford wasn't far from Bergen, the home-town of Jane Annetta Ames, whom he married at the Cranford Methodist Chapel on Thursday, 3 November 1870, when he was twenty-two and Jane (or Jennie, as she preferred to be called) was three weeks away from her twenty-sixth birthday. As he was a travelling salesman, sometimes needing to be on the road for days at a time, it was reassuring to know that Jennie's kin were fairly close at hand should she be troubled.

As the unofficial motto of the new township was 'Worth Makes the Man and Not Blood', it seems likely that if Joseph Sanford Elwell frequented either the large beer saloon or the shack of the Sons of Temperance, he was reticent about his forebears and those of his wife. He must have been tempted to speak of them, though. Both he and Jennie had ancestors who had served on behalf of the Revolution — nine altogether, including Onesiphorus Fisher of North Yarmouth, Maine, and Isaac Belknap from Woburn, Massachusetts, the commander of a company of New York Rangers — and the two lineages could be traced back to the Mayflower.

According to one genealogical school of thought, the name Elwell is a corruption of 'vale of Elle' — 'Elle' being a version of 'Aella', the name of the Saxon king who, from AD 559 till 588, ruled what became, roughly speaking, the East Riding of Yorkshire, England. Well, perhaps. Certainly, an early form of 'Elwell' was documented by 1327. In that year, a man called Adam De Ellewalle, a resident of the parish of Sedgley, near Wolverhampton, was assessed for 20 pennies in the National Defence Subsidy. Half a century later, one of his descendants, Adam Ellewall, was listed as a juror of Sedgley.

By the time the Mayflower sailed, Sedgley was a centre of the nail-making industry, and all but four of the twenty-five adult male Elwalls living there of whom there is any record were either nailers or workers in kindred trades. One of those facts, or the two together, may explain why the family became known as the 'Iron Elwells'. The association with ironmongery continued in the eighteenth century — even, for a short time after his departure from Sedgley, in the case of Edward Elwall, whose eccentric theological obsessions, loquaciously expounded on street corners in Midland towns and published in tracts, led to his being prosecuted for blasphemy in 1726. (The case did not go to the jury at Stafford Assizes, probably because Elwall had not been served with a copy of the indictment — which he subsequently derided as being 'near as big as half a door'.) Some thirty years after Edward Elwall's death in 1744, Doctor Johnson recalled for Boswell's benefit that

> Mr Elwal [sic] was, I think, an ironmonger of Wolverhampton; and he had a mind to make himself famous, by being a founder of a new sect, which he wished much should be called 'Elwallians'. He held that everything in the Old Testament that was not typical was to be of perpetual observance, and so he wore a ribband in the plaits of his coat, and he also wore a beard. I remember I had the honour of dining in company with Mr Elwal and Mr Barter. To try to make himself distinguished he wrote a letter to King George the Second challenging him to dispute with him, in which he said 'George if you be afraid to come by yourself, to dispute with a poor old man, you may bring a thousand of your black guards with you; and if you should still be afraid, you may bring a thousand of your red guards'. . . . Mr Elwal failed in his scheme of making himself a man of great consequence.

Most often, male children of the English Elwells were christened John; the name Joseph was chosen only infrequently. And there doesn't seem to have been a single Joseph among the American Elwells till the baptism of Joseph Sanford Elwell. Perhaps it was the name of an unrelated godfather. There is as much uncertainty about the reason for the name Sanford, which does not appear in the prior genealogy of the family.

However, it is reasonable to assume that Joseph Sanford Elwell's son was given the middle name of Bowne to please one or more of the several Quakers among the child's aunts and uncles. In the seventeenth century, John Bowne, an immigrant from Matlock, in the Peak District of England, who farmed at Flushing, just north of Brooklyn, had been punished by Peter Stuyvesant, the Dutch governor, for advertising his Quaker beliefs; the Bowne House, which was still lived in by descendants of John Bowne, had become a landmark.

Soon after Joseph Bowne Elwell's sixth birthday, he was taken by his mother to see the Bowne House. It was a walkable jaunt from his home, for in 1879 the Elwells had moved from Cranford to the Bedford Stuyvesant part of Brooklyn, then a neighbourhood mostly populated by people who could just, only just, lay claim to membership of the middle class. Joseph Sanford Elwell had lost or given up his job as a travelling salesman in New Jersey, and was now a commission merchant for a firm of general dealers on Front Street, close to where the Brooklyn Bridge to Lower Manhattan was being constructed. Working from his new home at 422 Gates Avenue, he spent long hours pottering about in search of buyers; but it was a rare week in which his commissions amounted to much more than his domestic expenses, because by now he had four children: as well as Joseph Bowne, there was a son named Walter and two daughters, Louise and Grace.

The family seems to have lived precariously during the next few years — always knowing where the next meal was coming from but hardly ever being quite sure of the source of the cash to pay for it. By 1880, Elwell Senior, now preferring the job-title of broker to that of commission merchant, was working for a different firm on Front Street; the family had moved to another house, No. 370, on Gates Avenue. Between 1881 and the spring of 1886 — by which time the family address was 313 Madison Street, two blocks south of Gates Avenue — Elwell Senior was a freelance representative, usually seeking orders for a number of small firms rather than for a single large company. Then, tiring of itinerancy, he got a job as a clerk in a branch office of the Norwich Union insurance society. Round about that time, the family moved yet again, to 1085 Herkimer Street, just south of the main Fulton Street, which cut through the centre of Brooklyn, running east towards the cluster of cemeteries that made up the city's largest verdant area and west towards the Brooklyn Bridge, which was now open to toll-paying travellers (one cent per pedestrian) to or from Manhattan.

Elwell Senior's employment by the Norwich Union gave stability to the family income; but it can hardly have meant much of an overall increase — certainly not sufficient to finance private education for Joseph Bowne Elwell. Therefore, one may accept the belief of a friend of the family that a comparatively wealthy relation of the Elwells paid for the boy to complete his education at a private school. The fact that the three other children were educated entirely at public schools (a term that in America means the opposite of what it does in England) causes one to suspect that the boy's middle name made him seem most worthy of subsidy to Quaker kin.

He entered Phillips Academy at Andover,[1] 20 miles north of Boston, in September 1886, when he was thirteen. His passing of the entrance examination for the English Department (as opposed to the Latin Department) does not necessarily mean that he was bright: the examination was held on the first day of the Fall Term, the start of the school year, and it is unlikely that the questions were hard, resulting in more than a few baffled candidates having to trudge home with their baggage and then hurriedly scout round for a school that accepted pupils who were less

---

1. The school is generally known as 'Andover' differentiating it from Phillips Academy at *Exeter*, New Hampshire.

knowledgeable or more flustered by tests than the fledgling Andoverians. The emphasis at Andover was on the twin virtues of discipline and conscientiousness. The printed 'conditions of admission' began as strictly as they meant to go on, by noting that 'students who wish to enter the Academy are required to furnish testimonials that they sustain a good moral character'. After bending a little — 'No age is prescribed for admission' — the conditions became peremptory again:

> Boys must possess sufficient maturity for the responsibilities of school-life here. The school is not a good one for boys who are idle, wayward, or averse to study. . . . The students are required to attend church regularly on the Sabbath at the Chapel erected for the joint use of the Theological Seminary and the Academy, unless excused to attend elsewhere, and also a Biblical exercise on Monday morning in the class-rooms. . . . Reports of the standing and deportment of the students are sent to parents or guardians at the close of each term; and at other times when occasion requires.

Even if Joseph Sanford Elwell contributed nothing towards the fees for his son (the cost of tuition was $60 a year, and there were three term-bills amounting to $63[1]), one may surmise, without thinking him niggardly, that he was not unhappy to read the particular request that

> parents will not furnish their sons with money beyond what is necessary for their ordinary expenses. Those who are supplied with much spending money accomplish but little in their studies, and are liable to form habits which require their removal from the school.

The cost of young Joseph's board and lodging at Andover would have adversely affected the family exchequer only slightly more than if he had been at home. Since he was one of the 'less well-off students', he roomed in Commons.

> There are sixty-four rooms in Commons for pupils, and two for teachers. Each room is designed for two persons, and has two single bedrooms connected with it. The rooms are furnished only with tables, and bedsteads for single beds. Bedding is usually brought from home. Stoves and other articles necessary to furnish a room can be obtained here at reasonable prices. The accommodations provided in Commons are very plain, and intended expressly for those who wish to make their expenses small. Persons who use tobacco must not apply for rooms in Commons. Each student is charged $3.00 a term for the use of his room. Students who room in Commons are required to board in Commons. The price of table board is at present $3.00 a week.

---

1. The present-day purchasing power of the 1886 dollar is about fourteen and a half dollars. In 1886, there were 4.86 dollars to the British pound. The present-day purchasing power of the 1886 pound is about thirty pounds.

Though Joseph Bowne Elwell was in the English Department, he lived in the Latin Commons; probably the English Commons was full. For most residents, the spartan nature of the accommodation must have acted as an incentive to be away from it as much as possible; yet young Elwell used none of the approved excuses for absence. He was not a member of any athletic team; he did not join the Philomathean Society, which held weekly meetings for literary improvement, nor the Society of (religious) Inquiry; he joined none of the several clubs or musical groups.

Perhaps he was a swot. (Unfortunately, the scholastic records of that period have been destroyed.) Or perhaps he spent much of his leisure time with students who, like himself, enjoyed playing cards — a pastime that, if not frowned upon by the school authorities, received no encouragement from any of the Andover clubs. (If there *was* a card-playing coterie in Commons, it seems to have been kept secret, not only at the time but afterwards: years later, when all sorts of people were volunteering snippets of information about Elwell to newspaper reporters, alumni of Phillips Academy, Andover, were conspicuously silent.)

Apart from the few details already mentioned about Elwell's time at the school, all one can say certainly is that, after being a Junior (4th class) in his first year, he was a Junior Middler (3rd class) in 1887–8 and a Middler (2nd class) in 1888–9. He did not return to Andover at the start of the Fall Term of 1889, when he would have been a Senior.

Why was that? Some writers have said that he was expelled; but none has stated, or even suggested, a reason. If he was expelled, the headmaster would almost certainly have written a letter of explanation to his parents — but there is no copy of such a letter, nor any other relevant document, in the headmaster's correspondence, which is kept in the department of archives at the school. There, then, is a negative reason for questioning the expulsion story. A positive reason is that, in 1919, Elwell sent his own son to Andover — surely an odd thing to do if he had left the school under a cloud. He told his son that he had resigned 'because of the strong stress on religion'.

But it is hard to accept that explanation (perhaps he meant that he had objected to the stress laid on a *particular* religion), considering that for half a dozen years after leaving school he was an active member of the Tompkins Avenue Congregational Church, just round the corner from where the Elwells were then living.

Yes, the family had moved again: to 247 Halsey Street, a few blocks north of Fulton Street. And while Joseph Bowne Elwell was at Andover, his father had left the Norwich Union. Having reverted to selling on a commission basis, he was now specializing in fish — contentedly, it seems, for he was still in that line of business in 1897, when his son Walter joined him as an assistant fish-hawker.

Joseph Bowne Elwell, who was sixteen when he left Andover, got a job as a salesman in a Brooklyn hardware store. He stayed there for some months, perhaps as long as a year, and then, following in some of his father's many footsteps, went into insurance, first as a clerk for a firm of brokers, subsequently as an agent, offering posthumous riches door-to-door.

On Sundays, virtually without fail, he attended the morning and evening services at the Tompkins Avenue Congregational Church, and he usually attended the prayer meetings on Wednesday nights. Though he had been determinedly unclubable at Andover, he persuaded the Reverend George Meredith, the pastor of the church, that a young men's club might help to maintain, even increase, the size of the congregation, and it was he who took on the task of starting such a club, enlisting members and arranging activities.

The activities included whist-drives.

The setting-up of the club was a turning point in his life.

He may have enjoyed a game of cards in the past, perhaps while he was at Andover; but it was in an austere church hall at the corner of Tompkins Avenue and MacDonough Street, seated uncomfortably on a rickety chair at an oilcloth-covered table, that he discovered that he had a knack for whist that set him apart from other players of the game.

It might be possible, if considered worth while, to itemize the gifts that, added together and enhanced by synergy, create a good card-player; but no one not a fool would be foolish enough to attempt to evaluate the gifts, to rank them, seeking to explain the difference between a good player and a brilliant one. All one can say is that the various abilities, whatever they may be, are bestowed by nature; most are intuitive, but some can be refined by practice.

Young Elwell's prowess at cards made him, if not popular, sought after as a guest at the homes of other players: at first, probably, the invitations to make up a four came from other Congregational young men, dissatisfied with the mere one or two card-playing nights a week of the club; but before long he was asked to ecumenical sessions. His circle of card-playing acquaintances grew; someone referred to him — casually, without being aware of a coinage — as a 'wizard of whist', the alliterative term caught on, and eventually was preceded by the *the* to become an especial epithet. By then, much of his spare time was spent playing cards; and no doubt he was occasionally playing during working hours, mixing business with pleasure by talking insurance between hands. Cards lured him away from the church: having, early on, lapsed from attending prayer meetings and Sunday evening services, he lost interest in the young men's club, and then, perhaps because he felt the need to sleep late on Sundays, gave up churchgoing completely.

In 1894 or '95, when he was just into his twenties, he joined the Irving Republican Club, whose premises were about a mile and a half north-east of his home, close to the Brooklyn cemeteries. Though he *was* a Republican, he would probably have become a member of the Irving Club even if he had been a Left-wing Democrat. He joined the club, not for a political reason, but because there he could learn and play the new-fangled game of bridge-whist — a variation on plain whist, but as different from that game as chess is from checkers.

Bridge-whist had been played by the British in Cairo, and maybe in parts of India, for some years before 1894, when Lord Brougham introduced it at the Portland Club of London. Among its differences from whist, the dealer or his partner could name the trump suit or elect to play no-trumps, the dummy hand was exposed, bids could be doubled and re-doubled, and the four suits were valued — in ascending order, spades, clubs, diamonds, hearts — and no-trumps had the highest value of all. In formulating the rules of bridge-whist, the Portland Club stressed the need for decorum (for instance, the person playing the first card was expected to enquire, 'Partner, may I lead?', to which the partner, if he didn't intend to double the opponents' bid, had to respond, 'Pray do.') — but the etiquette seems to have been merely a smokescreen around the fact that the doubling feature introduced the element of gambling, perhaps for very high stakes, into the staid game of whist.

Elwell took to bridge-whist as a duck takes to water. It is not known whether he had made side-bets when playing whist, or whether he had indulged in games of chance such as faro, but as soon as he had mastered the pre-play intricacies of bridge-whist, he played the game for money — at first, and on and off for some years, at the Irving Republican Club, and later (though not much later, for the game became the vogue in an amazingly short time, a matter of months) at other clubs and in the homes of abecedarian but already obsessed players of the game. Whereas, in the days of whist, he had picked and chosen his opponents, turning down the 'rabbits', he now sought people who were well-heeled and whose enthusiasm for bridge-whist outweighed their playing ability. There was a casual callousness about his demonstrations that fools and their money were soon parted; more than a quarter of a century before W.C. Fields expressed the advice, Joseph Bowne Elwell was gaining affluence on the basis of 'never give a sucker an even break'.

There were two overlapping reasons why bridge-whist became the most popular card-game. People who liked a flutter took to bridge-whist because the outcome of playing a hand was only partly dependent on the cards that had been dealt: smart bidding on one's own hand and in response to the esoteric messages from one's partner, or, conversely, the doubling of an opponent's bid, gauged as being over-optimistic, could bring points from an ostensibly poor deal. And as bridge-whist was an 'intelligent game', a not too demanding exercise for the mind, it was considered not only appropriate to but a necessary component of polite social gatherings. More than that, it became symbolic of status. The confidence to accede to a request to make up a four was as essential a part of the equipment of aspirants to, and members of, what would soon be called the Smart Set as mastery of the latest dance-steps, garments that were not yet at the height of decreed fashion, knowledge of 'in' words and sayings — and care not to use any of last month's.

Whatever one's reason for wanting to play bridge-whist, the game had to be learnt. And so — particularly in the early days, before the torrent of text-books — instructors were much in demand. Elwell cashed in on that. His reputation as a player helped, of course, but he had another advantage – perhaps an unfair one. Many of those who wanted to play bridge-whist were women; so were most of the tutors. Engaging the services of one of the latter — more often than not, a genteel spinster compelled to make her own way in the world — was decidedly unexciting; even downright depressing. On the other hand, tête-à-tête tuition from Joseph Bowne Elwell — young and personable, his dark blond hair shining without the apparent use of brilliantine, his fine, even teeth glistening when he smiled — was something to look forward to, something to talk (or perhaps whisper) about afterwards: it was, to say the least, *chic*.

Elwell's character was strangely dichotomous. Though he was a gambler, and though he could have earned his living entirely from cards, he continued to tout insurance. Until the turn of the century, that is.

'I don't remember where I first met him, but it was at some party.'

From that remark, made a score of years after the encounter, one might gather that Helen Catharine Augusta Derby Hanford was not much impressed by Elwell on first acquaintance. Perhaps, having just divorced William H. Hanford, Junior, a Long Island lawyer, she considered that once bitten was cause for being twice shy, and so was turning an uninterested eye to bachelors of about her own age — which, at the end of 1899, the time of the party, was twenty-three. Or perhaps, when she was

Helen in her late teens

introduced to Elwell, she tended to disregard him as a prospective beau, having been told no more about him than that he was a mere insurance agent who just happened to be rather good at that card-game everyone (excluding herself — she had never played cards in her life) was so enchanted by.

After all, she had a right to be hoity-toity. Admittedly, the break-up of her marriage of less than two years' duration had left her in rather straitened circumstances, causing her to reside — just for the time being, she insisted — in an apartment at the home of her friends, Dr David Myerle and his wife Lena, at 155 South Third Street, leading towards Gowanus Bay, on the western hem of Brooklyn. Putting financial endowment aside, it could be said that her parents had been only slightly over-optimistic in naming her Helen: her looks would not have been a hazard to the topless towers of Ilium — a touch too plump of features and form — but still, she had a serene, uncomplicated beauty. As important — to her, at least — was the fact that she was a Derby: a member of a family that would have been of the aristocracy if America had had one. Her uncle, Dr Hasket Derby, was a renowned eye specialist and surgeon, co-originator and president of the American Ophthalmologicial Society. He owned a mansion, set in grounds landscaped by himself, in the Hudson River Valley, north of New York City; the house was not far from Hyde Park, the home of Franklin Delano Roosevelt, who was a contemporary of the doctor's three sons at Groton School.[1]

Helen Hanford's first encounter with Joseph Bowne Elwell seemed unpropitious; but they met on subsequent occasions, at first by chance, then by arrangement. Romance entered into their association, and, perhaps before Elwell realized it, the meetings became courtship. They decided to marry. Either because Helen felt that she was marrying beneath herself, or because Joseph's parents had expressed qualms about his relationship with a divorcee, the ceremony was a quiet affair, conducted by John D. Wells, described as 'Minister of Christ', at the house on South Third Street on Saturday, 26 May 1900, and witnessed only by Helen's friends, the Myerles. The bride-to-be gave her name as 'Helen A. Derby'. After a wedding breakfast at Gage & Tollner's seafood and steak house on Fulton Street, the couple took a cab to the small apartment that Elwell had rented in Brooklyn Heights, overlooking New York Bay and Lower Manhattan.

They did not go away during the honeymoon. At Helen's insistence, Joseph gave her a crash-course in card-playing; and, except when he had a date with a rigorously all-male school, she accompanied him to the haunts of bridge-whist devotees and sat demurely on the outskirts of the play, afterwards quizzing him about his tactics in particular rubbers. Joseph must have been both relieved that marriage was not inhibiting his bridge-whist activities and proud, in a slightly condescending way, of Helen's quickness in picking up the rudiments of cards, her understanding

---

1. In 1913, one of the sons, Dr Richard Derby, married President Theodore Roosevelt's daughter, Ethel.

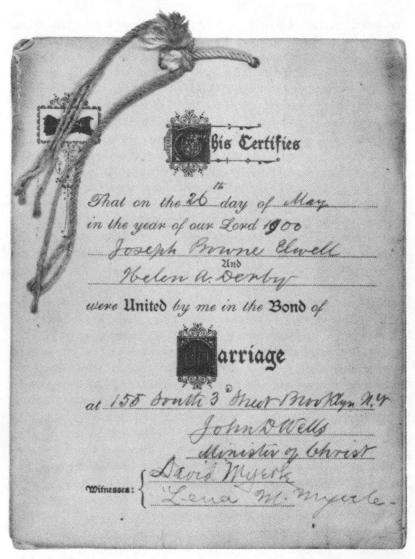

This Certifies

That on the 26ᵗʰ day of May in the year of our Lord 1900

Joseph Browne Elwell

And

Helen A. Derby

were United by me in the Bond of

Marriage

at 158 South 3ᵈ Street Brooklyn N.Y.

John D. Wells

Minister of Christ

Witnesses: { David Myerle
Lena M. Myerle

of the implications of his bids, doubles, and finesses. Far sooner than he had expected, he felt that the time was ripe to let her 'learn by doing', away from his overseeing and critical eye; all importantly, he had drummed into her the need to seek out and capitalize on the inherent weaknesses and the bad habits of others, partners as well as opponents.

It seems likely that, at the start of the marriage, Helen was less interested in the game of bridge-whist than in knowing how to play it. There is no doubt that she intended to push her husband towards _her_ objectives, so perhaps she decided that a knowledge of the game he played so well would come in useful.

She was careful to push without seeming to be pushy: to sow seeds in his mind, and then to express surprise, soon turning to enthusiasm, when they flowered. She wasted no time in putting this softlee-softlee approach into practice. One evening, while they were drinking coffee between games at a whist club, George Ehret, a wealthy Brooklyn brewer, came up to them and asked Elwell if he could spare the time to give his daughters lessons in bridge-whist. Elwell was about to say yes when Helen, the loving wife, chipped in, suggesting that his diary was already rather full. That caused Ehret to say that he was quite prepared to go above Elwell's usual tuition fee. As the Elwells walked home, Helen casually referred to Ehret, and just happened to mention that, at this time of the year, Newport, Rhode Island, was abundant with people far wealthier than the brewer . . . some of them, no doubt, keen to learn bridge-whist or to improve their play. Next morning, Joseph asked Helen if she would like to spend the summer in Newport. What a nice idea, she said, and without enquiring whether he needed to give his employer notice, went into the bedroom to continue packing.

They travelled by train to the fashionable watering-place on Narragansett Bay, a hundred miles north-east of Brooklyn, and booked into a decent hotel — rather than a rooming-house, which had been Joseph's idea until Helen, seeming to be thinking aloud, had wondered whether cheap digs would give the impression that he could be hired cheaply: Wasn't there a saying that one had to spend money in order to make money? She also suggested — only suggested, mind — that before he started looking for work, he should give her time to pay a few calls.

Using her maiden-name of Derby as an open-sesame, she gained access to the summer residences of rich families — a number of them from the Hudson River Valley, so she could also drop the name of Uncle Hasket — and, while sipping China tea, steered the conversation to the topic of bridge-whist: to the fact that her husband, the noted Joseph Bowne Elwell, might, just might, be persuaded to provide personal tuition. Oh, no, Joseph was not too proud to accept payment; as dear Uncle Hasket was fond of quoting from the Good Book, The labourer is worthy of his hire.

In the first week or so, the requests for tuition were few and far between; at this rate, the Elwells would not cover their hotel expenses. But, gradually, word spread through the Newport grapevine that Joseph Bowne Elwell, the wizard of whist, was in town; his first pupils chattered enthusiastically about him, remarking that he was not only the most brilliant card-player but also *sans pareil* as a teacher, lucid, patient, and confidence-boosting. A good type, too — related in some way to the Derbys, wasn't he. . .?

Each day, Joseph — or, more likely, Helen, acting as his social secretary — filled in blank spaces in his engagement book. If only as a means of increasing income, he would have liked to be *playing* bridge-whist, but Helen cautioned him that if he tried to join one of the several schools, he might be seen to be 'muscling in'. He had to bide his time, waiting to be invited — and when the invitation came, he must give the impression that he was thinking it over. Just as he was now being 'persuaded' to give tuition, he would be prevailed upon to play for money.

It was in the second or third week of the Elwells' stay in Newport that a note, with Helen's name on the cream-laid envelope, was delivered to their hotel by a grey-liveried chauffeur. The writer commented that the address printed on the notepaper — *Marble House, Newport* — was a temporary, summertime one, his family's main country residence during the rest of the year being just north of Hyde Park, in the Hudson River Valley, where he had occasionally met Dr Hasket Derby. He wondered whether Mrs Elwell's husband could be persuaded (that word again) to give tuition in bridge-whist to himself and his two sons. The signature on the note was that of William Kissam Vanderbilt.

The Vanderbilts, who owned, among other things, many large railroad companies, were the richest and most famous family in America.

One can guess that Helen and Joseph were euphoric; but perhaps their delight was edged with a fear that they were dreaming. Or that someone was playing a trick on them. Or, if they were not dreaming, not the victims of a practical joke, that Mr Vanderbilt might change his mind, be called away from Newport, be taken ill, be struck by lightning. For once, Helen did not even think of employing the softlee-softlee approach. While Joseph stared over her shoulder, she penned a reply; then she tipped a hotel messenger to deliver her note to the Vanderbilts' summer residence, high above the bay.

And then she and Joseph waited.

Not for long, though it must have seemed an eternity.

William Vanderbilt suggested a date, an hour, explaining that there were constraints on the availability of himself and his sons, for they spent much of their time on the family yacht. Helen confirmed the appointment, and Joseph, carrying two unused packs of playing-cards in the pockets of his best suit, presented himself at the house of all kinds and colours of marble exactly one minute before he was due.

When he returned to the hotel, Helen could see from his face that the session had been successful. He was excited as well as elated: excited because he was convinced that sixteen-year-old Harold, the younger of Mr Vanderbilt's sons, had the makings of a great card-player — excited because he and the boy (who was known, for some reason — versions of the derivation are at variance — as 'Mike') had sparked each other off by their communion of minds. That's good, Helen said — fine . . . but what about *Mr* Vanderbilt: how had *he* enjoyed the session? Oh, well enough, Joseph replied: both he and William Junior had gone along with Harold's desire to have further tuition — once a day if Joseph could spare the time.

A bandwagon started rolling. There was no need for Helen to put her shoulder to it. So many summertime residents of Newport wanted to keep up with the Vanderbilts that Helen was in danger of getting writer's cramp from entering appointments in the engagement book. And from filling in bank credit slips. The Vanderbilt connection gave *the* seal of approval to bridge-whist; to Joseph Bowne Elwell, too, of course.

All of a sudden, the young man from Brooklyn was a celebrity. To the *nouveaux riches*, keen to coax him into their drawing-rooms (their keenness undiminished, perhaps increased, by the higher fees Helen demanded of them for the pleasure of his company), Elwell's eminence as a card-player was a side-issue; the important thing was the vicarious association — almost superstitious, like touching a sailor's collar — with the local equivalent of the *ancienne noblesse*.

During the mornings and afternoons, Joseph taught. And so, eventually, did Helen, bowing to the pleas of people low on the social scale who, since Joseph was fully occupied, were willing to accept the second-best of being able to say that they were pupils of 'one of *the Elwells*'. She didn't let on that until her marriage, less than three months before, she might well have called a spade a club, never having played a game of cards in her life.

In the evenings, Joseph played. He chose the 'strong money' schools. He won consistently. But for his association with the Vanderbilts, and now with many of the lesser lights of Newport society, he might have been suspected of being a hustler; as it was, he was *expected* to win. On the comparatively few occasions when he lost, his opponents were almost disappointed, the spectators certainly so. To have played with Elwell was akin to having turned the pages for Rachmaninov: something to brag about in the manner that makes bragging most effective, which is casually.

A good many of the transient residents of Newport lived during the rest of the year in Manhattan; and in September, as the breezes from the Atlantic started to turn nippy, as the crescent of trees around the town became speckled with red and yellow, Helen, as usual thinking ahead, made sure that none of the Manhattan contingent of bridge-whist devotees departed before she had made a note of his or her address. In several instances, the address was volunteered. The day before the Vanderbilts left, Harold invited Joseph and Helen to spend the Thanksgiving holiday at the family mansion in the Hudson River Valley.

Before the Elwells themselves left, they had decided to return to the Brooklyn apartment only for as long as it took Helen to find and furnish a home — a base — in Manhattan, where the lucrative bridge-whist action was. If Joseph imagined that his wife would choose somewhere in a district in which property rentals were relatively low — Greenwich Village, for instance — he must have been surprised, even shocked, when she informed him that she had leased an apartment on the Central Park side of Park Avenue, at Sixty-Fourth Street, which was in a part of the town that, if not as fashionable as, say, Gramercy Park, to the south, certainly warranted being called 'swank'.

During the short period between the return from Newport and the move to Park Avenue, Joseph saw much of his family. His sister Louise had married and was living at Bayonne, New Jersey, but his parents, with his brother Walter and his younger sister Grace, were still living on Halsey Street. Since, without doubt, he dearly loved his parents, he must have been in something of a quandary, not knowing whether to speak excitedly or to be reticent about the sudden change in his fortune; he would have wanted his parents to be proud of him. but he would have feared implying a contrast between his own success and their signal lack of it.

Helen was proved right. Yes, again. Within days of the posting of the change-of-address cards, many of them to the Manhattan homes of Newport summer-residents, requests for tuition and invitations to play began to arrive. Usually, the suggested venue for a game was the inviter's home; but sometimes, if a male foursome was proposed, one of the several clubs in and around Fifth Avenue and Park Avenue was named — and more often than not in such instances, the place was the New York Whist Club, which was just off Fifth Avenue, at 13 West Thirty-Sixth Street. After being a guest at the club on a number of occasions, Elwell applied for membership and was at once accepted; he eventually became a director.

The club had strict rules on gambling, and members caught flouting them ran the risk of being expelled. Though the rules could be bent – for instance, by players agreeing among themselves, sotto voce, that the table-stakes should be considered mere tokens, to be multiplied afterwards, off the premises, in a settling-up between winners and losers — the deviousness, inconvenience and uncertainty of such ploys made them unappealing to certain wealthy members. Some time after Elwell joined the club, those men got together to discuss ways and means of assuaging their desire for virtually untrammelled gambling without hazarding their reputations.

The upshot was the formation of the Studio Club — a name chosen for no better reason than that it was unconnected with gambling. Meetings were held twice a week, usually on Wednesdays and Saturdays, in an old house, 384 Park Avenue, at Fifty-Third Street, that one of the members, a dealer in real estate, had acquired at a peppercorn rent. The membership was small, starting at a dozen and never rising above twenty or so. The members, with one exception, were tycoons or men of substantial private means.

The exception was Joseph Bowne Elwell, who was invited to join the club by Edric Bishop, the head of a Wall Street brokerage firm. Probably, Elwell did not accept the invitation without giving it some thought: on the one hand, he was confident of reaping impressive winnings from games in which skill played a part — on the other, he knew that he would have to stand his corner in games of sheer chance in which he, a David among financial Goliaths, would be perilously dependent on minimizing his losses when luck was running against him and, resisting an awful temptation, taking 'grab the money and run' decisions before winning streaks turned tail.

According to the journalist Frank M. O'Brien, Elwell's nerve was tested soon after he joined the club, on a night when baccarat was played. The amounts of money that could be at stake in this game were so enormous that even the high fliers of the Studio Club had agreed that no player could open the bank for more than $100. When it was Elwell's turn to be banker, he placed $50 on the table.

His bank stood up while each of the dozen players punted at it. It was one of those runs of winning cards more characteristic of baccarat or its foster-child, chemin de fer, than any other game. Finally Elwell's $50 had grown to $5,000. One of the players, the vice-president of a trunk-line railroad, offered to go banco. Elwell hesitated a second, and then drew the cards. The bank won. It now contained $10,000. The punter wanted to shoot for the $10,000, but Elwell took down half the bank and shot the remainder. He thus stood to win $4,950. The railroad man continued to punt $5,000 on each return until he owed the banker $60,000. On the next and last draw the railroad man won. Elwell passed his bank to the next player. During the rest of the evening he punted against the bank for small stakes, or as banker ventured $50 each time, but failed to get another run. At the close of the session, which was long after sun-up, he had won over $55,000.

Members might stagger from 384 Park Avenue with their billfolds empty, but at least their bellies were always replete. The club had a good cellar, and each night, marking an interim between the 'polite' play and the heavy gambling, waiters from Louis Sherry's restaurant on Fifth Avenue provided an elegant version of meals-on-wheels. Such arrangements were the responsibility of the club's factotum, an expatriate Englishman named William Barnes who either couldn't hold down a full-time job or, more likely, preferred the freedom of diversity. As well as being able to cope with most clerical tasks, including bookkeeping, he was a supreme 'contact man': if something was needed, he could be relied upon to think of an acquaintance who could provide it. A useful chap. A discreet one, too; or so he seemed. Fast-talking around an invariably jutting cheroot, Barnes was excessively spic and span: his dark hair, gleaming with macassar-oil, was brushed diagonally back from an impeccable centre parting; his spectacles were speckless; presumably ash fell from his cheroot, but never to mar his coloured waistcoat (which was what he insisted on calling what the natives called a vest).

Apart from the fact that when Elwell became treasurer of the Studio Club, Barnes had to account to him, the two men would have other, closer dealings.

Elwell's participation in games of chance for high stakes, first at the Studio Club and subsequently also at other places, was not entirely to Helen's liking. Admittedly, he won far more often than he lost, and the winnings were sometimes greatly in excess of what he picked up at bridge-whist, swelling their bank account and allowing her to indulge her collecting fancies — picking up Chinese porcelain figures and snuff boxes here, Sèvres ormolu vases and Limoges dishes there, until, as a visitor to their apartment afterwards remarked, 'the place looked like the French Embassy in Peking'.

Helen's concern was that her husband's image might be tarnished; hers, too. It was all very well for Joseph to play the *occasional* game of faro or baccarat (after all, the latter game had a royal cachet, as it were: the King of England continued to play baccarat despite having been pilloried by the press for his involvement, albeit innocent, in the Tranby Croft cheating scandal in 1891, when he was Prince of Wales). The important thing, Helen believed, was to ensure that Joseph's gambling for gambling's sake was kept very much in the background: remarked upon, if at all, as one of his pastimes, something that he did for pleasure rather than profit. Otherwise, there was the danger that he would be stigmatized as a professional gambler — or worse still, and perish the thought, as a hustler — and in no time at all, if either of those labels attached, the invitations to teach and play bridge-whist would diminish to an unlucrative trickle.

Helen had another of her good ideas. Thinking laterally, she reasoned that if the name of Joseph Bowne Elwell could be made almost synonymous with bridge-whist, then any talk about Joseph's other card-playing activities would be no more than an aside. And so she dropped a line to Charles Scribner's Sons, the long-established publishing firm on Fifth Avenue.

As soon as she heard from Scribners that they liked her idea, she broached it to Joseph. It needn't take up much of *your* time, she explained; I could do most of the writing if you could give me some notes — illustrative hands and that sort of thing — and once I had completed a draft manuscript, you could go through it, amending as you felt fit. Joseph's response was enthusiastic — especially so about the suggested title. It had a nice, authoritative ring to it: *Elwell on Bridge*.

He must have been pleased by the *look* of the little volume: measuring 6½ × 4½", 8 of its pages were preliminary to the 136 of the main text, which included 24 that set out the American Laws of Bridge ('Adopted November, 1902 . . . *Published by permission*'), a 3-page glossary, and a 4-page index; and so the book was a handy size, small enough to fit into gentlemen's pockets and ladies' purses, without bulging either. It was made outwardly pretty by its casing of dark green cloth, dimpled with gilt lettering and with a pictorial front: a white-framed panel the colour of card-table baize, on which was a dummy hand and a blank score-card, all picked out in white, black and orange. The innards were pretty, too: using off-white paper, all edges gilt, Scribners had gone to the expense of printing in two colours, orange in addition to black, the former discreetly embellishing the title- and section-introducing pages, and being used for sub-headings, as well as for heart and diamond symbols in illustrative hands (24 pages of them), examples of 'original makes' and opening leads, and tables showing the value of honours and tricks.

He (and the ghost-writing Helen, of course — to say nothing of Scribners) must have been even more pleased by the book's sales. Before its publication in April 1902 (thus pre-empting official adoption of the laws by half a year — but no one seems to have complained), the printer and binder were rushing through another impression, of a more optimistic number than the first. The optimism was soon shown to be pessimistic: further impressions were called for; then — till 1911 — new, slightly revised editions, and further impressions of *them*. By 1911, *auction* bridge (the third development of the game — whist: bridge-whist: auction bridge, which introduced 'competitive bidding', the aim being to keep the contract low since the declarer's side was credited with the number of tricks won rather than the number contracted for) was at least seven years old:

depending on which bridge-historian one believes, auction was first played in 1903 or 1904; certainly, in 1908 a code of laws was drawn up by a committee of members of London's Bath and Portland Clubs.

The immediate success of *Elwell on Bridge* caused Scribners to request sequels. And the New York *Evening Telegram*, all of a sudden keen to get in on the bridge act, to cash in on Elwell's fame, paid him well, having bartered with Helen, to explain do's and don'ts of the game, as exemplified by hands played at a major tournament in the city. With some slight tinkering, the newspaper articles became the second Elwell book, *Bridge Tournament Hands* (1904) — probably the one that Helen had least to do with, going by the comment of a modern expert on bridge that 'Elwell's annotations of the hands . . . show great skill at analysis'.[1]

In the same year, Scribners published *Advanced Bridge*, which seems to have been even more successful than *Elwell on Bridge*: there were seven editions in the six years till 1909. *Bridge Lessons* and *Practical Bridge* appeared in 1906, *Bridge Axioms and Laws* in 1907, and (rather slow off the mark, perhaps for a Helen-connected reason that will shortly be evident) *Elwell on Auction Bridge* in 1910; then there was a gap of a decade before publication of *Elwell's New Auction Bridge*.

As with so many — indeed, practically all — of the financial and numerical estimates conjured up by chroniclers of the rise and rise of Joseph Bowne Elwell, the guesses at what he made from the books are contradictory: the most diffident puts the annual income at $7,000, the most carefree seeks to amaze with the sum of $30,000. All one can say is that the books brought in a tidy sum.[2]

Soon after the publication of *Elwell on Bridge*,

Elwell was playing in *Mexico* when a spectator (they didn't say 'kibitzer' in those days) interjected a remark: 'Mr Elwell, you did something just then that's absolutely forbidden in your own book.'

'My book,' said Elwell, 'was written for beginners. I am an expert.'[3]

* * *

1. *The Official Encyclopaedia of Bridge*, edited by Frey et al, 3rd ed., London, 1977.

2. Scribners' correspondence with authors and their agents during the early part of this century is in the manuscript section of the library of Princeton University. A search carried out by the curator of manuscripts at the request of the Scribner's Son presently in charge of the firm revealed not a single note concerning the Elwell books: a lacuna that, according to a member of the firm, 'may be due to the fact that none of the top editors handled the bridge books. There would be little or nothing to write about, as is true today about books on crochet patterns and the like.'

3. *Odd Tricks* by Travis White, New York, 1934.

Mexico. That was just one of the faraway places where — invariably chaperoned by Helen in the early years of success — Joseph gave a few lessons at a high price and, for much more of the time, gambled for high stakes. The Elwells rarely ventured from Manhattan during autumns and winters; but at the start of nearly every spring they boarded a liner bound for Europe, and there flitted from one 'high-action' place to another — among those, London, Aix-les-Bains in France, Carlsbad in Czechoslovakia, Cologne in Germany. The transatlantic voyages — usually both ways on the *Mauretania* — were profitable parts of the trips, for, as Alexander Woollcott would comment, 'a lot of bridge flowed over the water'. Back in America by the middle of May, the Elwells stayed in Manhattan for only a short while (during which Joseph visited his parents, bearing gifts, discussed business matters with William Barnes at the Studio Club, and played some hands there, and Helen dealt with correspondence, paid bills, and bought summer clothes for them both) before travelling north, into New England — sometimes to spend a few weeks at Bar Harbor, the not merely self-styled 'playground of the rich' on Mount Desert Island, Maine, and always to enrich themselves at Newport, where, now ignoring the town's hotels as places of residence, they resided in a rented house overlooking the first-named of the three private beaches, Bailey's, Gooseberry, and Hazard's. In Newport, Elwell spent most evenings playing bridge at the Marble House – increasingly as the partner of young Harold Vanderbilt, with whom he was now far more than fine-weather friendly, for they played together frequently during the drab months, usually at the Vanderbilts' Manhattan mansion at 640 Fifth Avenue.

On Tuesday, 23 August 1904, in the house at Bailey's Beach, Helen gave birth to a son. It seems that Joseph was allowed no say in the naming of the boy, who, as the name Richard was favoured among the Derbys, was christened Richard Derby Elwell. Perhaps Joseph was more than usually complaisant in regard to this one of Helen's determinations, sheepishly keen to smooth away her scowl at a matter that had come, via gossip, to her notice. Shortly before the end of her confinement, he had left her (admittedly, cosseted by shifts of nurses) to spend a short while in Louisville, Kentucky — a while that may have been curtailed by the fact that as he was entering a cab outside the Galt House, Louisville's most fashionable hotel, a young woman had appeared at the doorway of the hotel, rummaged a revolver from her reticule, fired it at him, though not accurately enough to wound, and then disappeared from the scene of her disturbance, he having raised no alarm on behalf of apprehending her; immediately afterwards, at the hub of a crowd of onlookers and policemen, he had expressed perplexity at the woman's action and said that he was unable to give the least description of her.

The most obvious possible reason, though not necessarily the most likely one, for his trip to Louisville, in which and around which were an abundance of horse-racing courses and training stables, is that the seed had already been sown for his subsequent extreme enthusiasm for the Sport of Kings. To say that that *was* the reason would be as silly as to ascribe an Englishman's visit to Ascot to a desire for on-course betting, ignoring that place's unequestrian attractions to some: for instance, the fact that it is a notch in what parvenu locals speak of as the 'stockbroker belt'. Louisville, too, was a seat of brokers — saliently of tobacco and whiskey — and it may be that Elwell went there to dabble in commodity markets. He had for some time (since 1902 seems to be the best guess) been playing the markets, and not just the stock ones: playing them as astutely as he played cards — reckoning the odds, never wagering more than he could afford to lose, getting out while he was winning — and having the sense to know that the total of his gambling skills was but a slight addendum to the great advantage he enjoyed of being in eavesdropping earshot of the shop-talk of brokers and magnates who gambled for relaxation as well as at work.

The clearest difference between Joseph's and Helen's response to parenthood was that whereas he loved his son, she doted on the boy — doted in an exhibitive way, as if she feared that if she did not display the trappings of maternity, *people might talk*: might conclude that Richard Derby, begot unwittingly, was, to her, an irritating interference with her glamorous and exciting role as the wife of the famous Joseph Bowne Elwell. Looking ahead to the arrival of the child, she had told Joseph that they would need a larger apartment in Manhattan; and while they were at Newport in the summer of 1904, decorators worked in that larger apartment — at 746 Park Avenue, between Seventy-First and Seventy-Second Streets — and their belongings were moved to it, under the supervision of Joseph's mother, pleased to have a reason for outings from Brooklyn. Jennie Elwell was also given the task of choosing between servant-applicants paraded before her in an anteroom of the city's most reliable agency for domestics. She picked out a cook and a pair of maids — all to live in — and a char. A nanny, too? she had asked Helen. And had been told: Certainly not — there was to be no surrogation of responsibility for Richard Derby's upbringing; none at all. Joseph made no suggestions regarding the domestic arrangements; did not query any of the decisions. He simply ensured that there was a sufficient balance in the joint bank-account.

Helen's overt attitude towards all but one of the springs of their affluence — the exception was the royalties from Scribners — altered in an ashamed sort of way. It was a pity, she implied, that the revenues did not accrue from a *sound* occupation. Once Richard Derby was reacting to her baby-talk as if he understood, she informed him, and kept on informing him — irrespective of whether Joseph was present — that he, unlike his father, would follow a stable career: would be looked up to, not merely admired for a knack, by those from whom respect was a prize.

No longer was it unusual for the Elwells not to be seen together. For a few more years, she, with an at-first-bassineted Richard Derby, was proximate to Joseph during the Newport months; but he usually travelled alone on the springtime excursions to Europe; and it was a rarity — almost always something to do with the Vanderbilts — for her to leave her son baby-sat in the Park Avenue apartment in aid of a social cause. Joseph, feeling that he was simply the provider, not specially enjoyed by those he provided for, took to spending more and more time away from home. And found that the freedom pleased him.

I shall warn readers now, and not again, that Helen's reminiscences of Life With (and latterly Without) Joseph, post-1904, should be taken with a grain of salt; by the time she reminisced, she had a number of reasons for embroidering the truth. Speaking fairly generally, and of a period of about a dozen years, she said:

> It was a common thing for him to come home at six or seven o'clock in the morning, or even to stay out for a few nights without informing me previously. That he went out with other women, I am quite sure, but I never heard the names of any of my husband's women acquaintances. [From 1910] we lived in separate rooms. I saw him only occasionally, for we took very few meals together. His breakfast was sent to his room on a tray, and if he felt like coming home for dinner he would telephone and the cook would prepare it for him. He would come in at seven o'clock in the morning, or he would arrive at two: neither made any difference to him.

There was one *en famille* transatlantic trip. That was in 1909. An invitation that was of the nature of a Royal Command persuaded Helen that she and Richard Derby, who was close to his fifth birthday, should accompany Joseph to England, voyaging on the *Mauretania*. Arrived in London, the family put up at the then-exclusive Brown's Hotel, in Mayfair — the choice, probably, of Helen, who would have made it her business to know that Theodore Roosevelt, till recently President of the United States, had been married from Brown's in 1886, and that, only four years ago, Franklin Delano Roosevelt, a friend of her Derby cousins, had stayed there during his honeymoon with Anna Eleanor Roosevelt (her surname unchanged by marriage). In the first afternoon of the Elwells' stay in London, and in five or six following ones, Joseph took a hansom through

St James's Park and along the Mall to Buckingham Palace — there to give tutorage in bridge to King Edward VII, his friend Mrs George Keppel, and someone other than Queen Alexandra (who was not fond of games). There is no record of how the sessions went, nor of whether or not Joseph received a fee from the privy-purse: the enterprise was treated most discreetly — not, one surmises, because the King or Mrs Keppel or even the third player requested that it should be, but because Helen and Joseph feared that boasting of it might constitute a minor offence of *lèse-majesté*, deterring other kings or queens from following Edward's lead. The fact that Joseph Bowne Elwell had become Bridge-Tutor by Royal Appointment was not permitted noticeably to profit him.

Every so often, small scandals rippled the generally placid waters of the world of bridge. Top players were suspected of — sometimes even formally accused of — using underhand or under-table methods of transmitting messages to their partners. Such chicanery wasn't difficult; a vocabulary of sly signals was simple to coin, easy to use after slight private rehearsal. The way a hand was held; which fleshed hand it was held in; the subtle peeking of one card above the other dozen (so that the partner could count from left or right and know of, say, an ace of spades or the number of cards held in the suit the signaller had bid); even a blinking of the eyes; even — most audacious, this, and possible only if the opposing pair had diminutive and therefore dangling legs — a meeting of feet beneath the table, a tiptoeing intercourse between them: all of these stratagems, and many others, were employed — and watched out for by opponents, some of whom were made paranoid by concentration on trying to detect, to decode, esoteric quirks. Certain regular partners were so suspicious of other regular ones, and vice versa, that it was a condition of their playing together that all four persons had to sit bolt-upright, feet firmly on the floor beneath their respective chairs, mute but for bids (which had to conform to a formula), hands held tidy as fans, and needing to restrain from sniffing, belching, scratching, blinking, frowning, or smiling till the dummy hand was faced up on the table.

It appears to be a tribute either to Joseph Bowne Elwell's honesty or to his craft of artifice that he was never in danger of being drummed out of a bridge school or club. Of course, his connection with the Vanderbilts — in particular, with Harold, who from 1910, following his graduation from the Harvard University Law School, was Elwell's most frequent partner — may have implied innocence by association or stifled comment that, as well as being adverse to him, could have been misheard or misquoted so as to suggest accessoriality on the part of one or more of the Vanderbilts, a family that no one could afford to offend.

By no means all under-table leg-stretchings were to do with sleight-of-foot. Sometimes the motive for such motions was romantic — and, in that event, as likely to be directed towards an opponent of the other sex as to a partner of the opposite gender. The pursuit that has come to be called footsy only really got off the ground when variations on whist became the vogue. There is ño way of knowing the extent of bridge's responsibility as a shield for foot-fumbling overtures to courtship, but one is safe in saying that bridge, more than any other indoor game, has been a boon to manufacturers of, *inter alia*, bridal gowns and contraceptives.

Over the years, Elwell's ankles must have been bruised, his footwear scuffed, on countless occasions. Far less often, Helen's; but still not negligibly. Though she had become a home-body on account of mother-hood, that fact must not be taken to mean that she was often solitary, having settled Richard Derby down for the night. Ever-altering trios — some of bridge-pupils, some of people to ĥer standard at the game — kept her company in the Park Avenue apartment. During 1911, and perhaps previously, she was commonly partnered there by a man of her own age, called Charles Whaley. Near the end of that year, Whaley received a telephone call from Elwell — who, so Whaley long afterwards alleged, used 'such language' that he, Whaley, felt obliged to hang up the receiver. A week or so later, Whaley received a letter — 'ugly', he termed it — written by Elwell on Christmas Day. Straightway after tearing it up, he replied as follows:

J.B. Elwell, Esq.,
784 Park Avenue,
New York City.

Dear Sir:
I beg to acknowledge receipt of your letter of December 25, 1911. Your letter requires no answer, other than to say that it is both untruthful and impertinent.
Your suggestion as to where you can be found, namely at McCormick Bros.,[1] appears to me to be simply an expression of your desire not to meet me, as you are well aware that it is a suggestion that I meet you where you could hide behind the backs of friends.

---

1. A firm of stockbrokers whose Midtown-Manhattan office was in the Waldorf-Astoria Hotel on Fifth Avenue, between Thirty-Third and Thirty-Fourth Streets. (The hotel was demolished in 1929 so as to make space for the Empire State Building, which was completed two years later.)

I will be pleased to meet you at any time, at any neutral place, and if you will notify me when and where, I will meet you then and there. Any communication from you in the future must come through a third party or by letter. I will not discuss any matter over the phone with you. Vituperation or abuse over the phone is simply the act of a coward.

Yours, etc.,

CHARLES C. WHALEY

One gathers from that response that there were pistols-at-dawn implications from what Elwell had shouted over the telephone and scribbled on his ivory-hued, headed notepaper. Over-reactive, surely, considering that he and Helen had been sleeping apart for over a year: considering, too, that, without doubt though without conclusive proof of it, on some of the nights when he did not sleep in his own room, he was in bed, paired, in someone else's. The most likely explanation is that postulated long afterwards by Charles Whaley:

At that time, and later, Elwell was, or pretended to be, jealous of nearly every man who was on friendly terms with Mrs Elwell, and her card-table friends numbered scores. She and I had learned of Elwell's efforts to get evidence for a divorce, [which] failed completely because none could be discovered or successfully invented.

Shakespeare's John of Gaunt remarks of his sovereign: 'His rash fierce blaze of riot cannot last;/For violent fires soon burn out themselves;/Small showers last long, but sudden storms are short.' That, it appears, was true of Elwell so far as his long-range vituperation at Charles Whaley was concerned. Though the latter continued to play with Helen till – in 1913, it seems — he moved from New York to Knoxville, Tennessee, for what can only have been a business reason, since Knoxville was then the sort of industrial town that visitors spent weeks in on Sundays, Elwell made no more threats. Contrary to Whaley's comment that he was one of a number of prospective co-respondents in Elwell's temporarily-green eyes, not only at the time of the threats against him *but also later*, what little evidence there is indicates that Elwell's desire for divorce was a passing fancy, not to be rekindled till the late spring of 1920. According to Helen, when she and Joseph discussed the breakdown of their marriage,

I asked him if he didn't think it best we get a divorce decree immediately. After only a second's hesitation, he replied that he thought that would be an unwise step, because, he said, I was a great help to him. I realized very well what he meant. If I were divorced from him, he could perhaps have got into trouble with his women-friends and could have been sued for breach of promise. Although I do not know what the chances were, it could not happen while I was still his wife, and he knew it.

A recent photograph of 28 Liberty Street, Ridgewood

But in 1914, surreptitiously, Joseph began making plans for legal separation from Helen. He visited Europe in the spring of that year: his last visit there, as it turned out — in the following August the Great War began, to the great profit of America till, in 1917, that nation was forced to take a fighting part in the hostilities. Late in 1914, Joseph gave his parents the splendid present of a three-storey, timber-clad house, 28 Liberty Street, near the centre of the New Jersey town of Ridgewood (which, as the southerly Cranford had been, was being advertised to people of Brooklyn as A Healthy Place to Live), and, as well as arranging, with his brother Walter, for them to move there, transferred a large sum of money to their bank account. And in January 1915 he signed a will drawn up by his lawyer Frederick Ingraham, doing that in the presence of Milton Rosenberg, a friend since their childhoods in Brooklyn, and Hala Lack, a wealthy, bridge-obsessed widow who lived on East Eighty-First Street, close to the Metropolitan Museum of Art. The document read as follows:

> 1. I give, devise and bequeath all of my real and personal property, of whatsoever nature the same may be and wheresoever situate, unto my parents, Joseph S. Elwell and Jennie A. Elwell, equally, share and share alike, or to the survivors of them absolutely in case either of them shall predecease me.
> 2. I hereby nominate, constitute and appoint my father, Joseph S. Elwell, and my friend, Alfred H. Caspary [a banker with legal training who belonged to the Studio Club], executors under this my last will and testament, and I hereby request that they may qualify without giving bonds for the faithful performance of their duties.

3. I hereby revoke and cancel any and all former or other wills by me at any time made.

In testimony whereof, I, Joseph B. Elwell, have hereunto to this, my last will and testament, subscribed my hand and affirmed my seal this 11th day of January in the year of one thousand nine hundred and fifteen.

Some time before Sunday, 20 January 1916, he left the family home, moving to a larger apartment — a 'duplex', meaning that it was on two floors — not far south on Park Avenue, and taking with him all furnishings and fittings that were, as the forsaken Helen put it, 'in any way artistic and valuable'. Also before that date, which was when their separation became official, their respective lawyers (Helen's was a cousin of Charles Whaley) haggled over alimony. In her statement of claim, Helen reckoned the value of her husband's assets at the nice round sum of $600,000, and sought to bolster the guess by saying that he often made from $1,000 to $10,000 a night at bridge, adding that on one occasion his winnings amounted to $30,000, that he earned $18,000 a year in tuition fees, and that his royalties from Scribners averaged $7,000 per annum; she contended that, going by her sums, her demand for an annual allowance of $5,000 was eminently reasonable. Either her lawyer was less smart than Charles Whaley had made him out to be or — and this seems more likely — her estimates both of Joseph's earnings and of his *ostensible* capital were wide of the mark. (The word 'ostensible' is stressed because it may be that his gifts to his parents in 1914 were to some extent preparative practicalities rather than unblemished symbols of filial affection.) In the course of the lawyers' bartering, the $5,000 p.a. that Helen had hoped for was whittled down, down, down — till at last, fearing further whittles, she succumbed to $2,400 (a sum that, afterwards speaking of it, she usually prefixed with 'a mere'; its present-day value would be slightly less than $12,000), that to be paid to her in monthly instalments of $200, not by Joseph but by his father, who was instructed that no instalment following the first was to be posted to her till she had acknowledged receipt of the previous one. Joseph further agreed that each year he would provide $600 for Richard Derby's education (presently at the Buckley School on East Seventy-Third Street, Manhattan) and $200 so that the boy could attend a summer camp. According to Helen, speaking nearly five years later, when there was little chance of anyone questioning her recollection, Joseph agreed to the stipends on behalf of Richard Derby only on condition that she 'signed away' any rights she might have when he wished to buy or sell realty: 'I have heard that through this privilege that I, as his wife, granted him, he cleaned up a fortune.'

* * *

THE N.Y. CONSOLIDATED CARD CO.
M'F'RS OF PLAYING CARDS
AND PLAYING CARD ACCESSORIES - 222-228 W.14ᵗᵈ ST. N.Y. U.S.A.

BRIDGE

	♠	♣	♦	♥	NO TRUMP
One Trick	2	4	6	8	12
3 Honors	4	8	12	16	30
4 Honors	8	16	24	32	40
5 Honors	10	20	30	40	
4 Honors in one hand	16	32	48	64	100
4 Honors in one hand and 5th Honor in partner's hand	18	36	54	72	
5 Honors in one hand	20	40	60	80	
Small Slam adds	20	20	20	20	20
Large Slam adds	40	40	40	40	40
No trumps in one hand reduces Honors of adversary's	4	8	12	16	
No trumps in one hand increases Honors of partner's	4	8	12	16	

WE		THEY	
POINTS	HONORS	POINTS	HONORS
Elwell	30,000		
Hudson	20,600		
Smith	900		
C Potter	310		
Drake	21,190		
Bear		30,000	
White		28,000	
Kerr		25,000	
	51,810	83,000	
	21,190		
	83,000		

A score-card showing that Elwell won $30,000 at a bridge-playing session on 30 October 1911. The notes, in Elwell's hand, at the right of the card are of instalment-payments subsequently made to him.

Certainly, within a very short time — a matter of weeks, even before
Helen had moved from the apartment at 746 Park Avenue to a smaller
one, only six rooms, at 1187 Lexington Avenue, just a block east from Park
but leagues away in terms of fashionableness (she eked out her separation-
allowance by taking on more bridge-pupils, levying contributions towards
bed-and-board from certain guests from out of town, and making do
without servants other than a part-time char) — Joseph began wheeler-
dealing in the property market, restricting himself, or allowing himself to
be restricted, to realty in or convenient to the Floridian town of Palm
Beach, fifty miles north of Fort Lauderdale, and still farther north from
Miami. He had, over the years, during bridge-playing tours, paid many
visits to Palm Beach, and had found it likeable. But his liking of it was not
the main reason why he decided to speculate in property there: that was to
do with his friendship with Laurence Green, a member of the Studio Club
who, operating from a suite in the Waldorf-Astoria Hotel, had become a
millionaire from usury and from brokerage of real estate in New York City
— and, a thousand miles south-west as the crow flew, Palm Beach.
    Speaking in the summer of 1920, Green said:

> Four years ago, Elwell got the real-estate fever which was then sweeping the
> Palm Beach hotel colony. He built a very wonderful house on the Palm Beach
> lake-front, which would now be worth about $150,000. The house was small,
> but he furnished it exquisitely. He was very artistic. An offer came up for him
> to double his money on the house, and he accepted. He bought another piece
> of property, and six months later sold that, having about doubled his
> investment again.
>   Then I called him at my office one day and told him I had just the place I
> thought he wanted. Russell Hopkins had bought half of Hypoluxo Island, and I
> acquired the other half. The island is a wonderful dwelling-place, and since
> Elwell had a yacht, in which he could reach Hypoluxo in an hour from Palm
> Beach, and a fast car in which he could travel over the road in twenty minutes
> from social activity, I thought this place would suit him. He bought the half of
> the island 'sight-unseen'. I took a mortgage, at my suggestion.

Green went on, contrary to Helen's recollection of what she had 'signed
away':

> Elwell never took property in his own name. His deals were always made in
> the name of the Beach-Long Realty Company. He explained this to me once by
> saying that, under the laws of New York, his wife would have been a party to
> his deals, and he did not wish this. Since he could not do business without his
> wife's signature, he incorporated, his father taking one share and his chauffeur,
> Edwin Rhodes, another.

Vicariously piqued by what a rival real-estate broker had said of Elwell's
dalliances (to the effect that, during a period when he was staying, not at

Elwell at Palm Beach

one of his own Palm Beach properties, but at the Everglades Club, he had had concurrent affairs with a wealthy, widowed owner of a cottage on Sunset Avenue and with a leader of a local troop of Girl Scouts), Green snapped:

> There was never the breath of scandal in connection with his residence at Palm Beach.
> There's no doubt, however, that he was 'a ladies' man' in every sense of that expression. Elwell was not a man who seemed to select any special girl. He was

a man who exercised a remarkable influence over women. He was cold-blooded to an extreme, which, instead of repelling his friends of the opposite sex, seemed to attract them the more.

In a way, he was a poseur. He was not a gambler, but rather a good sport. He would bet on anything. His every obligation was met scrupulously on the day the money was due. There was no cheap intrigue about him.

Once he came to me and said: 'Green, I'm a plunger. I've lost $125,000 in the last two weeks, playing the market.' I told him to be careful and asked him whether he had provided against financial disaster. Then he told me that he had set up a trust-fund which assured him an income of $10,000 a year for life.

One wonders whether that conversation took place during the last months of 1917. If it did, Elwell's reference to a large loss may be some confirmation of the rumour, perhaps less strong than the recurrence of its being whispered suggested, that he had lost heavily as a consequence of the revolution in Russia, since a large holding of bonds from that country that he had acquired only the year before, then at what had seemed a bargain-price, were now, sans-Tsar, hardly worth the vellum they were printed on. And if that rumour was true, his in-that-case-understandable paranoia regarding the Russians, soon sparking a belief that they had reneged from the war against Germany, may have grown into distrust of almost all persons he encountered whose English was broken — and may explain why, by the end of 1917, he had joined the American Protective League, a sort of undercover vigilante organization whose members, most of whom were young businessmen, co-operated with agents of the Department of Justice (not, it seems, with the Department itself) in trying to unmask spies.[1]

Joseph's diverse busyness following his separation from Helen was, to lapse into new-fangled jargon, such as to give any workaholic a guilt-complex in regard to his own energy-deficiency. Tutor of bridge, player of that game and of others that required less skill, helper (in 1919) of the anonymous author of *Elwell's New Auction Bridge*, property developer and speculator, investor in stocks and shares, spy-catcher under the auspices of the American Protective League, honorary treasurer of the Studio Club, man-about-town (that, for some, a near-full-time avocation). The list is incomplete, and remains so even with the addition of *race-horse owner*.

It will seem odd to readers unenchanted by horse-racing, and perhaps to some who are, that Joseph — who, as a young man, 'enjoyed a flutter';

1. Brooklyn *Daily Eagle*, 17 June 1920: 'Three who were officers [of the American Protective League] said today that all records had been turned over to the Department of Justice and they could not recall whether or not Elwell had been responsible for the internment of spy persons as spies.'

who, when rich, wagered heavily; who eventually owned a stable of thoroughbreds — was not an avid racegoer. For him, horse-racing was an indoor sport: the horses and the men astride them were interesting only for their pasts — for the statistics they had gathered and, speaking of the horses alone, for their lineages. He knew perfectly well that those details, and others, generalized as 'form', were only slightly more reliable as guides for the picking of winners than a pin; that if form more often than not foretold, there would be no bookmakers. But still, and despite the fine-tuning of his gambling intuition, which should have set him far apart from the mass of punters, he was no different from them in that he pored over the small print in lists of runners, noting handicaps here, horses-for-courses there, before placing bets. That remained a morning routine, indicating a mixture of superstition and suspicion in him, when, favoured by owners and trainers, he was the recipient of horse's-mouth tips that certain runners in certain races were 'sure things' or destined to be also-rans. Gambling on cards was different: he could assess the strength of the cards he had been dealt in comparison with the strength of those dealt to a partner or to opponents, could decode the bids of others so that the cards faced away from him became almost as legible as those he was permitted to see: a hand of cards — *his* hand of cards — could be assessed meticulously, weighed with his partner's, and then, the two hands still physically separated but conjoined in his mind, weighed against the opponents', thus establishing with near-certitude the tactics, defensive or attacking, that would minimize a loss or enhance a win. Perhaps it was a wish to make betting on horses more akin to his almost exact science of gambling on cards — to have his own hand of horses, so to speak — that caused him in 1917 to join with a well-known 'turfman', William Pendleton, in setting up, on a fifty-fifty basis, the Beach Racing Stables near the Latonia track, which was then at Covington, in northern Kentucky, across the Ohio River from Cincinnati.[1]

William Pendleton, who may not have been elderly but certainly looked it, was burly of build; his ruddy complexion was emphasized by a large white moustache. Most of his acquaintances considered him good-humoured. Of his several homes, the closest to Manhattan was at the Long Island seaside resort of Far Rockaway, about a dozen miles by road from Brooklyn Bridge.[2]

1. The track, opened in 1883, was erased in 1939, following the sale of the property to Standard Oil of Ohio. Twenty years later, a new Latonia track was opened by the Kentucky Jockey Club at Florence, a few miles south-west of Covington.
2. Now the John F. Kennedy Airport is just to the north of Far Rockaway, separated from it by Jamaica Bay.

Elwell, astride one of his horses, with employees
of the Beach Racing Stables

Pendleton and Elwell appointed a trainer named Richard Carman, whose first purchase on their behalf was a costly one: a horse called Sunny Slope that was priced at $25,000. Carman was soon replaced by Lloyd Gentry, who had recently offered himself as a trainer after being for seven years a successful jockey, riding for leading owners such as Ben Jones, Rome Respess, and Colonel Edward Bradley. Within a month or so, Gentry bought some 'ready-made' horses and several yearlings of good stock.

Most of the horses of the Beach Racing Stables were entered only in races at tracks on the local circuit (Latonia: Keeneland: Churchill Downs: Ellis Park, and back to Latonia), but a few were boxed farther afield. (Sunny Slope was among the travellers. In 1918, its first full season and only accomplishing one, when it picked up a total of $11,263 in prize-money, three of its wins were at Belmont Park, close to Pendleton's home at Far Rockaway but 600 miles east-north-east of its own home at Covington.) Gentry's best buys were L'Errant, Sand Bed, The Ally, and, best of all, Flags, which in the three seasons from 1918 earned $26,464 from 49 starts.

When needing to spend days at the stables, Elwell lodged 100 miles south of them, at the Phoenix Hotel in Lexington — because that town, in the heart of the Kentucky bluegrass country, was the Mecca for wealthy Disciples of Equus, any of whom might let slip clues to the well-being of rivals to Beach horses, and some of whom could be fleeced at cards before bedtime.

At the end of the summer of 1919, Pendleton sold his share in the stables to Elwell. By then, Lloyd Gentry was tending and training sixteen horses. Elwell was also half-owner, with a Kentucky 'gentleman-trainer' named Phil T. Chinn, of a stallion wittily entitled Jusqu' au Bout and a brood-mare called Madge Brooks after one of Chinn's lady-friends, which were at Chinn's Himyar Stud, near Lexington. A suspicion whispered in that town had it that Elwell's half-shares were in lieu of losses Chinn had suffered at his hands during one long night of card-playing.

It would be reckless to make a guess as to whether or not Elwell showed an overall profit on his horse-owning ventures. Even if it were possible to estimate a subtraction of costs from the easily-estimated grand-total of winnings, sales and stud-fees, one would still have no idea of the extent of his wagering gains from inside knowledge of which of the horses stood a good change of being placed if spurred towards that end.

Elwell the One-Man Business Conglomerate employed surprisingly few personal helpers: none living in and only one who was always at his beck and call, he being a chauffeur, rarely troubled to make trips about Manhattan but earning his wage by virtue of the fact that he was required to be away from his home often and sometimes for weeks on end, driving his master to and from Palm Beach, Covington, Newport, and other places, and being handy to him, at any hour of the day or night, throughout the visits to them.

The chauffeur Elwell had shared with Helen was named Arthur Bishop; but soon after the separation Elwell sacked him (most likely, on account of Bishop's talkativeness to others of incidents *en route*) and took on a younger man, Edwin Rhodes, who lived with his equally young but more personable wife Katharine in a furnished apartment at 123 West Sixty-First Street. (Rhodes was the chauffeur, referred to by Laurence Green [page 37], who, like Elwell's father, had a single share in the Beach-Long Realty Company.)

Elwell made do with one domestic servant, who, when he was in Manhattan, arrived at half-past eight in the morning and, if he was then at home (she having checked that he was by communicating with him through the whistle-and-shout speaking-tube, generally known as a 'blower'), prepared breakfast before cleaning and tidying and shopping till the early afternoon — those chores uninterrupted unless he was home in the middle of the day and requested luncheon. The maid-of-all-work had instructions from Elwell that when breakfast or luncheon was just for himself, she was to serve it to him personally, but that when the meal was for himself and another, she had to transmit it via the dumb-waiter or, if he happened to be near the kitchen, hand it on a tray to him. During Elwell's absences from Manhattan, the woman's work was made slightly less unonerous by the addition of a daily task till a day or so before he was due back: the carrying of mail that had arrived since her previous visit to William Barnes, the English-born steward of the Studio Club — either at his office there or at his home at 149 East Fifty-Fifth Street — for him to read and then put aside if unimportant or acknowledge or post on to Elwell. Barnes did other odd jobs for Elwell (distinctly odd, some of them), both during the latter's absences and while he was in Manhattan.

The first of the maid-servants, Annie Kane, was a young woman, not long out of her teens, who hailed from the Irish province of Ulster. Though, like the first chauffeur, Arthur Bishop, she was a chatterbox, and garnished her chat with fruits of her industrious inquisitiveness, Elwell put up with her for four years, and would have put up with her for longer had she not felt obliged, in the autumn of 1919, to return to the place of her nativity, a cottage from which her father Augustine sold lamp-oils, in the hamlet of Carrickloughan, west of Newry.

Elwell turned to William Barnes to find a replacement of Annie, and Barnes, having turned to Carrie Nielson, a Swedish-born waitress at the Studio Club, effected the introduction to him of Marie Larsen, who, having pleased him by seeming to be in many ways antithetic to Annie, became his housekeeper (she insisted on being called that) on the first Sunday, which was the 5th, of October 1919. Originally Swedish, and still Lutheran of religion, Mrs Larsen was tall and well-built; in her mid-thirties. If she had ever broached her constant expression of solemnity, she might then have looked pretty: pictures of her call to mind theatre-people's condemnation of any dour play as being like Strindberg but without the jokes. She seems never to have appeared hatless in public, indoors or out, nor to have worn any hats other than black-straw brimmed ones that hid all but the ear-muffing chignon of her hair, which was darker than one would expect on a Scandinavian. Her husband, who had anglicized his given name from Anders to Andrew, had become a butler straightway after migrating to America, but, following conscripted service in the wartime army (or, as the Americans say, having been caught in the draft), had switched to butchery, and now hacked and served in a shop at 899 Third Avenue, where Mrs Larsen also served from three till six in the afternoon, Monday to Saturday. The Larsens, who were childless, lived not far from the shop, in a diminutive apartment at 324 East Fifty-Second Street.

So: a housekeeper, a chauffeur, and William Barnes, whose contributions were too inconstant to be given a title. That was the complement of Joseph Bowne Elwell's Manhattan retinue.

By the time Mrs Larsen entered his employ, he had moved west from Park Avenue: across Central Park, and past the intersection of Amsterdam Avenue and Broadway that is called Sherman Square: to a house about 100 yards farther on from the square, on the south side of West Seventieth Street:

Number 244.

The houses on the block were all of a size — three storeys, plus a loft, above a basement — but of several complexions, brownstone predominating. Four embanked stone steps rose to the front double doors of the grey-faced Number 244, which Elwell rented from its owner, a lawyer named Bernard Sandler. From the topmost step, the Hudson River, separating Manhattan from the eastern coast of New Jersey, was glimpsable.

The first eight feet of the hall of the house was made a vestibule by a door that distance from the double doors. Like each of them, the inner door framed a panel of glass, but of the mottled, translucent sort. Like them, it had a lock.

Past the inner door, on the left, were stairs, bulbously balustered, leading upwards. In a crook formed by the side of the stairs and a jutting wall was a door opening on to steps to the basement, the windows and doors of which, front and back, were protected by grilles of curled iron bars about an inch square.

The first doorway to the right beyond the vestibule led into a reception room; the door was of a folding sort, known to some as a 'concertinant'. On the outside and at the bottom of the room's wide windows, facing the street, was a grille similar to those below.

Beyond the reception room, not connecting with it, was a slim lavatory, and then a store-room, just as slim. (The identical slimness of those two rooms suggests that they had started off as one; but the fact that neither had a window suggests otherwise.) The farthest room on the ground floor (I shall call it that in the British way, though Americans start counting storeys at once) was the kitchen — the windows of which, looking on to a forlorn garden, a space for washing-lines rather than flowers, had a grille like the one on the windows of the reception room.

The first floor (second to Americans) was thrice-divided. As used by Elwell, the front room, stretching across the house, was used for the playing of card-games in general, the teaching only of bridge. The dining-room was at the back. Between the two rooms, in the area next to the staircase (to the right of it if one was climbing to the top floor), was what some present-day people would call an 'open-plan', or even 'ranch-style', living-room.

On the top floor were two bedrooms: the larger, Elwell's, at the back; the other, at the front, for guests. A passage from the landing separated the rooms. At one end of the passage, near the landing, were a bathroom and, facing that, a closet. The other end of the passage became, as it were, a T-junction with another passage, against the uninterrupted wall of which was a long table on which Elwell kept bottles of liquor and weakeners of it, glasses, a cocktail-shaker, and other appurtenances of what the Prohibitionists, scenting victory, damned as the Demon Rum.

Of those guests of Elwell's who openly partook of his hospitality, the most frequent were William Barnes, who came chiefly to discuss business matters, and Harold Vanderbilt, who came with two others to play bridge or alone to rehearse with Elwell the licit deceits of bidding.

Elwell sometimes entertained — but was more often entertained by — a banker named Walter Lewisohn, who, having been born on 7 January 1880, was seven years younger than himself. The two men were markedly dissimilar in appearance and mien: Elwell, six feet tall, fair-skinned, and with light brown hair (which was noticeably thin at the front by 1919), had all the social graces that were inferred by the unwary to signify that he lacked ruthlessness, and his smile — ranging, always aptly to the cause of amusement, from a slight crinkling below his blue eyes to a full-faced show of delight that revealed his glistening, regular teeth — charmed men and women alike; Lewisohn, a dark-haired, sallow-skinned man of medium height, stoop-shouldered and inclined towards pudginess, either had never felt the need to fashion disguises of his ruthlessness, or, having felt the need, had failed to satisfy it.

Walter Lewisohn was one of the three sons (the others were named Oscar and Frederick) of Leonard Lewisohn, who, with *his* brother Adolph, had amassed enormous wealth from the mining of copper on their behalf. Walter Lewisohn was well-provided with sisters, among whom were a wife of a sometime United States Assistant Treasurer, the two spinsters who founded and financed the Neighbourhood Theatre in Manhattan, and the wife of Sir Charles Solomon Henry, who was temporarily a Member of Parliament and continuously a banker in England, where she lived with him — grandly, whether in an elegant house between the Malls of St James's, London, or in a mansion near Henley-on-Thames.

Walter and his brother Frederick were the sole partners in the family's banking business near the southern tip of Broadway, and were members of the New York Stock, Coffee, and Copper Exchanges. Millionaires at birth, they had swollen their respective fortunes, which would have increased only extremely without their assistance, through further investments and the provision of funds at high rates of interest and under the protection of mortgages. Walter's wealth was visible in all of his several homes — particularly in the Manhattan one, a joining of buildings at 154–156 East Sixty-Third Street, which was a treasure-dome of artistic things that he had bought on his understanding from experts that they could only grow in monetary value.

His wife Selma, whom he had married in 1911, when she was twenty-two, he thirty-one, had not needed to marry him for his money, for she was the elder daughter of Maurice Kraus, who had come to America from Austria in 1859 and thenceforth prospered exceedingly, ostensibly as a banker. Selma's sister, her junior by more than three years (having been born on 18 April 1891), was called Viola — perhaps after the character in *Twelfth Night*, but more likely with reference to the sort of fiddle, since the Kraus family was music-loving. (One is not exact in calling the Krauses Kraus, for during the Great War the parents of Selma and Viola, keen to be considered loyal Americans, had officially anglicized the family-name to Cross. Since it seems that no one who has so far written of individual members of the family has bothered with the changed name, I shall, to save confusion, stick to Kraus.) The sisters, so said a journalist specializing in vignettes of personages of Manhattan,

> are both beautiful women of what may best be described as the distinctly feminine type. Though there is a difference in their ages, they look much alike. They have the same soft, dark eyes, set wide apart, pointed nose, full-lipped mouth, and rounded chin, and the oval of their face is framed in wavy, reddish-brown hair that is no small part of

Selma and Walter Lewisohn on the porch
of the Breakers Hotel, Palm Beach

Viola Kraus

their attraction. They are slender, though
with well-rounded figures, about 5 feet 4
inches tall, and weigh perhaps 120 pounds.
[When the sisters were last observed,]
Viola wore a dark-blue serge walking frock
trimmed in white, a veil depending from
her small hat. She had on black stockings
and French slippers. Mrs Lewisohn also
wore a blue frock trimmed with red worsted
tassels and a terra-cotta coloured hat, with
brown stockings and French slippers with
interlaced straps over the insteps.

Walter and Selma Lewisohn had known Elwell since shortly before their
marriage. Their first encounter with him was at a bridge-party, and the
relationship remained wholly social till 1916, when Elwell, away from
Helen, started to seek advice on and help with financial deals from Walter,
as he did — and in some cases already had done — from other 'money
men' of Manhattan. The assistance that Elwell received from Walter was
not all to do with stocks and interest rates: some of Elwell's purchases of
works of art were instigated by Walter, divulging his appraisers' prophesies
of leaping values of the work of particular artists or of types of art; Elwell's
renting of 244 West Seventieth Street was initiated by Walter's introduction to him of Bernard Sandler, the owner of the house, whose law office
was at 150 Broadway, close to the far more imposing headquarters of the
firm of Lewisohn Brothers (Bankers).

Viola's first meeting with Elwell was at a dinner-party that she attended
with her sister and brother-in-law in an hotel at Palm Beach in 1912. She
was then twenty-one, and Elwell thirty-nine. There is no doubt about the
year and place of the introduction; but hardly any previously printed
statements concerning the relationship that grew between them can be
taken as God's truth.

Viola lived with the Lewisohns till 1915, when she married Victor von
Schlegell, who was thirty-six and looked every bit as one would expect of a
man with a name like that, for he was blond, tall and erect of bearing, and
took such care of his clothes that they resembled batman-tended uniforms.
But for the absence of a ritual duelling-scar, one would have put him down
as a graduate of the University of Heidelberg. Actually, he had been born
in the state of Missouri in 1879, and, his family having moved north to the
city of Minneapolis, where his father practised law and was a judge in a
probate court, he had studied civil engineering at the University of
Minnesota, but without graduating. His lack of formal qualification had
not stopped him, straightway after settling in Manhattan, from becoming a

member of the Engineers' Club there. By occupation (which was not interrupted by the war), he was a vice-president of the United & Globe Rubber Company, whose offices were in the Equitable Building at 120 Broadway. How many vice-presidents there were of that organization seems never to have been publicly announced, and so, considering that some American companies are like armies with as many colonels as privates, there is no way of telling whether Vice-President Victor von Schlegell (called Von by those he permitted to do so) had a strategic post or a subordinate one, or occupied a sinecure.

Viola did not long enjoy being Mrs Von Schlegell, and she went home to the Lewisohns in September 1919. Subsequently, Von Schlegell agreed to the fabrication of evidence for a divorce on statutory grounds, the first decree for which was granted by a referee at White Plains, New York State, on 10 March 1920. The defendant, epitomizing perfect gentleman-liness, said of the wronged party: 'She is a lovely woman. The trouble was that I was thirty-six and still a bachelor. I was too fond of clubs, perhaps, and did not give her the attention she should have had from a husband.' Even before the hearing, Viola reverted to her unanglicized maiden-name.

At about the time that Viola separated from Von Schlegell, the Lewisohn circle was enhanced visibly by the arrival within it of Leonora Hughes, who, in that lingeringly poetical era, was said — and not only by her publicity agent — to be the sort of woman who is put into the world for men to write poems about. 'Hughes', though not particularly Irish, was probably her real name; 'Leonora' was almost certainly of her choosing. But it was suitable. She was breathtakingly beautiful of tresses (which were auburn), features (excepting her nose, which was a mite too wide), and form (which was modishly slighter than was the mode before the war) — and any man capable of unconcentrating his gaze from components and viewing Leonora whole was given a sublime synergistic treat.

Five years before (that is, in 1914, when she was sixteen), she had given up telephone-operating in her native Flatbush part of Brooklyn to be a chorus-dancer in cabarets at Manhattan clubs, Murray's at first, followed by the Sixty, and then the McAlpin. While at the latter place, she had met Maurice Mouvet, a New Yorker of Belgian parentage who was then partnering his ex-wife in a dancing act — Maurice & Florence, his name pronounced Moreesse — that was the main attraction of the floor-show in the red-and-gold dining-room of the Biltmore Hotel on Madison Avenue at Forty-Third Street. Captivated by Leonora's loveliness, Maurice had asked her to become his partner, she had accepted, and he had given Florence three weeks' notice, during which time he and Leonora had spent the days rehearsing the waltzes and fox-trots that on the twenty-second

Leonora Hughes

The Biltmore

The Waldorf-Astoria

night formed the act of Maurice & Leonora. The act was well-received at the Biltmore — as it was subsequently at other Manhattan hotels, and then at hotels in London, Paris and Deauville. Just prior to the 'Triumphant Return' of the act to Manhattan, there was a scurry of publicity, from which emerged a lasting description of Leonora as 'the dimpled wisp of grace from Flatbush'. Late in 1918, she took time off from Maurice to appear, but only just, in a film called *The Indestructible Wife*, made by the Select company. Her part, that of 'Julia', was negligible, penultimate in the cast-list, separated from space by that of 'The Butler'.[1] While hoping for bigger things on the silver screen, she resumed her terpsichorean way of earning a living. Following some out-of-town dates, Maurice & Leonora were booked into the Waldorf-Astoria.

It was there that Walter Lewisohn saw her. And was conquered. He became whatever the hotel equivalent of a stage-door Johnnie is known as. Flattered by the attentions of a man of such wealth, Leonora accepted an invitation to his Manhattan residence like a shot. There is no record, not even a slight indication, of whether she was disappointed or virginally relieved to find others there: among them, his wife and sister-in-law and a renowned bridge-player. Before long, she was a frequent guest at the Lewisohns' homes, and often — when she was not entertaining publicly herself — a member of their party at theatrical first-nights, at gala dinners, at balls in aid of Jewish charities.

Neither Selma Lewisohn nor Viola Kraus was glad of her company. Walter Lewisohn was — as the new saying had it — mad about her. Joseph Bowne Elwell was taken by her, too.

As he did not expect to live for long at 244 West Seventieth Street, he had not taken much trouble to display his decorative assets. Some were in darkness, stuck, higgledy-piggledy, in the slim store-room.

The greatest of the assets was a painting, said to be by Rembrandt, of Christ carrying the Cross. Elwell had paid $17,000 for it, having been made confident of its provenance, partly from the fact that it had belonged to an aristocratic Peruvian family for nearly a century, but more so from the presence on the back of the canvas of a document, carrying the seal of the Peruvian Government, that attested that the painting had once hung in a palace in Lima but had been taken from there when the monarchy was overthrown in 1825. A similar document was attached to a sheet of copper that was painted on both sides, each by a different hand — one of the paintings, carrying the signature of Willem Wissing (1656–87), court-painter to England's Charles II and James II, was claimed, though it was called 'The Princess', to be a portrait of William of Orange. Among the

1. She was not mentioned in either of the two reviews, both intended to help cinema-owners to decide whether or not to book the film, that appeared on one page of *Motion Picture News* of 1 March 1919. The owners cannot have been helped by the duplexity of the reviews. Whereas the longer of them was enthusiastic, to the extent of saying that the film was 'one of the season's treats', the other considered that 'anybody who looks for life and vigour in a photoplay may beg and pray for the Sennett comedy that might be next on the bill. . . . The well constructed subtitles have worked overtime to put some ginger into it . . . but hardly with much success. By dressing the programme with some lively short stuff, you may be able to get by without any serious kicks. The picture is clean. Length, 5 reels.'

other thirty-five paintings was a riparian scene by the Frenchman, Charles-Emile Jacques (1813–94), and a portrait of a small girl by the Austrian-born but America-preferring August Friedlander (1856–97).

Further to such pictorial assets were many other desirable things. For instance: several dinner-services, including one of 75 pieces from Limoges; a First-Napoleon banquet suite, consisting of a buffet, a pair of crystal closets, an extending table, and six chairs, that had cost Elwell $6,000; a semi-nude bronze figure of Faith by Matthew Moreau; a host of Chinese vases, some of the Ming period, and collections of porcelain and of jade figures that Helen had garnered, piece by piece, over many years; a loving-cup of sterling silver that had been presented to Elwell by the Newport Golf Club; mahogany cases in which were ranged full-leather-bound sets of the works of Dickens, Fielding, Flaubert, Scott, Smollett, and (his presence would excite surmise) Wilde; also — even more splendidly covered — a set of the Elwell books on bridge (that in addition to the cloth-bound set that, with forty or so bridge-books by other hands, filled a shelf in the card-room).

Elwell's favourite possession would have been unregarded by visitors with appraising eyes; demeaned as an example of the bric-à-brac of his life. It was suspended from an electric-light bracket on the hall side of the reception room, a foot or so above an upright armchair of gilded timber and crimson plush: a plain-framed printing of Kipling's 'If — ': probably the only poem that Elwell knew by heart, and certainly specially cherished by him for the first half of the third stanza of requirements for being a Man:

> *If you can make one heap of all your winnings*
> *And risk it on one turn of pitch-and-toss,*
> *And lose, and start again at your beginnings*
> *And never breathe a word about your loss;*

None of Elwell's possessions was insured, and so he was fortunate on Thursday, 4 December 1919, when the house was entered by burglars. Three of them — they waited till Mrs Larsen had left at two o'clock in the afternoon, then scuttled down the steps to the basement area at the front — prised away the rusted grille over the door, forced the lock, and moved through the basement and up the steps to the hall. But a neighbour had noticed their intrusion, had telephoned the police station on West Sixty-Eighth Street. They were still in the hall, confused by the embarrassment of riches as to what to take, when a posse of constables led by Detective Sergeant Thomas Donohue effected their arrest. They were white-skinned denizens of an area around the far-west of Sixtieth Street that was inhabited mainly by black people, and was on that account known as San Juan Hill, referring to a place where Negro soldiers fought bravely in the Spanish-American War. All three burglars were imprisoned, each for the strangely particular term of forty-two months.

Elwell arranged not only for a new lock to be fitted on the basement-door and for the broken grille to be replaced by a freshly-fashioned one, but for all of the grilles, front and back, to be examined and, where necessary, repaired or substituted.

And while he was about it, he arranged for new and stronger locks to be fitted to the front double doors and the door at the end of the vestibule. Each of those locks had a catch which, when applied, allowed the door to be opened simply by turning the handle.

There is uncertainty about the number of keys that were provided for those locks.

Elwell pocketed one set.

A second set was held by Mrs Larsen.

Probably there was another; possibly others.

Elwell had a dreary Christmas and New Year, being laid low by what seems to have been influenza. There was a lot of it about. He was visited by, *inter alios*, William Barnes, Harold Vanderbilt, Walter and Selma Lewisohn, and his son, Richard Derby (now fifteen years of age, a pupil of Phillips Academy, Andover), who went away better off by fifty dollars, given to him on the understanding that he would not mention it to his mother. Viola Kraus had herself driven to West Seventieth Street — but, so she subsequently professed, did not go into the house to comfort the sick man but stayed in the limousine while the chauffeur delivered magazines, a novel, and a hamper of delicacies.

Elwell was quite recovered of health long before the first week of February 1920, on a morning in which his chauffeur, Edwin Rhodes, collected one of his two cars, a Packard roadster, from the Chatsworth Garage at 213 West End Avenue, and drove him south, to Palm Beach.

In the following four months, Elwell was more away than at home. One can attach only a couple of precise dates to his itinerary: afterwards, Edwin Rhodes, who was with him or close to him for most of the time, either was not asked to diarise or was unable or unwilling to.

Certainly, on Monday, 23 February, Elwell was in Palm Beach (whether or not he had been there constantly since the start of the month, I cannot tell), and in the evening of that day he celebrated his birthday with a party at the Breakers Hotel. Chatting to guests — one of whom was a recent acquaintance, a young woman named Florence Ellenson who had come to the seaside from her home in upstate New York to convalesce from illness

— he sighed that he was well into the middle years of life, admitting to gauche questioners that he had reached the age of forty-five. Actually, of course, he had reached that age two years before, and was now forty-seven.

Before leaving Palm Beach, early in March, he learned from Florence Ellenson that she would be spending the summer as a stewardess on the Van Noy Interstate Company's steamer *Horizon*, plying Lake George, and asked her to keep in touch, saying that he intended to visit Saratoga Springs, south of the lake, in mid-June, and would like to escort her to the Adirondack Mountains when she had a day off.

It may be that Elwell left Palm Beach earlier than he had intended. Edwin Rhodes subsequently said that

> there was a scene in a garage the day before Mr Elwell left. He told a woman that he could associate with her no longer, because her husband suspected him and had made threats against him. The woman charged that Mr Elwell was advancing an excuse for a break with her, and became hysterical in her reproaches. . . . He departed the following day on his way to Lexington, Kentucky, by train, directing me to drive the car there alone.

By the end of March, he was staying at the Phoenix Hotel, Lexington, and spending most days at the Beach Racing Stables at Latonia. His trainer, Lloyd Gentry, had wintered the horses at the Idle Hour Stock Farm belonging to Colonel Edward Bradley, who had become a frequent companion of Elwell's, both in Kentucky and in New York City, where the colonel had a home. All of the horses were now back at their home-stables, and Gentry was preparing all but one of them for the Latonia Summer Meeting, which was scheduled to start on Saturday, 5 June, and to continue for more than a month. The comparatively leisured horse had been sold to a man named Winfrey for $5,600 — $5,200 by cheque, and the remainder covered by Winfrey's tearing up of an IOU from Elwell.

Towards the end of April, Elwell returned to Palm Beach; but stayed there briefly, it seems — for little longer than was needed to complete negotiations over the sale of his power-boat to a wealthy resident, John Rutherford, with whom he agreed the price of $8,000.

Thence back to Lexington, which was now cacophonous of speculation about the new racing season. This time, he made the acquaintance of a girl called Anne Russell Griffy, who came in from her father's farm at Versailles (one of several towns near Lexington with unoriginal names: there was also a Paris, a Frankfort, a Winchester, a Richmond, a Lancaster). Miss Griffy would recall:

> I was introduced to Mr Elwell at a social function prior to the Lexington spring racing. I saw him three times in Lexington and once at Louisville, that latter meeting being merely by chance. I last saw him in Lexington on the

night of Friday, May 28. He had come that evening, he said, from Louisville by train. I had been to a lawn fête with a number of friends, and came upon Mr Elwell in the lobby of the Phoenix Hotel. I told him I was going to a hospital the following week for an operation upon my tonsils.

At least two days before that last meeting with Anne Russell Griffy, Elwell had written to his wife. (Yes: although during the past months, in Palm Beach and in Lexington, he had told new female acquaintances — including Florence Ellenson in the former place — that he was a divorcee, he was still married to Helen.) The letter, which reached her on 27 May, was only the second she had received from him since their separation (during which time they had never met): in the previous October, he had written to her concerning their son's change of school, from Buckley to Andover. In the second letter, he asked if she would be 'willing to secure a divorce' from him, and, assuming such willingness, suggested that they should repair, separately, to the town of Reno, Nevada, which had made Divorce While You Wait its main industry.

According to Helen, speaking three weeks later, her response to the letter was as follows:

> Realizing that it would be best if we received the final decree, I wrote him my willingness to bring an end to our marital unhappiness. I also told him in my reply, which was mailed to 244 West Seventieth Street, that the lease on my apartment would expire in October 1920, and urged him to answer through my attorney, W. Gibbs Whaley, what immediate steps he could take. I wanted to know how the trip [to Reno] was going to affect the lease.

In other, not dissimilar words, she expected that her agreement to a divorce would be financially agreeable to herself.

On Tuesday, 1 June, Elwell arrived back in Manhattan, where among the names dropped in the talk of the town were those of Cole Porter, composer of a song entitled 'Old-Fashioned Garden' which had a tune that was easy to remember and a lyric that Mr Porter would soon want to forget; Babe Ruth, recently purchased by the New York Yankees from the Boston Red Sox for the phenomenal sum of $125,000, tribute to his new-found knack of swatting baseballs into the bleachers; F. Scott Fitzgerald, replete with optimism following his marriage to Zelda Sayre and the success of his first novel; and Man o' War, a big red three-year-old horse that had come second in one race (that at Saratoga) but had been first past the post in the other eleven.

Within a fortnight, those names would be temporarily lost in a commotion of comment and conjecture about Joseph Bowne Elwell: a din that would not disturb him.

MIDNIGHT FROLIC

On Monday, 31 May, the day before Elwell's return, a workman hired by Robert Silverman — ostensibly long retired as a real-estate agent but still dabbling intermediarily from his apartment in West Ninety-Second Street, near Riverside Drive — strapped a For Sale board to the railings guarding the front basement area of 244 West Seventieth Street.

When Elwell entered the house, Rhodes following with the first instalment of luggage from the car, Mrs Larsen confused words of dismay about the board with words of welcome that were as invariable as one of her Lutheran prayers whenever he had been away. But he was casual about the board, unsurprised by it. Among the mail that William Barnes had posted on to him, there had been a letter from Bernard Sandler: legalistic of content but unctuous in tone, it had advised him of Sandler's intention to sell the house — not as an investment, allowing the possibility of Mr Elwell's continued tenure under new ownership, but as a residence of the new owner; since the question of Mr Elwell's purchase of the above-mentioned property had already been mooted by his Obedient Servant, and at the aforementioned time rejected by Mr Elwell, he was now within the terms of the leasing agreement, requested to quit the premises forthwith.

Elwell had not replied to the letter. And his only apparent reaction to it, and to the subsequently strapped board, within a day or so of his return was to mention the matter to Walter Lewisohn — who murmured regrets, saying that he felt a certain responsibility since he had introduced Sandler to Elwell, but explained that he held no sway over the ejecting lawyer, whom he never met socially and rarely did business with.

On Thursday, 3 June, Sandler telephoned Elwell and arranged for a prospective buyer and his wife, escorted by the aged Silverman, to look over the house at a certain time next day. Punctually on the Friday — according to Sandler's part-hearsay account —

They did call. Silverman told me that although they rang the bell and knocked on the door, they were unable to get in for about an hour. Silverman then went to a telephone and called me up. It had begun to rain, and he had left the man and woman in the doorway of the house next door. About the time he called my office, another call came in from the Elwell home. Mrs Marie Larsen, the housekeeper, wanted to know why the parties who were to inspect the house did not appear. She said Mr Elwell was waiting for them. After a telephone conversation with me, Mr Silverman returned to the house and rang the bell. Mrs Larsen opened the door, telling them that Mr Elwell was waiting for them and had just come in.

Mr Silverman afterwards told me that he saw an empty champagne bottle and two empty glasses on a table in the reception room. He said Elwell greeted them and showed them through the house. They saw no woman other than Mrs Larsen in the house, and Silverman says no one entered or left the house during the hour that he and the prospective buyers were trying to gain admittance.

All of which raises several suspicions, a couple of alternative ones being that Mrs Larsen was a tardy potwoman or that she and Elwell, he keenly obstructive of Sandler's objective, whiled away an hour of intended delay by splitting a bottle of Bollinger in the reception room, whence the incommoded and eventually moistened trio could be covertly observed through the lace-curtains.

If one goes by William Barnes's outline of Elwell's daily routine (which one should not if one accepts Barnes's assertion that he rarely visited Elwell at home, and then only briefly),

> His habit was to get up at about eight o'clock or 8.30 in the morning and have his breakfast at home. Then he usually went to his broker's to look at his stock transactions. He was generally in bed by one o'clock.

In the short period after the day when Elwell temporarily repelled the prospective buyers, known unique, unusual or at least irregular insertions in or alterations to his routine may be itemized as follows:

On Saturday the 5th, in the morning, he visited his bank, apparently solely for the purpose of depositing funds, including a cheque for $5,200 from Mr Winfrey, part-payment for the horse that the latter had bought from him. Directly afterwards, Rhodes drove him to the Lewisohns' country estate, Elwood Park, inland from the New Jersey seaside resort of Long Branch, where, in the afternoon, he played golf with Viola Kraus, who was a devotee of that game, and in the evening played bridge with her and the Lewisohns. He stayed the night (as did Rhodes, in the servants' quarters), and

on Sunday the 6th, at noon, having played another round of golf with Viola, set off towards home. When Rhodes had driven thirty miles, about half the journey, and was steering round an awkward corner near Woodbridge, a wheel came away, and the car finished up in a shallow ditch. It was as well that the accident happened where it did, at a place requiring a fairly slow speed, else both driver and passenger, to say nothing of any other proximate road-users, might have been injured. Elwell, shocked into a bad temper, blamed Rhodes for not having checked the car following its intensive usage in the four months till the previous Monday; and Rhodes, while unbolting the spare wheel, blamed the mechanic at the Chatsworth Garage who was supposed to have given the car a full servicing on the Tuesday. Still, there were only a few bumps and scratches to the bodywork, no harm done internally, and Elwell was delivered to his door less than half an hour later than he had expected to be.

On Monday the 7th, for an undetermined time, he entertained at home 'a young woman of fair complexion' — that slight description coming, not from Mrs Larsen, who by the end of the week had forgotten the occasion, but from Joseph Wagstaff, a driver for the Black & White Taxicab Company, who answered a call from 'Elwell' of 244 West Seventieth Street at 2.20 on the Monday afternoon, and drove a 'lady fare' to the 800-or-so part of Madison Avenue, where there were several small shops, at her request waited, then took her to the intersection of Park Avenue and Sixty-Sixth Street, received payment of $3.10 plus tip, and drove off without noticing or for long remembering the direction in which she walked.

On Tuesday the 8th, Elwell lunched at home with (Mrs Larsen's description, this:) 'a little, short, fat, dark-haired, pretty girl of about twenty-four, who wore a grey dress that was trimmed with fur at the bottom'. Elwell had not told Mrs Larsen that he was expecting company. 'At about noon,' she was subsequently caused to remember, 'the doorbell rang and Mr Elwell himself admitted the young woman. He directed me to set lunch for two, so I went out and came back with chops, tomatoes, and strawberry shortcake, a meal on which I was complimented by Mr Elwell, who seemed to be in high spirits. He served it himself, taking it upstairs from the kitchen on a tray. The young woman left in a taxi-cab. Shortly after her departure, Mr Elwell himself went out.'

On Wednesday the 9th, in the afternoon, he attended a wedding reception at the Plaza — an hotel that, what with its unconfined frontage on the south side of Central Park, was as rewarding to alfresco gapers as to wonderers within: years after 1920, Zelda Fitzgerald, recalling Manhattan then, would be delighted by the especial memory of 'girls in short amorphous capes and long flowing skirts and hats like straw bathtubs waiting for taxis in front of the Plaza Grill'. Returned from the reception,

Elwell took off his cutaway and striped trousers, changed into a grey suit, and having asked Mrs Larsen to fold the formal attire into a chest containing his winter wardrobe, left the house again. During the day, he made three telephone calls from the house, using either the telephone in the reception room, on a table in the corner to the right of the door, or his bedside set — which, being an extension from the telephone downstairs, was also designated Columbus 9689. Two of his calls were to numbers in New Jersey — one in Plainfield, the other in Bound Brook, both places close to Cranford — and were on behalf of his father, who had expressed a wish to locate a friend from his early commercially-travelling days. The other call was to a number — never to be publicly disclosed — in the Flatbush part of Brooklyn.

On Thursday the 10th, when Mrs Larsen arrived at the house at the usual time of 8.30, Elwell was already astir, sitting in the upright armchair between the door and the telephone-table in the reception room. He was wearing a black and purple dressing-gown over red silk pajamas, and black slippers that were gaily tasselled at the instep, and was engrossed in his morning mail. After eating a hearty breakfast, he bathed and dressed, and then returned to the reception room to deal with correspondence, a task that was interrupted by a telephone call from Florence Ellenson, who was speaking from the New Jersey seaside resort of Asbury Park, where she was staying with friends during the short time left to her before she was due to start stewardessing on Lake George. She told him that she intended to be in Manhattan the next day, and he, saying that he hoped they could meet, promised to call her before 8.15 in the morning, the time when she had to leave her friends' house to catch the train. He had hardly replaced the receiver when, dead on eleven o'clock, Edwin Rhodes arrived to drive him to the Belmont Park horse-racing track, on Long Island. There, Elwell lunched in the club-house. And so, though at another table, did William Pendleton, his ex-associate at the Beach Racing Stables, who had come the short distance from his home at Far Rockaway by cab. Elwell left in the middle of the afternoon, prior to the last race, and arrived home with ample time to spare — sufficient to include a nap if he wanted one and was not prevented from dozing by the presence of a visitor — before sprucing himself up for a rather special evening engagement.

The notion that Elwell may have napped — or may at least have wanted to — stems from Mrs Larsen's subsequently reported observations and surmises:

> He was restless and sleepless throughout the week, though not in bad spirits. He was always a heavy smoker [of cigarettes of Virginian tobaccos, blended to his taste at a shop near the Grand Central railroad terminal], but he was

smoking more than ever. In the past, he was nearly always in bed when I arrived, but for most of the last few days he was already up when I arrived. I found on his bed each morning for several days a handkerchief which was folded and soaked with perfume. It was Eau de Cologne, No. 4711. I thought that he had put it on his forehead when he went to bed because he had a headache. He may have been disturbed by the painters and carpenters at work next door [to the west] when they started at eight o'clock each morning, or he may have been affected by the very hot weather.

The outdoor temperature was 68°F at eight o'clock on the night of Thursday, 10 June, when Elwell, toppered and tailed, stepped from the elevator on the top floor, the fifteenth, of the Ritz-Carlton Hotel, on the north-western corner of Forty-Sixth Street at Madison Avenue. Scott Fitzgerald would write about a diamond as big as this Ritz — a place that was very big indeed, its front (similar in style to those of the other Ritzes in the world) almost as long as it was tall: a place of 300 elegantly-appointed rooms and suites, and with, among other amenities, a roof-restaurant, the Ritz Garden, that could accommodate 400 diners — who in the unlikely event that they all at the same time wished to dance to the strains of the Ritz-Carlton Orchestra, could do so on the central rink of parquet without feeling crowded.

From a guide to the best eating-places in Manhattan, this reference sandwiched between references to the Athena Restaurant, 832 Sixth Avenue at Twenty-Ninth Street ('. . . the genuine White Greek cheese is grand, and for dessert there is Yogourt, in both the ten- and fifteen-cent portions, and you might as well know right now that Yogourt is something that looks too terribly like sour milk. A la carte. Terribly, terribly reasonable.'), and Lee Chumley's, 86 Bedford Street, Greenwich Village ('Lounge of the Literati: ladies and gentlemen who, albeit they bow to the arts, positively salaam to the cashier!'):

> You enter the huge, oval-ceilinged, facet-walled dining-room of the Ritz-Carlton. . . .
> Here, afternoons and evenings, you'll find the world's most expensively gowned women and the world's most leisurely men — ambassadors, financial giants, ladies who set the fashions and ladies who merely copy them; polo players and the less crusty, fusty members of the Union League; Dukes and Counts and debutantes and dandies and dowagers and divas. . . .
> No culinary offering stands out for the simple reason that all stand out; no one thing is to be recommended above all others, because they are all to be recommended — which is a great bit of encouragement for those Ritz-Carlton connoisseurs who speak no French, for thus are they enabled to point to anything on the wholly French menu, and be assured of getting something — anything — and getting it better than most anywhere else. . . .

The Ritz-Carlton

It would be almost a case of lily-painting to tell you that the Ritz is expensive!

Expense was no object to Walter Lewisohn, who would foot the bill for the Thursday-night dinner for himself and four companions: two ladies — his wife and her sister Viola — and two gentlemen — Elwell and an Argentine newspaper-publisher named Octavio Figueroa, who had come from Buenos Aires on business (which he could conduct without an interpreter) and was staying at the Ritz-Carlton. The three-to-two sexual imbalance of the party makes one wonder why Lewisohn had not invited the lovely Leonora Hughes, who was certainly in New York City, perhaps staying with her parents in Flatbush, and, so far as her dancing partnership

The Ritz Garden

with Maurice Mouvet was concerned, not otherwise engaged. Perhaps the dinner-reservation had originally been made for four, but at the last minute Lewisohn had got his social secretary to telephone the restaurant (the number of which was on the Plaza exchange, a sort of advertisement for that other hotel that must have miffed the Ritz's publicity manager), asking for a fifth place to be laid, that for the recently-arrived Señor Figueroa.

Another apparently slight puzzle arises from the fact that whereas in the past, whenever Elwell had been asked out by the Lewisohns, he had met up with them at their home, on this occasion he joined their party at the place of the outing. Perhaps that had been his idea, prompted by uncertainty when the invitation was extended about the time of his return from Belmont Park.

In any event, the Lewisohns, Viola Kraus, and Octavio Figueroa were already seated at a table on the perimeter of the dance-floor but well away from the orchestra when Elwell, having left his top-hat in the cloakroom, became a member of the party.

So the two lady-members subsequently said, the dinner was not intended to be celebratory: it was coincidental that today was the day when Viola's divorce from Victor von Schlegell became absolute, leaving her free, if she so wished, to become someone else's wife.

It may be that she was not noticeably joyful prior to about nine o'clock on this her independence day; but there is no doubt that by then, an hour after Elwell's arrival and occupancy of the chair next to hers, she was decidedly tetchy. The sequence of incidents is obscure, but she either took a dainty propelling pencil from her purse and wrote with it on the nearer of Elwell's starched shirt-cuffs, and then, scowling, whispered a series of remarks at him while he concentrated on the cuisine — or she whispered and then wrote. Or she whispered, then wrote, then resumed the whispering.

The coincidence of the dinner's being on the day of her divorce was made comparatively slight soon after nine o'clock, when ostentatious chuckling from a nearby table drew the Lewisohn party's attention to another diner:

None other than Victor von Schlegell.

He, much amused, called out something to the effect that, no matter what the law had decided, he and Viola seemed to be magnetically attracted to each other.

Viola didn't appreciate the joke.

Nor did Von's companion, a pretty and petite young woman who was wearing a dress of black chiffon. (That the dress was of chiffon is immaterial, but you should note for future reference that the chiffon was black.)

Post-prandially, the members of the Lewisohn party danced — in the meticulous style insisted upon by Vernon & Irene Castle, who, never mind that the leader had passed on precipitately, were as renowned, as revered, as partners on the dance-floor as were Elwell & Harold Vanderbilt as partners at the bridge-table. Since Selma and Viola were outnumbered by the males, they danced most often — Viola once with her brother-in-law, a couple of times, presumably to paso-dobles, with Señor Figueroa, and, seemingly having let bygones be bygones so far as Elwell was concerned, frequently with him. Twice during excursions by Elwell and Viola, they came close to the also-dancing Von Schlegell and his lady-friend. On one of those occasions, Von panted, 'Hello, Joe,' and on the other, 'looking at Mr Elwell, clipped his fingers against his forehead and away, much in the manner of an army rookie attempting his first salute'. The description of that gesture was given some days later by his friend. According to some sedentary spectators, also questioned afterwards, Elwell smilingly acknowledged either the gesture or the spoken greeting; according to others, he ignored both. Reverting to Von's recollective friend, she said, speaking more generally, that 'Miss Kraus was decidedly expressionless, sort of wooden-faced, every time I caught sight of her during the evening'.

At eleven o'clock — by which time Von and his friend had long since departed, he without bidding farewell to his just-ex wife — Elwell, having received acquiescence from the other members of the party to his expressed desire to extend the evening into the small hours, suggested a move from one Manhattan pinnacle to another: to the Aerial Gardens above the New Amsterdam Theatre. His suggestion assented to, he left at once to make arrangements at the theatre (a favourite haunt of his, to the extent that he was sure that even if the House Full boards were displayed, he could inveigle 'management seats'), leaving the others to follow, reaching the theatre before 11.30, the time when the curtain went up on the *Midnight Frolic*.

A cab was hailed for him, and one may suppose that the driver went four blocks down Madison Avenue, turned right on to Forty-Second Street and drove on, passing the New York Public Library on the left, and having crossed Broadway and Seventh Avenue, at the southern edge of Times Square, pulled up some seventy yards farther on, in the stretch of Forty-Second Street that its equivalent of a chamber of commerce glorified as 'the centre of the theatrical universe, standing for revelry and rapture'. After alighting and paying the fare, Elwell crossed the street to the New Amsterdam, a building more than twice as tall as its older neighbours, its façade fashioned from limestone and terra-cotta.

To those who considered the Art Nouveau style of decoration lovely, the New Amsterdam was a lovely place. A few days after it had opened with a production of *A Midsummer Night's Dream* in October 1903, the New York *Times* had commented:

> In the New Amsterdam, Art Nouveau, first crystalised in the Paris Exposition of 1900, is typified on a large scale in America. The colour scheme is of the most delicate reseda green and dull gold. . . . The allied arts of painting, sculpture and architecture have, through their exponents, combined to produce a result that astonishes and delights, and whose effect and feeling are that of permanence, durability, and extreme beauty.

There were two theatres within the New Amsterdam, one above the other. The main theatre, the lower, had 1,702 seats disposed as stalls or in curved ranks on the two balconies (which, innovatively, did without supporting pillars) or in the boxes — six at each side of a stage that was among the largest and best-equipped in Manhattan. The auditorium of the

rooftop theatre,[1] the Aerial Gardens, was much smaller — a stalls area and a single U-shaped balcony (also regardless of pillars) which, together, made space for about 500 tiered seats. The rear of the stalls area, which was on the Forty-First Street side, was made up of windows, and these were swung open when the weather was fine, giving some impression of an open-air theatre.

1. Rooftop theatres were particular, if not peculiar, to Manhattan — a symptom of the fact that, as it was an island, its acreage finite, it created a need, so far as many latterday financiers of buildings were concerned, to 'think tall' — and to ensure that every cubic foot of architectural space was gainfully used.

The most famous of the rooftop theatres was atop the first Madison Square Garden, at the corner of Madison Avenue and Twenty-Sixth Street, a site purchased from the Vanderbilts. The main reason for its fame after Monday, 25 June 1906, was that, on that night, during the opening performance of *Mamzelle Champagne*, and just after a comedian had sung a ditty called 'I Could Love a Thousand Girls', it was the scene of the shooting to death of the designer of the entire building, Stanford White, by Harry Kendall Thaw, a mad millionaire made madder by the knowledge that White had had a relationship with his, Thaw's, beautiful wife Evelyn, *née* Nesbit.

Since 1913, the New Amsterdam had housed productions by the great showman Florenz Ziegfeld, and had also been his administrative headquarters (for there were eleven storeys of office-space in the building). And since 1915, while successive, and always successful, editions of the *Ziegfeld Follies* had occupied the main theatre, the Aerial Gardens, with part of its stalls area polished as a dance-floor and the rest dotted with chairs-surrounded tables, on which 'light refreshments' were served, had been the venue for various *Midnight Frolics*.

The glittering rooftop showplace . . . became a world-famous attraction. Even Nijinsky came in one night during his 1916 American tour. . . . Many of the *Follies* stars appeared simultaneously in the *Frolics*, often resulting in their doing two completely different shows a night. It was on the Roof that Fanny Brice introduced 'Rose of Washington Square' and 'Second-Hand Rose'.[1]

The smaller theatre served Ziegfeld as an experimental laboratory . . . for testing out new songs, skits, girls, stage effects — anything at all. Eddie Cantor was first a rooftop baby. And so was Norma Terris, who later became a star in Ziegfeld's *Show Boat*, after proving her mettle at sixteen [in 1920] by singing a song of remarkable impermanence called 'Life is Just a Tiny Little Mushroom'. Ziegfeld's most important find up at the *Frolic* was the young lasso-twirler, Will Rogers . . . . Ziegfeld saw him in New York vaudeville and asked him up. Rogers was the perfect contrast to all the fluffy girls and citified comedians and did more to broaden and Americanize the Ziegfeld shows than any other single performer. Again and again the same people took the midnight elevator ride to see him twirl his ropes and toss off his sly ad-libs — at least they sounded like ad-libs. His fans included everybody from President Wilson to Diamond Jim Brady.[2]

1. Joel Lobenthal, contributing to *The New Amsterdam Theatre*, The Theatre Historical Society of America, San Francisco, 1978.

2. Tom Prideaux, in *New York, N.Y.*, American Heritage, New York, 1968.

Elwell, with five tickets held like a poker-hand, was waiting in the entrance to the New Amsterdam when the others of his party arrived. He and they — his guests now — passed beneath a carved panel, a sort of comic-strip version of the story of Faust, into the foyer: a miniature art-gallery, the amber light from its row of chandeliers adding pronounce-ment to the friezes on both sides — scenes from Wagner on the right, from Shakespeare on the left, over the elevator-doors of cast-metal adorned with floral designs in relief that were as in keeping with the perceived dictates of Art Nouveau as were the chandeliers.

The ascension to the Aerial Gardens was part of the fun of the *Frolics*: 'These late-hour fiestas exuded such snooty glamour that many people felt the elevator ride was the height of sophisticated euphoria. They were squeezed in with the best people.'[1]

Disembarked, and having severally checked temporarily unrequired belongings, the Elwell party moved through a slight lobby — a pretty place, decorated with sky-blue and gold plasterwork — and into the Aerial Gardens. Preceded by an usher-cum-waiter, the party moved to a table, and Elwell told the attendant what 'light refreshments'[2] to bring.

Since a *Frolic*, as well as being something to see, was something to be seen at, it is probable that, Señor Figueroa excepted, each member of the party recognized and/or was recognized by a number of others in the audience. But the only instance of reciprocal recognition that was subsequently reported was between Elwell and a well-connected young

1. Prideaux, *ibid.*

2. In the Aerial Gardens, 'light refreshments' was a euphemism for the already-euphemistic 'alcoholic beverages'. Though the Volstead Act, prohibiting the sale and consumption of any drink containing more than ½ of 1% of alcohol, had come into effect throughout the United States on 16 January, it was observed in few previously licensed premises. (Indeed, like a Welsh Sunday writ large, Prohibition had effects contrary to its 'noble' intentions: Andrew Volstead's Act, the Eighteenth Amendment to the Constitution, gave a marvellous fillip to the organization of crime: chiefly by courtesy of gangsters, more booze was imbibed during its Prohibition than in equivalent time-spans of legal unconstraint.)

The isolated Aerial Gardens — accessible from ground-level only via the elevators or, awkwardly, fire-escapes — seemed well-nigh immune from surprise raids by enforcers of the 'dry law'.

(The same seemed to be so of the similarly-situated Ritz Garden. But on the night of Friday, 12 July 1924, a deceitful battalion of Prohibition Agents entered that restaurant and, the leader having announced its presence and purpose, proceeded to arrest half a dozen wine-waiters, presumably slow-witted since they were still toting bottles, and a Mr Edwin Goodman, the sole patron among the four hundred present who had not thought to spill his drink, while the Ritz-Carlton Orchestra extemporized the plaintive 'What'll I Do?', its saxophonist every so often appending a voo-hoo-dee-oo-doo of musical mournfulness apropos of the warranted intrusion.)

woman who as recently as October 1919 had sacrificed her maiden-name of Elizabeth Clarkson, and possibly her maidenhood, upon her marriage to William Mayhew Washburn, who had done brave deeds, acknowledged by medals, as an officer of the American Expeditionary Force in France but, following his homecoming, had settled into a life of unremitting pleasure, subsidized by doting and, more important, wealthy kin. Elizabeth Washburn had been acquainted with Elwell for six or seven years, having been introduced to him by relatives of hers to whom he was teaching bridge. So far as is known, the acquaintance had never progressed beyond the casual; according to Elizabeth, she had been Elwell's guest but once, and then observably, at a dance that he had hosted in Palm Beach. Again according to Elizabeth, their acknowledgement of each other at the *Frolic* (mutual waving or mere smiles across the intervening tables? — whichever, the tacit greetings were noticed by Viola Kraus) was of the 'long time no see' sort, for it was nearly a year since they had been within acknowledging distance.

Even so — and though her wedding to William Washburn had been an unheralded, quiet affair, attended only by close relatives of bride and groom — Elwell, somehow learning of the wedding, had sent a present of a cheque for $200. The cheque had been paid into the Washburns' newly-opened joint bank account.

However — according, this time, to *William* Washburn: 'on our return from the honeymoon last January, we checked over our wedding presents, and I noticed the Elwell cheque again. I told my wife that, since I was not personally acquainted with Elwell, I did not think the present should be accepted. I drew another cheque for $200, and my wife sent it to Elwell with an explanatory letter.'

William Washburn was not with his wife at the *Frolic*. Nor had he been with her earlier that night, though she had given a dinner-party at their home, attended by his elder brother and the brother's wife and a man of whom the only information subsequently made public was negative, that being that he was 'in no way related to the Washburns'. The dinner-party seems to have been ill-fated: apart from the fact that the intended host did not turn up, at the last minute the table again had to be re-arranged owing to the sudden indisposition of a woman-invitee. The three invitees who did arrive had planned to go on to the *Frolic* with the one who didn't. Elizabeth agreed to complete the quartet, and before doing so left a note for William, in case he returned before two in the morning and wondered where she had gone.

Did Elizabeth and Elwell acknowledge each other's presence in the Aerial Gardens before the *Frolic* began, during the show, or after the performance, while the pit-orchestra played music for dancing? There seems to be no information on that point.

Nor as to whether Viola's hushed spat with Elwell was virtually continuous from its inception at the Ritz-Carlton — or, truced for a time, was renewed, no more audibly to the others, before all of the party descended as part of the cramming of an Art Nouveau elevator to street-level, strolled together through the Shakespearian/Wagnerian foyer, and waited while one of the New Amsterdam's corps of blue-and-gold-uniformed, tips-reliant doormen, thinking that he was acting on behalf of all five, competed with colleagues for the attention of a cab-driver.

One or the other: Viola's hostility was virtually continuous or renewed.

And it may explain why Elwell did not enter the eventually-captured cab. Perhaps he felt tired from straining his ears to catch the tenor of the nagging, did not fancy further strain.

When Philip Bender, owner as well as driver of the cab — an Overland, freshly painted green — set off (to drive, first, to the Lewisohns' home on East Sixty-Third Street, and then to the Ritz-Carlton, there to allow Octavio Figueroa to alight and to receive payment from him for the dog-leg journey plus a pleasing tip of 40 cents), Elwell was still standing just beyond the canopy of the theatre: one smart figure among a decreasing many, all of whom glistened with the light falling from hundreds of yellow bulbs that spelt, more than once, the words

NEW AMSTERDAM
ZIEGFELD
and
FOLLIES.

Elwell would be claimed to have been seen, at various times from a quarter to two on the Friday morning, at all sorts of places by all sorts of people. Here is a sampling, very roughly chronological, of the sites of the supposed sightings:

A dance hall; a whist club; the Biltmore Hotel; a café (in which he was with a young woman); a gambling den; on one of the West-Forties streets (where he was engaged in a brawl); another café — the Montmartre, on Broadway at Fiftieth Street (sharing a table with two men and a woman whose description bore no relation to that of the woman in the other café); Pennsylvania Railroad Station, between Seventh and Eighth Avenues at Thirty-Third Street (the sighter insisted that 'Mr Elwell met two parties at the station at five o'clock, city-time, Friday morning, the station clocks registering an hour earlier'); entering a cab in Times Square (also at five, now in the company of two women, neither of whose descriptions tallied with either of those of the women said to have been in his company, each in a different café, closer to 1.45).

All of those sightings, and all but one of those that I have not mentioned, can be disregarded, I think — on the grounds that they were among the early symptoms of a soon-to-be-widespread wish to 'get in on the act', or that they were optical illusions occasioned by the sleepiness of not-normally-nighthawk eyes, or that they were instances of one of the multifarious usual defects in eye-witness evidence, that being that witnesses who *have* seen some one or some thing at some time tend to assume that the date of the sighting was that which has been publicized in regard to the person or incident.

The sighting that was most probably actual seems to have been pooh-poohed in some quarters for the simple reason that the sighter was a Negro: one of New York County's assistant district attorneys would be quoted as saying that 'no tall man of light complexion [like Elwell] would be safe from identification by a coloured chauffeur' — which is an interesting reverse version of the comment, generally applied by whites to blacks, that 'they all look alike to me'. The assistant district attorney used the word 'chauffeur' in its wide sense, meaning a man who drives a motor-car for a living. The black chauffeur in question was a cab-driver named Edgar Walters, whose always-nocturnal paid travels took him, in yo-yo fashion, from and back to a rank near Times Square. The fact that inquirers about Elwell's movements on the Friday morning approached Walters, rather than he them, is a good start towards believing his statement, which was to this effect:

At about 2 a.m., when he was cruising near the New Amsterdam, he was flagged down by a 'male fare' who asked to be driven to an address on West Seventieth Street. (Walters believed that, only a few nights before, he had picked up the same man and taken him to the Hotel des Artistes, on Fifth Avenue. When he voiced that belief, neither Walters nor any of the inquirers was aware that Elwell frequently dined in the artistically-decorated grill-room of that hotel.) The journey north was interrupted at Sixty-Sixth Street, where Walters' passenger bought a *Morning Telegraph*, the New York paper that was the daily vade-mecum for local addicts of horse-racing, from a kerbside news-vendor. Having slightly misheard his directions, Walters pulled up outside 204 West Seventieth Street — whereupon his passenger called out, 'This is not the place. Drive two doors west of the apartment house.' The 'two doors west' was No. 244: Elwell's house. Walters identified a photograph of Elwell as that of the passenger — who, he recalled, had added only a dime to the fare of 60 cents.

Additional to the reason already suggested for the pooh-poohing of Walters' account by some, there was the fact that, when asked to describe the passenger's apparel, he searched for words and finally came up with no more than 'a business suit'. Well, that was proof-positive, wasn't it, that the coloured chauffeur was lying? After all, there was no doubt that Elwell was wearing dress-clothes. 'A business suit' — laughable. No point in asking the man what he meant by that — whether he meant, for instance, the sort of clothes still worn by some tycoons (Walter Lewisohn among them) who conducted their business in and around Wall Street: or any suit that wasn't casual: or any suit unlike the one that he wore for *his* business.

And then — oh no, not trying to confuse Walters — he was shown a fuzzy snap of Victor von Schlegell. Was that anything like the early-morning passenger? Take a good look, now — notice that *that* man is clean-shaven, light-haired, six feet tall . . . just like Elwell. *Could* it be the passenger? What's that? A *slight* resemblance, you think? That'll be all, my man. There's the door. Find your own way out.

Since *Total* Recall is a conceit of science-fiction, any eye-witness whose evidence extends beyond a glimpse and yet faultlessly follows the known facts must be eyed with suspicion. Even if one subtracts Walters' sartorial error and the confusion imposed upon him by the presentment of the snap of Von Schlegell from the strength of his original account, one is left, it seems to me, with a statement so strong that it could be denied only by a stronger statement. There was none.

And so, relying somewhat on the Holmesian dictum that 'when you have eliminated the impossible, whatever remains, however improbable, must be the truth', I — and you, I trust — can be almost, if not quite, sure that Elwell got home by about a quarter past two.

THE MORNING AFTER

I t had been a sultry night, and would be a scorching day, though a partly-clouded one, with the temperature reaching 90°F soon after lunch-time.

Even by 8 a.m., at about which time Mrs Marie Larsen left her apartment on her way to work, a thermometer in Battery Park, facing across the bay to the Statue of Liberty, gave a reading of 70°. The mark would have been a notch or two higher but for a westerly breeze of 9 knots.

Mrs Larsen had the breeze in her face as she walked to Broadway, there to board a street-car for the journey of about a mile north to Sherman Square — roughly the same distance as she had walked.

Alighting, she hurried along West Seventieth Street. Even so, she arrived at her workplace a few minutes later than she was supposed to. Close to 8.35, she afterwards — long afterwards — reckoned.

While still outside the house, she heard the carpenters banging next-door, in No. 246. 'Enough din to wake the dead,' she thought testily on behalf of her master.

The front double doors were locked.

Mrs Larsen used her fairly new key to open them, and after walking into the vestibule, closed the doors behind her.

She smelt smoke. Not the kind that alarms with thoughts of an accidental fire. Cigarette smoke, she guessed.

She bent to pick up the pint of milk and half-pint of cream from the tiled floor, unperplexed by how they came to be in the vestibule though the front double doors had been locked.

The inner door, that leading to the hall — it, too, was locked. She opened it with her other key.

Closing it quietly behind her, she walked along the hall (tutting the while at the racket from next-door) and into the kitchen, placed the milk and cream on the centre table (thinking that she must remember, and soon, to set them in a bowl of cold water and drape them with a muslin doily, else they would go sour), removed her redundant wrap and hung it over the back of a chair (not on a hook, which might give it an unsightly dent), tied on a pinafore, and, still hatted, retraced her steps along the hall, intending to have the reception room tidied before Mr Elwell whistled through the 'blower' for breakfast.

The door of the room was open.

As Mrs Larsen made to enter the room, she was surprised by an unaccustomed reflection in an ormolu-framed mirror hanging on the far wall, above the mantelpiece.

There was someone in the room.

Mrs Larsen apologized for having very nearly intruded. Then, hearing no reply, but a sound of some strange sort, she ventured through the doorway and, prepared to apologize again, peeped to the right of it.

The bald-headed man, who was wearing only a pair of red silk pajamas, nothing on his feet, was sitting in an upright armchair of the type that is sometimes provided for consorts of sovereigns of unimportant nations; the visible timber of the almost regal chair was daubed with gilt, and the swollen upholstery was of crimson plush, unevenly faded and flattened.

The man's eyes were shut, but the lids quivered, as if in response to a nightmare. He was noisily fighting for breath, his mouth gaping to reveal that he was left with just three teeth, none contiguous.

A cone-shaped hole, never less than the diameter of a .45 bullet, was burrowed through his head, starting, obscenely symmetrical, midway between the top of his eyebrows and the place where, in his younger days, there had been the apex of a widow's peak.

Blood trickled quite neatly from the hole in the forehead. Gouts of it were humped, like the wax seals of a practising clerk, on a letter open in the man's lap, and on the letter's envelope and three unopened ones that had spilled on the carpet, near his bare feet. Also on the floor, between the spilt mail and the windows, 30 inches from them, was the cartridge of the bullet that had made the hole.

There was nothing neat about the emission from the exit-wound. Portions of it rested in resemblance of an ungainly, unravelling ruff on the man's shoulders, and the glistening mess was pricked with splinters of bone and dimpled with lumps of brain-tissue. On the part of the wall behind the exit-wound, and seeming to be suspended from the ragged pit in which the bullet was lodged, there was a swag of blood, mottled in places with brain-tissue that the blood had affixed, and around its perimeter were many red exclamation-marks, two or three of those that had been spurted highest staining the glass that protected the copy of Kipling's 'If — ', giving awful emphasis to the poet's same punctuation at the end.

Perhaps after doing a mite of tidying, though not of her intended sort, Mrs Larsen hastened (which is not to say that she ran) from the house. She did not follow the mode of shrieking 'Murder! Foul Murder!': did not raise her voice at all. Even considering the extreme provocation, such attention-drawing would have struck her as being embarrassingly aberrant.

There were two milk-carts plying the block: one belonging to the Borden Milk Company; the other, driven by a man with the either memorable or easily forgotten name of Jost Otten, belonging to the Sheffield Farms. Otten, it appears, could have done with disciplining by an exponent of the fairly new but already so-called science of Time & Motion: earlier in the morning, he had delivered dairy products to customers on the block — *opening the closed, and so obviously not locked, front double doors of No. 244 in order to place the milk and cream in the vestibule, and closing them again, at about half-past six* — and had then started trundling back, stopping at each house where he had delivered, hoping to extract payment for that and previous mornings' deliveries. By about twenty to nine, when Mrs Larsen returned to the street, he was once more near No. 244.

(Apparently Mrs Larsen locked the front double doors behind her. That would have been characteristic of her carefulness.)

From the last of Otten's subsequent statements:

> Mrs Larsen approached me and said: 'Get an officer quick!' She did not tell me what the trouble was. I jumped out of my wagon and asked Mr Fisher, superintendent of the apartment house at No. 236, to telephone for an officer, and he said he would.

But according to one of Mrs Larsen's subsequent statements:

> I said to the milkman, 'Hurry and call the police. Mr Elwell has been shot.' He did not go or make a move, so I went to the policeman by the drugstore [in Sherman Square] and told him to call an ambulance.

Instead of doing as he had been told, the policeman — Patrolman Harry Singer, Shield-number 8557, who was attached to the local 28th Precinct — stared for a moment at the teller's retreating figure, then sought to catch up with her.

From the last of Otten's subsequent statements:

> I saw Mrs Larsen come down the street, followed by an officer. I headed them off in front of No. 236 and asked Mrs Larsen again, 'What's the matter? What's the trouble?' — but all she did was make an excited gesture; she did not

say anything. Then she and the officer went into the house. I stood outside. He no sooner got in when he came rushing out, and he said, 'Give me a hand with this fellow — he can't live very long.'
    I rushed in and saw the man. . . . The officer told me to get an automobile, and I went out, and there was an auto standing in front of No. 236, and I asked the chauffeur would he take the fellow away, and he kind of reluctantly started to back up his car, and I rushed back to the house again.
    The body was so close to the wall that I could not get a purchase on it to help the officer lift it, and I think I pulled the chair away from the wall for that purpose. I was just about to lift the body with the officer, I being at the head and he at the foot, when the officer said:
    'What's that, a bullet-wound in his head?'
    I replied:
    'It appears to be a bullet-wound.'
    He said:
    'We better leave it.' (the body)
    So I walked outside and stood in front of the house. My wagon was still across the street.

While Otten was feeling relieved that his wagon had not been hijacked, Patrolman Singer thought back to Mrs Larsen's approach to him, and decided that what she had told him to do then was a good idea. He asked her if he might use the telephone in the reception room, and she said that he could try to make it work — a comment explained by the fact that the apparatus was loose from its hanger. She added, either to Singer or to one of the policemen who arrived later, that the telephone had been in that state for a day or so: incoming calls were unaffected by the damage, but sometimes perseverance was needed in making connections — though the extension telephone in the main bedroom was altogether fit. She didn't know whether Mr Elwell had arranged for a repairman to come; he hadn't asked her to see to it.
    After some jiggling, Singer got through to his station, insisted on speaking to Captain Thomas Walsh, outlined his predicament, and was told to stay where he was, without touching anything, and that, separately, an ambulance and some detectives would be at the house before long.
    From the last of Otten's subsequent statements:

> [While keeping surveillance on the milk-wagon,] I saw three fellows coming out of the Elwell house. . . . The three men looked like stevedores or truckmen. I had not seen them go into the house and had not seen them in the house while I was in there.

(The District Attorney of New York County would claim that the trio of visitors of artisan appearance were early-arriving and soon-departing detectives. Well, perhaps two-thirds of the trio was constabularian, but the

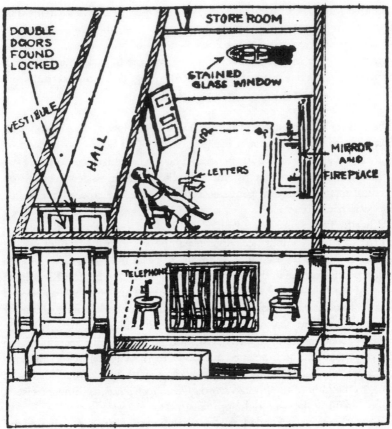

A rough plan that appeared in the New York *News* on Saturday, 12 June 1920

remainder was George Gernant, a mechanic at the garage where Elwell kept his cars, who, happening to be passing when Otten came down the steps, divined from his milk-white countenance that something was amiss so far as one of the Chatsworth Garage's best customers was concerned, and decided to pop in to see if he could help.)

Otten's statement, continued:

> When these three men came out of the house, one of them said: 'That is a funny thing — they can't find the gun.' That was the first I thought of it being a murder. Then I remembered that I had seen no gun while I was in there.
> I stood around talking to customers, but none of them said anything that struck me as important, except a Mrs McCarthy of 243 West Seventieth Street, who said she had read a piece in the paper about Elwell coming home with a bride, and that she had not seen any bride around anywhere.

Either Mrs McCarthy was more observant, retentive, of news items than anyone else who took an interest in the case — including newspaper employees who were paid to read proofs or issued pages of their particular papers — or her mythic-marriage-making was the first blooming of what, by the end of the day, would be an effluent springtide of stunted truths and downright lies about Joseph Bowne Elwell.

The call for an ambulance was received at the Flower Hospital on East Sixty-Fourth Street at 8.55, at least a quarter of an hour after it was first known that an ambulance was needed. Though detectives got to the house before the ambulance, let us, for the sake of trimness, concentrate on medical matters for a few pages — remembering that, meanwhile, much else was happening.

Elwell, still just alive, was taken to the Flower Hospital, tended routinely on the way by an ambulance surgeon named Brennan. No sooner was he there than it was decided that he ought to be at the larger Bellevue, the oldest public hospital in the United States, overlooking the East River from where First Avenue was met by streets around Thirtieth. He was booked into Bellevue at 9.19, and a doctor treated him for shock while waiting for him to die. There was no reason, other than a bureaucratic one, to be precise about the time of his death, and so in a centre section of the delivery note that accompanied his body to the City Morgue, someone scribbled, 'died in less than hour after admission', and at the foot of the note, to the right of the printed words *Death took place at*, someone else, a more careful writer, entered 'approx. 10.00 a.m.'

That Elwell was regarded as a very important victim is indicated by many facts — one being that Dr Charles Norris, vast and grey-bearded, so nautical in appearance that he gave the impression of being marooned when in dry surroundings, went to the trouble of going to 244 West Seventieth Street, simply to view the reception room. And he wasted no time in getting there: he missed seeing the dying man by only a few minutes. The unusualness of such an outing by Norris is expressed on the report-form that he subsequently completed: he needed to cross out the word 'Assistant' from the printed *Assistant Medical Examiner* below the signature-space, and insert the word 'Chief'. Norris had been appointed as the first[1] Chief Medical Examiner of New York City two and a half years

---

1. From *It's Time to Tell* by George P. LeBrun, as told to Edward D. Radin, New York, 1962:

   'Although technically [Dr Norris] was the second man to hold the office, he always has been considered the first . . . because he was the first qualified man, and a fresh breeze blew through what was once the coroner's office. . . . I believe that some of the coroner's

before, in January 1918, and had lived up to his few peers' expectations. As well as looking around the reception room, which was crowded with detectives by then, and taking some measurements (without using a rule), Norris had a few words with Patrolman Singer and, by eavesdropping on detectives' chatter, learned why the public face of Elwell, whom he had once met socially, was more complete than the face of the man who was now being transported to one hospital or another. Upstairs, in Elwell's bedroom, there had been noticed, among other private possessions of his, a *toupee* — no ordinary, off-the-peg sort of toupee, but a crowning achievement of a bespoke-wig-maker: more perfect, even, than its resting-place, a block chiselled at the top in imitation of the contours of Elwell's cranium. And, submerged in misted water in an ampulla of cut-glass, a contraption of *false teeth*, three fewer than a set, that must have taken a dental artificer weeks to match with the slight reality and then to engineer — that must have required practice at uniting by Elwell — that caused one detective, quite toothless himself, to wonder why on earth Elwell, left with three true teeth, had not had them extracted, thus making entire space for uncomplicated dentures.

If one presumes that the cartridge had not been picked up, then Norris bent to peer at it. He observed indentations on the base: the number 17, or the digits 1 and 7, and a circle, which indicated to him that the cartridge had been filled with smokeless powder. (Had he heard that Mrs Larsen, when she first entered the house, had smelt smoke in the vestibule?) Though a detective assured him that there was no sign of the weapon — not in the reception room, at any rate — he looked for it. But he did not find it either.

By the time that Norris returned to the morgue, which was conveniently close to Bellevue, Elwell's body was there. Norris himself carried out the autopsy; but just to be on the safe side, in view of the importance of the subject, he arranged to be observed at work by two other pathologists, an Assistant Medical Examiner named Benjamin Vance, and Dr Otto

---

physicians were graduates of diploma mills rather than reputable medical schools. There were a few whose medical ability I so doubted that I would not have trusted them to prescribe an aspirin for a common cold. These men were political appointees selected for their ability to swing votes and not a scalpel.... The new mayor appointed Dr Patrick Reardon, a former coroner, as chief medical examiner, and explained that Dr Reardon's appointment was strictly a temporary one, which could be made legally for thirty days, in order to give him time to study the qualifications of the various candidates.... Dr Norris was not a political appointee; in fact, his only flaw was an almost pathological dislike of politicians; to him, they were all bad. His appointment had been demanded by the people because he was so eminently qualified. He was recognized as one of this country's outstanding pathologists, had taught the subject at the Columbia University, and had been director for many years of the Bellevue Hospital laboratories.'

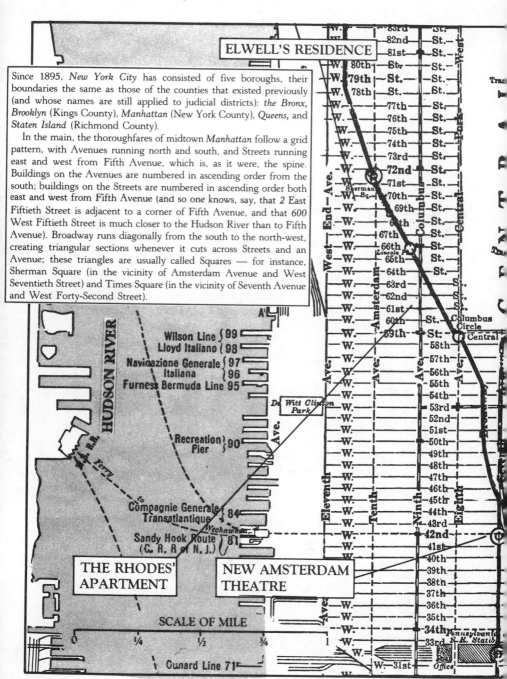

ELWELL'S RESIDENCE

Since 1895, *New York City* has consisted of five boroughs, their boundaries the same as those of the counties that existed previously (and whose names are still applied to judicial districts): *the Bronx, Brooklyn* (Kings County), *Manhattan* (New York County), *Queens*, and *Staten Island* (Richmond County).

In the main, the thoroughfares of midtown *Manhattan* follow a grid pattern, with Avenues running north and south, and Streets running east and west from Fifth Avenue, which is, as it were, the spine. Buildings on the Avenues are numbered in ascending order from the south; buildings on the Streets are numbered in ascending order both east and west from Fifth Avenue (and so one knows, say, that 2 East Fiftieth Street is adjacent to a corner of Fifth Avenue, and that *600* West Fiftieth Street is much closer to the Hudson River than to Fifth Avenue). Broadway runs diagonally from the south to the north-west, creating triangular sections whenever it cuts across Streets and an Avenue; these triangles are usually called Squares — for instance, Sherman Square (in the vicinity of Amsterdam Avenue and West Seventieth Street) and Times Square (in the vicinity of Seventh Avenue and West Forty-Second Street).

HUDSON RIVER

Wilson Line { 99
Lloyd Italiano { 98
Navioazione Generale { 97
Italiana { 96
Furness Bermuda Line 95

Recreation } 90
Pier

Compagnie Generale } 84
Transatlantique

Sandy Hook Route } 81
(C. R. R of N. J.)

THE RHODES' APARTMENT

NEW AMSTERDAM THEATRE

SCALE OF MILE

Cunard Line 71

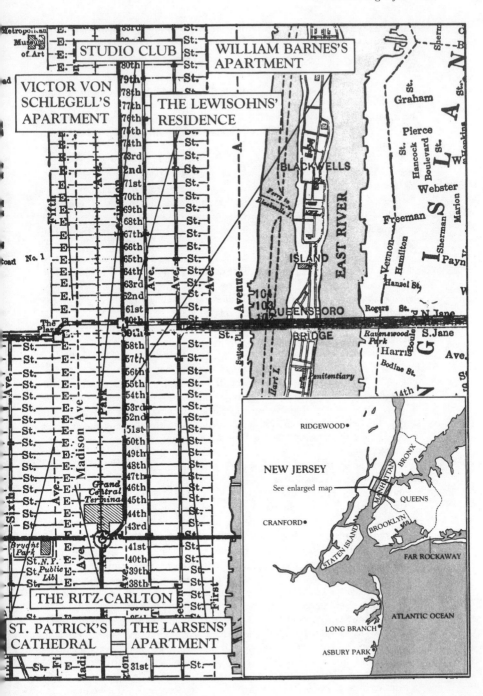

Schultze, a short but almost globular man, once a coroner's physician and now Medical Assistant to the District Attorney of New York County. Extracts from Dr Norris's autopsy report:

Body is that of an adult male, 6' in height; weight 185 lbs.; appearing to be in the late forties; well nourished; well developed; muscular development fairly well marked. Chest flat in front. Only a few thoracic hairs; pubic hairs are feminine in type and scanty. There is no semen present on the penis or on the scrotum.

The hair over the top of the head is very scanty. The line of growth of the hair is placed unusually far back and corresponds to a coronal line drawn from the front of both ears. The forehead is very large, round and prominent.

Heart: There is a large excess of fat in the mediastinum, and an excess of epicardial fat.

Stomach: empty except for a small quantity of brownish black fluid. The mucosa is well preserved.

About 2" above the elbow joint of the right arm, there are two very superficial, reddish coloured abrasions involving only the outer cuticle. They measure approximately ¼" in length by less in breadth. [Author: They were probably caused by Jost Otten when he and Patrolman Singer were trying to lift the body, an attempt curtailed by the latter when he noticed the bullet-hole, or by an ambulanceman, or, prior to Elwell's death, by a hospital-worker.]

Head:

A large wound of exit is situated in the scalp 1" to the left of the sagittal or midline of the skull and 1 to 1½" above the external occipital protuberance. The wound is shaped like a cross with two bars of nearly equal length; transversely it measures .9", the sagittal or antero-posterior branch measuring .8" in length; the lower branch or the sagittal bar is the smallest, being .3" in length. The edges of the wound are somewhat ragged, especially the anterior left flap. Beneath the scalp there is found a large hole in the skull with freely moveable fragments.

Wound of entrance: In the sagittal or median line of the forehead, commencing at a point 1.8" above the bridge of the nose, there is a bullet wound of entrance of the skin, measuring in an anterior-posterior direction .5" and crosswise .4". The general shape of the wound is quadrilateral, with radiations or lacerations of the skin at the four corners of the wound and a fifth laceration in the middle of the left border of the wound.

In the skin of the scalp about the bullet wound and in an area measuring crosswise 3" and antero-posterior 2½", there are a considerable number of small reddish, pinhead-sized spots. A few of these spots, when viewed by a hand lens, are black in colour. Thirty of these marks were counted to the right of the wound of entrance. The majority are present in an area situated .6 to .7" to the right of the wound of entrance, occupying an area the length of which follows almost exactly the sagittal length of the wound; they are much less numerous on the left side of the wound and there are none in an area ½" crosswise posterior to the upper border of the wound; the furthest powder-mark is situated 2" from the centre of the wound in a line drawn at an angle of 45 degrees from the sagittal line of the skull and posterior to the wound. The edges of the wound of entrance show no burns, and no powder-marks were visible, even with hand lens. There is no powder smudging, except for the powder-marks described above, or burns of the skin of the forehead. Relation of the bullet wounds to each other: The bullet wound of exit is situated an inch to an inch and a half above the bullet wound of entrance, the measurement being taken by drawing a plane perpendicular to the line corresponding to the length of the body when in an erect position.

CAUSE OF DEATH: BULLET WOUND OF SKULL AND BRAIN. HOMICIDAL.

The penned underlining of that last word may have been provoked by Norris's discovery, soon after the record of his findings had been typed, that Dr Otto Schultze, the DA's man, whom he had invited to observe the autopsy, had previously looked at the body — and had telephoned the DA and at least one newspaper reporter, proclaiming that Elwell had committed suicide. Schultze seems to have gone off at half-cock. Supposing that his proclamation was reported accurately, its wording indicates that he had not thought to ascertain whether the weapon that had fired the fatal shot had afterwards been found somewhere proximate to the victim. Admittedly, an absence of a weapon is not a sure sign of murder — but still, such an absence does, in most people's minds, require a reasonable explanation so as to make an accusation of suicide tenable.

Dr Norris issued a counter-proclamation. Indeed, so angry was he that he issued more than one: issued them whenever newspaper men were in earshot. His separate explosions are here combined into a single report:

Elwell was drilled through the head, right in the centre of his forehead. There was about three inches of powder grains around the wound, but no powder burns, indicating that the gun had been held at least four or five inches away. He could never have inflicted that wound himself. No man can hold a .45-calibre gun that far away and shoot himself through the head. I can say fairly positively that the muzzle of the weapon was held not more than three feet from his forehead, and probably not more than one foot.

[Author: Norris seems to have known what he was talking about. One of his first actions as Chief Medical Examiner had been to collect types of firearm and discharge them into diverse materials, from different angles and distances, and to assemble his observations as a database of facts concerning visible effects of gunfire.]

I do not believe that a .45-calibre automatic [Author: as opposed to a revolver, from which used cartridges are not ejected] can be fitted with a silencer, but there is nothing in the nature of the wound to support or demolish the idea that one was used.

The upward trajectory of the bullet, causing it to exit an inch or so higher than its entrance, might be taken as an indication that Elwell had his head thrown slightly back and was looking past the muzzle of the weapon into the eyes of his slayer. The circumstances, in my opinion, prove that Elwell was not taken by surprise — at least that the presence of the man or woman in the house was not a surprise to him. He might have been shot without knowing that he was about to be shot. On the other hand, he might have been sitting there, trying to induce the murderer not to shoot. There are no indications one way or the other on that point.

Schultze, making the best of a bad job, issued a statement (and apparently insisted that it be printed verbatim, without omission of the opinionative parenthesis):

> Dr Otto H. Schultze, one of the greatest experts in the United States on the causes of violent death, has studied the circumstances of the shooting in connection with the nature of the wound, and agrees with the conclusions of Dr Charles Norris.

Enough said. Indeed, the presence of the parenthesis made it more than enough: excessively more.

You will recall that Dr Norris arrived at 244 West Seventieth Street only a few minutes after the tenant had been taken away in an ambulance: shortly after nine o'clock, then. In his report on the visit, he noted that he had 'met Detective Finn, Ptl. Singer and detectives from the 28th Precinct'. No mention of the presence of either Captain Thomas Walsh, the senior detective of the 28th Precinct, or Captain Arthur Carey, the head of the New York City Police Department's Homicide Bureau — whom Walsh, anticipating a case of homicide on the basis of what Patrolman Singer had told him over the wonky telephone, had arranged to be informed.

Yet both of the captains were about the house.

Both had arrived, by separate routes, before Elwell's removal. In a few days' time, Walsh would be criticized for not having had the victim photographed as he was found: unfairly criticized, for if he *had* delayed the departure of the ambulance until snaps had been taken, he would probably have been criticized more fiercely on the grounds that, but for the delay, Elwell's life might at least have been prolonged, maybe sufficiently for him to have named his assailant, or even saved, thus diminishing a case of murder to one of attempted murder.

And Carey certainly saw the body in the chair. He examined the soles of Elwell's feet — and having coupled their cleanliness with more general underfoot facts (that the flight of stairs leading to the bedrooms was carpeted; that the lower flight and the floor of the hall were not), concluded that Elwell had done little barefoot walking in the recent past.

It seems likely that though Walsh and Carey were about the house when Norris was there, they were in different parts of it, pursuing separate objectives.

There was no love lost between them.

Walsh, like many other 'general' detectives in the city, objected to Carey's rather condescending manner, envied him for the excellent results he achieved from his publicity-seeking. Carey, whose rather condescending manner *was* a sign that he held himself in high esteem, believed that, as a specialist — commander of what had first been called the Homicide *Squad*, then the Homicide Bureau, since the summer of 1908 — he was perfectly entitled to save his own legs by using 'utility officers' as leg-men. He made it irritatingly clear to Walsh and others that 'murder . . . is a subject which requires the attention of detectives who not only are interested in this special field of investigation but who are equipped for the job by special training and a natural bent'. Another of his dicta — this one spoken without causing offence — was that 'the smarter murderers are, the harder they fall'. The Elwell case did not cause him to add the word 'usually'.

Walsh and Carey were about the same age; the latter had been born, in America but to Irish parents, the father a uniformed one of 'New York's Finest', in July 1865, and so was close to fifty-five at the time that concerns us.

In appearance, the two men were not greatly dissimilar. Walsh sported a moustache; Carey didn't. Walsh usually wore a dicky-bow; Carey hardly ever did in preference to a vertical tie of sombre hue that, perhaps to him unwittingly, emphasized the shining white of his Eton collar. Carey has been described thus:[1]

> He is of average height and build, quick in movement and restless. He might be taken for a man in any walk of life, and this, of course, is the unfailing requisite of the successful man of his calling who must be all things to all men, and at the same time remain inconspicuous. His hair . . . has not greyed, which disposes of the presumption that a man long engaged in unravelling the tangled skeins of the phenomenon known as murder has an inordinately worrisome job. His face too is boyishly plump and almost unlined. His hands are thin and soft, his fingers taper, which invites the surmise that he has artistic ability. . . .
>
> His eyes are blue and constantly in motion. They seldom betray eager interest. . . . A most noticeable quirk in his deportment is that he never turns his back in the presence of someone about whom he knows little. This may be charged to caution.
>
> And he bears the inevitable 'tag', that mannerism with which the inventors of the fictional sleuths invest their manhunters. Carey is possessed of two

---

1. By Howard McLellan, who collaborated with Carey on the latter's *Memoirs of a Murder Man*, New York, 1930. The style of the pen-portrait will remind anyone who has read *Bleak House* of Dickens's description of the fat-fingered Inspector Bucket, a character modelled on the London police-inspector, Charles Frederick Field.

voices. Now his speech is soft and sympathetic, almost soothing, but in the twinkling of an eye it shifts, becomes shrill and demanding, penetrating. . . . This duality of voice is paralleled by another uncanny 'tag'. When his voice is soft and soothing his face is alight with a pleasant smile. Suddenly a hand moves quickly to his forehead, covers it, then comes slowly down across his face. With this movement the smile vanishes. His features become stern and unyieldingly serious. . . .

Outside, on the manhunt in the field, he betrays another characteristic mark. He comes for the first time upon the scene where murder has been done. He looks about with an all-inclusive glance at the body of the victim, the setting, and invariably in a quiet voice remarks:

'Well, this is the picture I get.'

We know most of the components of the picture Carey got from his all-inclusive glance around the reception room. One that has not been mentioned may be important:

A *Cogswell* — which is described in a dictionary of furniture as 'a 20th-century easy-chair with a fully upholstered back and seat, and a low upholstered platform. The sides are not enclosed. The arm stump rises from the platform and carries an overstuffed arm pad.'

The upholstery of the Cogswell in the reception room was doubly damask, being a figured linen the red colour of a damask rose.

As Carey entered the room, the Cogswell was ahead of him, diagonally facing the almost regal chair, and a yard or so from the far left-hand corner.

That 'yard or so' was peculiar, Mrs Larsen had already told a detective, only when he had invited her to comment: normally, the Cogswell was tucked into the corner, making it a fireside chair.

The detective had theorized that the displacement might mean that the criminal had pulled the chair out so as to hide behind it prior to Elwell's entrance. He imparted the theory to Carey, who straightway made it his own.

Carey's all-inclusive glance also took in two dead cigarettes, both of which had died without being stubbed. One was in an ashtray on the table beside the almost regal chair. Subsequently, an anonymous friend of Elwell's was reported in the press as saying that a detective had told him: 'The cigarette, of Elwell's usual brand, made to order for himself, had been lighted at the wrong end, indicating probable mental stress' — in Elwell, presumably, though the fact that he was a heavy smoker, and that his especial cigarettes were not cork-tipped, rather goes against the idea that he was customarily pernickety about lighting his cigarettes at the right end (always supposing, of course, that the maker wrapped them in paper with a printed device at one end, showing that that was the right end, the other the wrong).

The second cigarette-end impressed all of the detectives (or perhaps all but one). It rested on the mantelpiece, had burnt itself out on coming into contact with the polished rosewood. It was not one of Elwell's own brand: the police were so impressed by its evidential value that they kept its make secret. When first observed, shortly after nine o'clock (Mrs Larsen, remember, had arrived at about 8.35), it was moist from its smoker's spittle. Had it been left behind by the criminal? Had he or she (after forsaking the Cogswell hiding-place?) talked with Elwell while both smoked cigarettes, Elwell his own brand, the criminal his or her over-the-counter sort? The mind-picture of a conversation brought to an end by a .45 bullet, before either of the speakers' cigarettes was ready for stubbing, was generally pleasing among the detectives. During the investigation, the Vital Cigarette kept popping up in police statements. The mystery surrounding its make made it seem as vital a clue as the axe-blade in the Borden case, as the robin's-egg-blue notepaper in the Molineux case (in which Carey had been involved). None of the detectives would ever admit that, almost certainly, it had been left to burn out by one of their number. Of course, if that were not so, it *was* an extraordinarily significant clue: there can have been few people in New York, let alone of Elwell's acquaintance, who were such slobbery smokers that cigarettes discarded by them for at least twenty-five minutes, when the outside temperature was over 70°, still showed signs of their salivation. One wonders why a Wanted notice was not broadcast, seeking information regarding the whereabouts of a person who, though almost surely bibbed, could not travel far without dribbling a trail rather like a snail's.

The letter, dappled with blood, that lay open in Elwell's lap was from Covington, Kentucky: from his trainer, Lloyd Gentry, reporting on the fitness of horses of the Beach Racing Stables that were running in races during the long Latonia summer meeting that had started on the previous Saturday. So far, only two of Elwell's horses had run: L'Errant had finished fourth in the fifth race on Monday, and (as Elwell would have known, probably before looking at the results pages of the *Morning Telegraph* that he had brought home with him) Free State had been placed in the third race yesterday.[1]

Gentry's letter held no apparent clues towards an explanation for the shooting of its recipient. But the fact that it and the three unopened letters had been delivered and — virtually without doubt — picked up by Elwell

1. If, in the letter, Gentry was optimistic as to the chances of the next two horses that were running, in separate races on the following Wednesday, betting detectives taking his words as tips would be disappointed: DeClasse finished eleventh in the second race, and Flags came in tenth, and last, in the fifth.

was very important indeed. That was soon realized by the detectives, one of whom was despatched to Postal Sorting Station N, at Broadway and Sixty-Ninth Street, there to ascertain the name and present location of the postman. In those days, when a main aim of public services was to serve the public, there were several postal deliveries each day. By the time the detective got to the sorting station, the postman who had done the early-morning round including the far-western blocks of Seventieth Street was out on another round. Guided or at least accompanied by the superintendent of the sorting station, the detective found the postman; the superintendent, nicely free from pride, took the postman's satchel and continued deliveries from it; and the detective hurried the postman to what was, by then, the murder-scene.

The postman, Charles Torrey, had delivered mail thereabouts for a quarter of a century. Asked to think back to that day's early-morning round, he stated:

> I delivered at 244 West Seventieth Street at about, well, between 7.20 and 7.25 o'clock.
> I tried the storm door [he was referring to the front double doors] and found that it had not been locked. This was unusual, because on every other occasion that I had tried it, I had always found it locked. [*Author: Which makes one wonder why he persevered in trying it.*]
> I had always been in the habit before that of shoving the mail under the bottom of the storm door. There is quite a space which permits quite a thick envelope to enter. But on this occasion I found the door unlocked, and I turned the knob that opened it and threw the mail, some four or five letters, into the vestibule, and closed the door. I did not drop the catch on the lock.
> I heard no sound in the house and I saw no person in or about the house. I rang the bell twice to indicate that I had left mail. I did not blow a whistle as I am not in the habit of blowing a whistle in that street.
> I then continued down West Seventieth Street, delivering the mail from house to house up to West End Avenue, the corner. Then I turned and started to deliver mail on the uptown, or odd-number, side of the street, and I arrived on the opposite side of the street, just across from 244, at about 7.40 a.m. I did not then see any person going into the house or coming out of it. I am certain of this, because in delivering mail to A.W. Baird at 239, which is just opposite the Elwell house, I go up the stoop to deposit the mail, and I always turn — but, in turning, I did not see anyone come out of 244, and, in fact, I did not observe anything out of the usual.

And so the police had the beginnings of a time-table that, omitting the word 'about' in relation to the times, looked like this:

6.30   Jost Otten delivers milk and cream. (Front double doors *unlocked*.)
7.25   Charles Torrey delivers mail. (Front double doors *unlocked*.)

8.35 Marie Larsen arrives (front double doors and inner door locked) and finds Elwell shot through the head, one letter of the early-morning mail in his lap, its envelope and three unopened ones on the floor near his feet.

Dr Norris, when asked, guessed that the shot had been fired between 8.20 and 8.25. The sole basis for the guess was another guess: that Elwell could not have survived the injury longer than a hundred minutes: he died at about ten o'clock — ergo, the wound was inflicted no earlier than 8.20. It seems probable that if Mrs Larsen had turned up, say, half an hour later than she did, Norris's reckoning of Elwell's staying power would have dwindled by thirty minutes.[1]

---

1. In his book *Mostly Murder* (London, 1959), the great Scottish pathologist Sir Sydney Smith recounts a case that throws doubts on Norris's guess(es):
'An elderly professional man walked out of his private hotel in Edinburgh one winter evening and . . . returned the next morning at half-past seven and rang the bell. When the maid opened the door she saw that he was wearing his overcoat and hat, and carried his umbrella over his arm. She also noticed considerable bloodstains about his face. Alarmed, she called her mistress. The old man, however, said, "Don't worry. I will go upstairs and have a wash." He placed his umbrella in the hall-stand, hung up his hat and coat, and walked upstairs to the bathroom, where he collapsed and lost consciousness. The police were told, and he was taken to hospital. He did not regain consciousness, and died three hours later without having made any statement.
'There was no mystery about the cause of death. The man had been shot in the head. The bullet had entered under his chin. . . . The wound tracked upward, passed through the brain, which was severely damaged, and came out on the left side of the frontal bone of the skull. The exit-hole was one and a quarter inches in diameter, and its size and shape suggested a .45 revolver bullet. . . .
'The police . . . followed a trail of blood to a public garden on the opposite side of the street. In these gardens was a shelter, and on the seat in this they found a .45 revolver, later identified as the property of the dead man — and in front of the seat a large pool of blood. A bullet-hole, surrounded by fragments of brain and bone, was observed in the roof of the shelter just above the seat. . . .
'It had begun to snow at six in the morning, and a track of footprints and blood-spots was clearly outlined in the snow from the shelter to the grass in front, continuing in a circle for about 165 yards, and returning to the shelter. . . . An examination of the bloodstains inside and outside the shelter and of the tracks in the snow indicated that the wound must have been inflicted some time before six o'clock. It seemed that after shooting himself he had rested in the shelter with his head hanging forward, and thus had produced the pool of blood in front of the seat. Then he had walked round the gardens and returned to the seat, where he rested again for a while. Finally, at half-past seven, he returned to the hotel. . . .
'I am quite certain that in such a case many of us would be prepared to give an opinion that the injury would lead to instant unconsciousness and rapid death. Yet it is established without a shadow of doubt that this person, after shooting himself, remained alive for several hours, walked about for a considerable distance, made his way home, carried out definite purposeful acts, and spoke reasonably and intelligibly before consciousness was lost. It is a striking example of what can be done after a severe injury to the brain.'

Newspaper reporters of the case (and subsequent writers of articles about it) would turn Norris's guess as to the time of the shooting into the 'fact' that Elwell was shot between 8.20 and 8.25. The closer the time of the shooting to the arrival of Mrs Larsen, the more dramatic the story — to the extent of causing readers to shiver on behalf of Mrs Larsen, who, if she had been punctual, might have bumped into the exiting murderer, might have been bumped off by him or her.

The literary aggrandisement of the Norris Guess so that it became an Accepted Fact would make one of the small mysteries of the case seem more mysterious still. The small mystery was that no one outside the house heard, or afterwards remembered hearing, the bellowing explosion of the .45 automatic. Most peculiar, that. The police made house-to-house inquiries. So did reporters. Neighbours quizzed one another. But the oft-repeated question never once received the unsurprising answer. The small mystery grew a little when a detective, emerging from the house, mentioned that though, despite the heat, the windows of the reception room had been kept closed, one could hear from within, and without straining one's ears, the sound of footsteps in the street — why, he had even heard, word for word, the conversation of two female passers-by! Even more peculiar, then, that the explosion had gone unnoticed.

But the small mystery seemed further expanded, to at least twice its proper size, by the ostensible narrowing-down of the time when the shot *ought* to have been heard — by, for instance, the decorators working in the house next-door from 8 a.m. (and loitering outside for five or ten minutes before that starting-time); or one of the roundsmen (among others, the two milkmen, a deliverer of journals, a deliverer of groceries); or the street-cleaner, Charles Spratley; or an Italian, known to his customers only as Joe, who washed down stoops at the fee of a dime a dousing (according to Mrs Larsen, the stoop of No. 244 was wet when she arrived — but according to Joe, when told what Mrs Larsen had said, he had been nowhere near the stoop that morning: so perhaps there really was something to the police belief, based on the damp cigarette-end, that the killer was an extravagant drooler); or one of the many people who, between eight and half past that hour, walked along the street on their way to work.

Idées fixes have a way of engrossing the mind away from alternatives. It doesn't seem to have occurred to anyone that the unhearing of the explosion within fifteen minutes of Mrs Larsen's arrival might mean, not that the small mystery was enlarged, but that the gun was fired earlier in the morning — when fewer people were outwardly about, when more of the neighbours were sound asleep, and, perhaps specially significant, before the arrival of the decorators of No. 246, some of whose workaday

A posed photograph of Jost Otten outside 244 West Seventieth Street

noises, none as noisy as the noise from a .45 automatic, were aggravatingly audible in No. 244.[1]

The focusing of attention on the guessed period had the effect of deflecting attention from the important part of the evidence of Jost Otten — which was very important indeed. His statement that the front double doors were unlocked at 6.30 a.m. was strongly supported by the fact that when Mrs Larsen arrived two hours later, the milk and cream he had delivered were *inside* the vestibule. If he hadn't put them there, who had? If he *had* put them there, it stood to reason that the doors were unlocked at 6.30.

One cannot feel as confident that the doors were still unlocked at 7.25, when Charles Torrey delivered the mail. Torrey's assertion that he had always found the doors locked when he had tried them in the past, but found them unlocked on that particular morning, suggests a choice between three possibilities: that 'always' was an exaggeration or that he was a man of stupid habits or that he was just plain stupid. None of the possibilities allows entire acceptance of his statement. *If* one believes it — and if one *cannot* believe that Elwell, returning from his night out, unlocked the front double doors, then *lifted the catch*, walked through the vestibule to the inner door, unlocked it, then *lifted the catch*, and, with the house now quite unnecessarily insecure against intrusion, unconcernedly went upstairs to his bedroom — then consequently one believes that the murderer was in the house at 7.25.

The more sensible belief in Otten's statement means that one also believes that the murderer was in the house at 6.30 — for two simple reasons, one being that the front double doors, unlocked at 6.30, were locked some time before Mrs Larsen arrived, the other being that, apart from the murderer, the only person who could have locked them after 6.30 was Elwell. If, inexplicably, Elwell lifted the catch on the lock as soon as he returned from his night out or at some time between then and 6.30, why on earth should he have bothered to *drop* the catch at some time after 6.30? On the other hand, if the murderer used keys to enter the house or, having knocked or rung, was admitted by Elwell, he or she, thinking ahead to the possible need for a hurried exit, might have lifted the catches on the front double doors and the inner door — and, when leaving, dropped the catches so as to delay, if only by a minute or so, the discovery of the crime.

1. The other next-door house — the one to the east: No. 242 — was unoccupied. Its tenant, the well-known operatic soprano, Anna Fitziu, was away on a concert-tour in South America.

It is, I think, not only permissible but necessary for full understanding to refer at this point to the keys to the doors at the front of the house — though, in doing so, I shall mention some information that did not come to light till the investigation was several days old.

When, early in the investigation, Mrs Larsen was asked how many sets of keys there were to the front double doors and the inner door, she said that, so far as she was aware, there were two — hers, which she had used to unlock the doors when she arrived that morning, and Elwell's. That answer, she was soon afterwards told, was wrong: Elwell had two sets — the set that he carried and a spare set, found in a vase on the mantelpiece in his bedroom.

Was *three* the definitive answer, then?

Well, no. Among the factors complicating the key-accountancy were the following:

1. The identity of the locksmith who changed the locks following the attempted burglary in December 1919 was never surely established. (The probable reason for the uncertainty is that press speculation that the murderer had acquired a duplicate set of keys was rife before official attempts were made to find the locksmith; and he, fearing a charge as accessory before the fact, decided that a still, or even lying, tongue made a wise head.)

2. Elwell's chauffeur Edwin Rhodes said that the locksmith, whoever he was, had handed him the 'master set', he had handed the keys to Mrs Larsen, and she, after trying them, had handed them back, saying that they were useless, and 'demanding' replacements; and so he had ordered replacements from another locksmith, who, less security-conscious than he should have been, had left them under the mat at the top of the stoop.

2a. None of the above references to Mrs Larsen was true, she said.

3. But, speaking of keys left under the mat, she recalled that, just before Christmas, Elwell had left a set of keys under the mat so that William Pendleton, his former partner in the Beach Racing Stables, could let himself in 'on a matter of business' while he, Elwell, was absent.

3a. Apropos of the above recollection, Pendleton snapped: 'Perfectly absurd! Mrs Larsen doesn't know what she's talking about. I have not seen Elwell for eight months or more, when I had dinner with him one evening.' [Even if that had been true, which it wasn't, it was no answer: Mrs Larsen had not said that Pendleton had seen Elwell — on the contrary, she had said that it was *because* Elwell was otherwise engaged that he had left the keys under the mat.] 'I never was very intimate with him, for I am a family man and could not afford to run about with him.'

(Pendleton's snappishness is understandable considering that Mrs Larsen's recollection had been retailed by the press as addendum to stories implying that he was near the top of the investigators' list of person suspected of having murdered Elwell.)

4. According to Arthur Bishop — who had been chauffeur to Elwell and his wife, and to Elwell alone for a short while after his separation from Helen — Elwell had 'often' left keys under mats for 'his many' visiting lady-friends. Maybe he had grown more cautious over the years; maybe, post-burglary, he had never left keys under the mat outside 244 West Seventieth Street — not even for William Pendleton. But supposing he had not changed his keys-leaving way, it would have been simple for a visitor to procure a counterfeit set of keys — by arriving so early as to allow time to pop, with one set of keys, to a locksmith, and to return with two; or, having thought to bring a piece of plasticine, or some such cast-making substance, by making impressions of the keys, such impressions to be copied in iron at any time at all.

5. A week or so after Mrs Larsen had been scolded for saying that there were two sets of keys, the scolding on account of the discovery of a set of keys in a vase on the mantelpiece in Elwell's bedroom, one of the detectives thought to try the discovered keys in the locks, and found that they did not fit — they were not a spare set of the present keys but an undiscarded set of the previous ones.

Of course, it is possible that there *were* only two sets of the new keys — and that, if there were further sets, either licitly or slyly made, none of those was used by the murderer. The front double doors — and, for that matter, the inner door — may have been unlocked all night, perhaps even from before Elwell's return from the *Midnight Frolic*. Or they may have been unlocked by Elwell at some time following his return but before Jost Otten delivered the dairy produce. An embellishment of the latter possibility is that a pre-6.30 ring of the bell caused Elwell to unlock the inner door by lifting the catch, and (having peeked to ensure that the caller was either someone of respectable-artisan appearance or someone with whom he was extremely intimate, for, being proud of his prepared visage, he would not have wanted anyone else to espy him without his toupee and dentures) to walk through the vestibule to the front double doors and lift the catch on the lock, thereby allowing entrance to the person who would murder him. Having committed the crime, that person departed, dropping the catch on each of the locks as he or she did so. There seems no doubt that the murderer entered and exited through the front doors: the police found the outside door of the kitchen locked; Mrs Larsen said that she had not touched it since her arrival.

The investigators never did establish whether or not there were more than two sets of keys to the doors at the front of the house. Their efforts in that regard were dogged by reporters; were hampered by some reporters' efforts to come up with keys-finding scoops. After a week or so, during which press accounts of investigations by diverse bands of investigators were almost invariably stippled with references to keys that, 'according to reliable sources', *had* been found, might be findable, or had been 'destroyed by the anonymous culprit', no newspaper reader can have had the foggiest idea of the exact plurality of still-suspected keys that one reporter, speaking of species of clue, audaciously singularised as 'the key to the great mystery'. As confused as were readers of any of the papers, including the New York *Times*, a reporter for that paper compared the Elwell case to a best-selling novel by Earl Derr Biggers, described by its publishers as 'an unusual tale, full of unexpected happenings'. The novel was entitled *Seven Keys to Baldpate*.

Having glanced around the reception room, Captain Carey toured the rest of the house, following in other detectives' footsteps.

In the basement, he observed that, front and back, the doors were locked, the windows clasped, the grime on the panes not impressed by a single fingermark. He learnt that one of the other detectives, venturing from the house, had examined the grilles on the windows and doors, and the locks on the latter, without finding an indication of tampering.

On the ground floor, nothing arrested Carey's attention other than that the outside door and windows of the kitchen were secure.

The next floor was even more unrewarding to his various glances. One of the other detectives had already removed an item from a drawer of the desk in the front room, Elwell's den. Some of the remaining contents of the desk would interest, if not the investigators, then newspaper reporters: even some newspaper *readers*.

A further climb, bringing Carey to what he would describe in his reports as 'sleeping quarters, etc.', was worth the effort. Having strolled along the passage from the landing, he was confronted by the drinks table in the passage running at right angles. He may have reflected that Elwell, like most people in America, himself included, had not taken the Volstead Act too seriously.

He entered the rear bedroom, the larger of the two: Elwell's.

Another detective, one of Captain Walsh's men, was using the extension telephone on the bedside table. Mrs Larsen, whom the detective had not told that she might sit, was hovering nearby. The detective had in front of him the item removed from the desk in Elwell's den. An address-book. The detective had been guided to it by Mrs Larsen when he had asked her about Elwell's next of kin and main business assistant; was consulting it so as to call Elwell's father, at his house in Ridgewood, and William Barnes, at his apartment on East Fifty-Fifth Street.

The detective was not presently concerned with the many other entries in the book. But during the investigation, almost all of the persons named and found to be alive, whether in Manhattan or elsewhere, would be interviewed — at home or at a place of work, at the scene of the crime, or in the premises of law-enforcers; some would be interviewed more than once, and for some of those the respective interviews would not be in a single setting; some of the interviews would be conducted so fiercely as to be worthy of being called, as they were by eavesdropping or invited reporters, 'third-degree sessions'.

Never mind that Elwell's address-book was bisexual of entries: reporters' leading questions about it were rewarded with police quotes — or 'no comments', which were more rewarding still, for they set no boundaries around reportorial surmise — and, before long, the presence of women's names became 'a concentration upon the distaff'. That phrase, too subtle to satisfy for more than a few editions, grew by easy, all too easy, stages into the assertion that the address-book was a *Love List* (which in those days, when the word *gay* was uneuphemistic, could only mean that the lister was of the sex opposite to those listed). Reporters, having learnt while still cubs that the best way of giving authority to a concoction is to invent supporting statistics, contradicted one another as to the number of names on the Love List: 400 seems to have been the ultimate, but the favourite was 53 — simply because, counting the Joker, that was the number of playing-cards in a pack.

But, as I have said, the telephoning detective was unattentive of all but two entries, neither for a woman in Elwell's life, when Carey entered the bedroom.

Almost always when he had entered bedrooms on business relating to murders elsewhere, he had noted, first, the beds. Even if that had not been so, he would almost certainly have given precedence to the bed in Elwell's bedroom — would have had little choice, since the bed was more eye-catching than any other piece of furniture in the house. Massive stump-legs upheld the base for the double-sized mattress, at the head of which was a scroll-topped board of polished mahogany; a semi-crown, also of mahogany, was screwed to the wall a yard or so above the bed, and draping from it on each side to each end of the head-board was a pleated length of lavender-coloured satin; the bedspread, also of satin, was wide-striped alternately in purple and black.

A corner of the spread was turned back, revealing that the pillows and sheets were of silk, but it was clear that the bed had been lain on rather than slept in. On the floor beside the bed was a *Morning Telegraph*, that day's, folded to a page itemizing the runners and riders in that day's horse-racing fixtures.

Writing long afterwards, peculiarly in the present tense, Carey noted other mute recipients of his all-inclusive glance around the bedroom:

> [Elwell's] toupee and false teeth . . . are on a chiffonier. . . . His dress clothes are hanging upon the back of a chair four or five feet from the foot of his bed. On a small table near by is a whiskey flask. On a couch is about four hundred dollars in currency, a watch, pin, and other jewellery.

Carey's slight recitation is added to, and tinctured by, a snippet that appeared in the New York *News* five days after the murder — the writing of a reporter who, with similarly police-favoured rivals, had been allowed to view Elwell's bedroom:

> Effeminacy was evidenced in the boudoir pillows of filet lace on the red couch . . . the upholstery of rich velvets, and the fittings of his dressing-table, which was laden with expensive perfumes and powders.

Reverting to Carey — and to his strangely present tense:

Piecing together what has been observed up to this point the picture is a little more complete. Elwell probably lay upon the bed in his pajamas with blouse open,[1] reading the racing news. . . . For some reason he arose, probably quite suddenly, for the newspaper was thrown upon the floor. He went downstairs in his bare feet. . . .

Mrs Larsen has been looking through the house and finds that nothing is missing. If robbery were the motive of the slayer it is evident that the plan miscarried. Yet robbery cannot be dismissed from consideration.

Again I refer to patterns in my mind. They tell me that house-breakers, especially those who rob unoccupied residences, are frequently surprised in the act and kill or wound their discoverers, hurrying from the house without carrying anything away, especially when the weapon they use is a pistol whose report may be heard throughout the house and on the outside. We proceed a little farther with the picture. What probably happened was this: Elwell, with his mind on his race-horses and the races that were to be run as shown by the *Morning Telegraph*, learned that the morning mail had arrived. It was customary for him to receive weekly letters or reports from Gentry, his trainer. His mind therefore was on his horses as he lay upon the bed. He threw down the newspaper and went downstairs.

1. Elwell's pajama-jacket was unbuttoned at the top when Carey arrived. But the unbuttoning was almost certainly a result of the brief efforts of Patrolman Singer and Jost Otten to move him.

This and subsequent cartoons are from issues of the New York *News* between 14 and 20 June 1920.

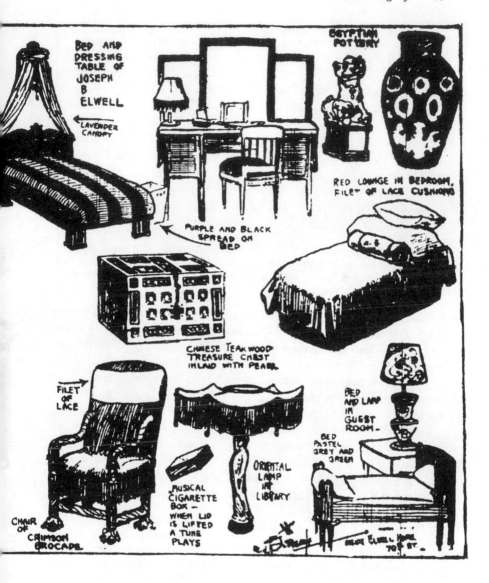

BED AND DRESSING TABLE OF JOSEPH B ELWELL

LAVENDER CANOPY

EGYPTIAN POTTERY

RED LOUNGE IN BEDROOM, FILET OF LACE CUSHIONS

PURPLE AND BLACK SPREAD ON BED

CHINESE TEAKWOOD TREASURE CHEST INLAID WITH PEARL

FILET OF LACE

MUSICAL CIGARETTE BOX — WHEN LID IS LIFTED A TUNE PLAYS

ORIENTAL LAMP IN LIBRARY

BED AND LAMP IN GUEST ROOM —

BED PASTEL GREY AND GREEN

CHAIR OF CRIMSON BROCADE

BED ELWELL HOME 70 ST.

Carey walked out of Elwell's bedroom. The patterns in his mind should have been like the patterns in a kaleidoscope, unresistant to change by outside influence. They were not. His patterns were fixed — immutable except for embellishment. If he had heard of E.W. Hornung's remark that 'there's no p'lice like Holmes', he had decided that he was exceptional to it; if he had heard of Holmes's dictum, 'It is a capital mistake to theorize before one has data', he had ignored it: he had broken the basic rule of all sorts of investigation, that one must not deduce any of the answers before one knows all of the questions. His further investigations in the Elwell case would be directed towards confirming the patterns in his mind rather than seeking the solution to the mystery.

Carey entered the room at the front of the house. What he saw — or rather, sees — is

. . . a guest bedchamber. The bed is made up. It has not been slept upon. The window in this room is locked and dust upon its sill indicates it has not been opened in some time. In a closet is found a number of women's garments — lingerie.

That word 'lingerie' would please the reporters no end. What with two other French, and therefore naughty-sounding, words — 'boudoir' and 'negligee' — they only needed some padding words, any would do, and they had a story that no news editor could refuse. It was lovely that, as the words were French, they could be printed in italic — meaning that they were foreign, not that they were pointed out for the benefit of salacious readers. None of the reporters cared that the traces of femaleness in the guest bedroom indicated that female guests had slept there — while Elwell slept in the other room. The reporters' style of composition would be aped, though usually more sparingly of italics, by most subsequent writers of articles on the Elwell case: by Russel Crouse,[1] for instance, in *Murder Won't Out* (New York, 1932), a book that Alexander Woollcott had urged him to compile:

It was a bedroom furnished, obviously, for a woman. There was a sort of oriental splendour about it. On the dressing-table were all the powders and unguents that are the modern feminine complexion. In the closet were filmy feminine garments — lingerie, pink pajamas, négligé, boudoir cap, slippers.

---

1. Himself a New York reporter in 1920 — though never, it appears, of the Elwell case. He would become exceedingly rich from his collaboration with Howard Lindsay in the writing of the play *Life with Father* (the first Broadway production of which ran record-breakingly for over seven years from 1939, and which ran for just over a year in London from the summer of 1947) and from his collaboration with Lindsay in the presentation of Joseph Kesselring's comedy *Arsenic and Old Lace*.

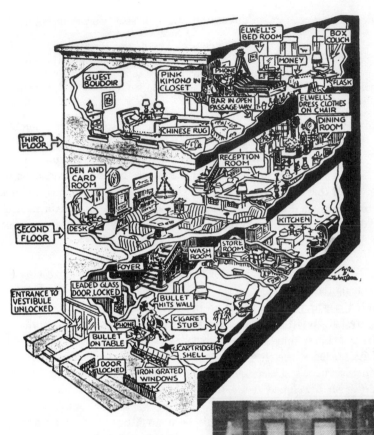

(*top*) A drawing, by no means
accurate, that illustrated an article
by Sidney Sutherland that appeared
in *Liberty Weekly* in 1929

(*bottom*) 244 West Seventieth Street

Mr Crouse goes on to discuss an effect of such purple reporting:

> In the twinkling of a winking eye Elwell, the [bridge] lawgiver, was forgotten. Solon became Don Juan. What might once have been whispered was shouted now. It was something about which a sophisticated New York could talk without blushes. The last remnant of Victorian reticence had gone away to the recent war and never come back.

Having glanced around the guest bedchamber, Carey risked smirching his dapperness by climbing into the loft, hoping to find evidence that a specialist burglar, a loft-worker, had made a downward entrance into the house. But the scuttle on the skylight was intact. Noting footmarks on the dusty floor that were of sizes different from those that he had just trodden, he made a mental note to tell Captain Walsh that he and his men really should know better than to plod markedly in places unvisited by experts like himself and, speaking modestly, a couple of others.

At a quarter past eleven (Elwell had been dead for about seventy-five minutes), the telephone in the reception room rang. Captain Walsh nodded meaningfully at Mrs Larsen. The meaning was that she was to take the call and, if the caller asked to speak to Elwell, to find out who was calling, saying nothing to suggest that Elwell was permanently unavailable.

Mrs Larsen should have been rehearsed. As it was, she picked up the phone, listened, and then, quite forgetting to ask who was calling, blurted out that Mr Elwell had 'met with a terrible accident'. The caller hung up.

But not on any sly account. The caller was Florence Ellenson, who earlier in the morning, at her friends' home in Asbury Park, had waited for Elwell to phone her, as he had promised on the day before: 'It worried me because he was always so punctual. I left Asbury Park on the 8.30 train, arriving at the Pennsylvania Depot in New York at 11.10, New York time. I called his home. The housekeeper was very nervous, and I became so, too.' And so she put down the public phone, and sought a taxi to take her to 244 West Seventieth Street. The cab-driver's name was Jacob Strauss.

Already, the steps at the front of the house and the railing guarding the basement area were hidden by reporters and cameramen: the first of many day-and-night shifts of them. All of them — no exception — wore straw boaters. They looked like a small unsporting version of the Henley Regatta. Despite the heat, hardly any were in shirt-sleeves. A rough sketch of the pressmen whiling away their stints is given by four of five items that helped to fill an Elwell-gossip column in the *News*:

Pennsylvania Station

A score or more of reporters and photo-graphers grace the vicinity. Some of the reporters seem very 'edgy'. One wonders if among them there may be some Edgar Allan Poe who will reconstruct the truth about the tragedy and bring the murderer to justice. It has happened before.

* * *

A famous writer, who refers to reporters as 'small fry', declares that, in a dream, it was revealed to her that Elwell was shot by some one whom he did not know.

It is a strange world indeed.

Out of the past she came again —
Revenge was within his grasp —
He would crush her —
He wanted to see the anguish in her eyes —
Her sobs would be music to his ears —
He planned to trample her beauty —
See THE NEWS tomorrow for further news
of THE WOMAN HATER.[1]

1. Author: In case you are as confused by this item as I was when I first saw it, I should explain that it referred to a fictional serial-story.

A note of love and romance enters the plot. She has red hair and blue eyes. All the reporters, special writers, photographers and detectives are in love with her.

She is greeted with acclaim. There is rivalry to see who shall win her smiles. She is Miss Joan Larabee and she is four years old.

How pleasant it is in the midst of this story of gaming, deceit, illicit love and crime to find this little ray of sunshine.

* * *

Much excitement is caused by the 'discovery' of spots, which appear to be blood, on the front steps. But the hope that a clew has been found proves futile when detectives pronounce the spots paint.

The cab carrying Florence Ellenson slowed down, and she saw the crowd of pressmen: 'When the chauffeur opened the door to let me out of the car, he said: "Don't you know that there was a man murdered here this morning?" When he told me this I could barely believe it, and I was afraid at first to leave the car. I was nervous: I became hysterical. As soon as I recovered myself, I went into the house, where a detective met me.'

The *News*:

Detective Sergt. Tom Donohue [who, in December, had led the posse of policemen who arrested the burglars] comes out of the house and is pounced upon.

'Tom, for the love of Mike, tell us who the woman is,' pleads one tall young man.

'What woman?' innocently asks Donohue.

Florence Ellenson: 'The detective showed me a chair and said: "Do you know that Mr Elwell was murdered while sitting on this chair this morning?" He then quizzed me, and I was so unnerved at the news of Elwell's death that I hardly knew what I was saying.'

Having concluded that Florence exhibited the fluster of innocence, the detective told her that she could leave, and called a cab for her, using the phone in the reception room. (That phone was now giving no trouble on outgoing calls. It must have been mended by a handy detective, for if a repairman had called, the *News* would surely have noticed him. The reporter from the *Times* could hear the detectives *making* many calls, some to 'far-distant places'. Though he may have been more dog-eared than his rivals, the fact that the phoning was audible to him was an addition to the things that seemed to complicate the puzzle of why the explosion had not been heard by an outsider.)

Florence Ellenson was the first among the first women-visitors to the house following the murder to be given a false name, intended as a protection against press harrassment, in official bulletins on the investigation. The false name (or *nom d'amour*, as one French-preferring reporter put it) was rather flimsy: 'Miss Ellis' — eventually deciphered by the press, but not until Florence was stewardessing on the steamer *Horizon* on Lake George. One of several egg-or-hen questions that cannot be answered is whether the eye-witness who professed to have seen Elwell meeting 'two parties' at Pennsylvania Station at 5 a.m. on the day of his death[1] so professed before or after the appearance of press reports that 'Miss Ellis' had arrived at the station at 11.10 a.m.: perhaps because of the eye-witness's statement, the police checked Florence's statement — and found it honest in respect of the time of her departure from Asbury Park and the time of her arrival at Pennsylvania Station.

Florence Ellenson may not have been the first woman-visitor to the house following the murder. At some time between about half-past nine and midday, another woman called.

I have assumed that the last *News* item I quoted — that which includes the plea from a tall young reporter to Detective Sergeant Donohue, 'Tom, for the love of Mike, tell us who the woman is' — applied to Florence Ellenson. But I may be wrong. Donohue's reply — 'What woman?' — may have been truly innocent: perplexed. But it seems likely that the woman-visitor other than Florence arrived — and departed — quite early in the day, before many reporters were outside the house.

She walked through the open doors and started up the stairs just as Mrs Larsen was coming down. The two women knew each other. Some days later, when Mrs Larsen was at last forced to recall the diagonal encounter, she said that the visitor 'came up all excited, and said, "Oh, what accident, Mrs Larsen?" and then, without waiting for an answer, continued up the stairs to the first landing — where, seeing detectives (apparently for the first time following her arrival), she either spoke to one or several or straightway turned on her heels and exited from the house.

Her identity will be revealed in due course.

Elwell's father (who was now seventy-two) and William Barnes had

1. See page 70.

Reporters outside 244 West Seventieth Street

been telephoned at roughly the same time. Though Joseph Sanford Elwell had had to come all the way from Ridgewood, New Jersey, he arrived only a few minutes later than did Barnes.

Emerging from the house after being questioned by detectives, Barnes was only too happy to be questioned by reporters. He gave the impression that he didn't mind what they said about him so long as they got the nature and small extent of his part-time employment by Elwell right: No matter how the reporters pronounced *valet*, he had certainly not been Elwell's — and, excluding this morning's visit, he had only been inside the house half a dozen times. That low number was hard to reconcile with the certainty of subsequent assertions: 'Elwell would always take off his toupee and remove his false teeth just before going to bed. From my knowledge of him, it would be absolutely impossible for him to do that if there was anyone in the house with him. It shows positively to me that he was ready for bed when he went to the door in answer to the bell and that he was not expecting a visitor. . . . He was a man who would not show any more fear or excitement in a case of this kind than he would in looking across the table at an opponent in a card-game.'

Elwell Senior told detectives that he was sure that his son had never owned a gun. Shown a blackjack that had been found in a drawer, he said that his son had bought it five or six years ago, 'when a man paying attention to his former [sic] wife had threatened him'.

Leaving the house, Elwell Senior refused to talk to the assembled reporters. Later, however, the carefree libelling of the dead man by those reporters and others caused him to issue a brief statement:

Joseph Bowne Elwell was the best son anyone could have in the world. He always provided well for his mother and me in our advancing years, and he was considerate. He was entirely self-made. We had little to give him. All racing and the like is a gamble. Why single him out as bad if he made big sums on his horses?

Helen Derby Elwell was not asked to the house on the first morning of her widowhood. She heard the news from reporters. Asked for an epitaph, she spoke with a bitterness that she would regret when, thinking practically, it occurred to her that *de mortuis nil nisi bonum* was sound advice considering that her parents-in-law were the sole beneficiaries of her husband's, Richard Derby's father's, will:

Vanity and bad rearing account for his peculiar behaviour. His gambling and racing activities ruined our domestic happiness. He was a piker. When it came to a showdown he was afraid to come across. He chased the phantom of impossibilities. He claimed incorrectly to be a broker. Each new face was a new possibility for Joe. He was a chicken-chaser.

If by 'chicken-chaser' Helen meant that Elwell was more attracted towards young women than towards older ones, she received excessive support from William Olcott, a former district attorney and a present member of the Studio Club, who visited the house on the Friday morning and, when leaving, told reporters that Elwell had revised a precept of Sir William Osler's into the declaration that 'women should be chloroformed after reaching the age of thirty'.

Unaided, surely, by the confetti of remembrances of Joseph Bowne Elwell, a writer for the *Times* would sum up *his* view of the man:

. . . Should even the murderer come forth tomorrow and confess, the curious life and mental and moral makeup of his victim would still remain planted in the popular imagination.

New York is full of 'types' and 'characters,' but they all fall into several general classifications. The 'rounder' type, the 'bachelor' type and the gambler type are well known. They have common characteristics. The 'society butterfly' type is equally well known and as easily classifiable.

Elwell was all these — plus something more. It is just that plus that puts him as a type in a class of his own. It is just that plus that forbids designating him as a 'rounder', a 'gambler', or a 'society butterfly'.

He had character. He was intelligent. He was suave. He knew the meaning of *savoir faire*. Everybody knew him. He apparently had no enemies. His characteristics on the surface were as clean-cut as a cameo.

And yet this man whom everyone called 'Joe' lived an odd and mysterious life. Beyond the race-track, the stock market, the whist table, the cabaret, the touring car Elwell, there was another Elwell — an Elwell who deliberately left his wife and son to shift for themselves, and chose to live alone in a big house; an Elwell who bobbed up unexpectedly anywhere and disappeared like a jack-in-the-box; an Elwell within an Elwell, so to speak; a secret, a remote, even a misanthropic Elwell.

In Palm Beach, in New York, at Belmont Park, who ever met the real Joseph Bowne Elwell? The veil that surrounds his murder may never be pierced until the police have got on the track of that other Joseph Bowne Elwell, of whom his friends knew nothing; that other, mysterious Elwell, who was cloaked by the everyday Elwell as completely as Dr Jekyll hid Mr Hyde.

He was a man of masks. Men such as he who are invariably suave and polite are always masked.

What was he hiding?

There is another side to the Elwell mystery. Before we entered the war, New York was America's greatest all-night city. The bars, the restaurants, the cafes, the cabarets, the dance halls, the 'Bohemias', and many gambling 'joints' ran for twenty hours out of twenty-four, and some doors never closed. In those days a man of the Elwell type attracted no attention. They were common enough. They lived, practically, in the public eye.

The 'all-night town' is gone — ostensibly. It is gone for the great masses of men

and women. But there is still a subterranean
all-night town that goes on just the same.
The type of man of which Elwell is an
example is the type that invites crime.
Charm, money, solitude. These three things
combine to draw, by a subtle psychological
law, out of their lairs the criminal and
perverse instincts of this supreme mystery,
the human being. . . .

By one o'clock in the afternoon — or, to put it another way, by the time
that Elwell had been dead for three hours — the police investigators had
learnt only a little about the 'society butterfly' side of the victim's life.
They did know that Elwell had planned to go to the Ritz-Carlton the
night before. Florence Ellenson had said that, during her conversation with
him on the phone, he had mentioned a date at the Ritz. And William
Barnes had said that Elwell had told him the same thing. No doubt some
of the detectives had recognized the probable importance of putting two
and two together: *a night out at the Ritz-Carlton* plus *the night-out clothes
draped over the back of a chair in Elwell's bedroom* might equal *assessment of
the maximum time that Elwell had spent in the house before the arrival of Mrs
Larsen.* It appeared to be just a matter of asking his companion or
companions at the Ritz-Carlton the time of his leave-taking.
Barnes had given the police the name of the person who had extended
the invitation to Elwell:
Mr Walter Lewisohn.
A name to conjure with. The name of one of the highest and mightiest
in Manhattan. In America.
No one had telephoned Mr Lewisohn; no one had sought him at his
office or at his home. Perhaps none of the score of detectives (an actual
score: two reporters had counted them and come up with the same answer)
had been able to tear himself away from whatever he was doing.
Shortly after one o'clock —
But no; let us have Captain Carey's version:

The bell of the telephone on the table in the reception room rings.
'Get that call!'
A detective steps to the telephone.
'Yes, this is Mr Elwell's home,' says the detective. 'Who is calling him?' The
detective jots down the name and address of Walter Lewisohn, who is the
speaker at the other end of the telephone. He is a member of one of New York
City's most prominent and wealthy families. He advises the detective that
Elwell had an engagement with him to go motoring with Mr and Mrs
Lewisohn and friends at 1 p.m. today. It is past that time. They have not heard

from Elwell. They were out with him the night before and at that time today's engagement was agreed upon.

The detective states that Elwell cannot be seen. The telephone receiver is replaced upon its hook. And that detective hurries to talk with Mr Lewisohn.

The final sentence of Captain Carey's account is factually faulty in a Mohammed-and-the-mountain sort of way — that is, unless one assumes that the detective did hurry off, intending to talk with Mr Lewisohn, but not fast enough to reach his destination in time to carry out his intention. Within a quarter of an hour of the telephone call, Walter Lewisohn arrived, chauffeur-driven in one of his cars, at 244 West Seventieth Street. He was accompanied by his wife and sister-in-law, and the three of them were chaperoned by Walter's lawyer, Lyttleton Fox, a partner in the firm of O'Brien, Boardman, Parker & Fox.

The Lewisohn party remained in the house (glimpsed in Elwell's den by reporters standing across the street, taking a breather from the crush) for nearly three hours, till soon after four o'clock. During that time, Inspector John Cray of the Detective Division, the most senior officer in the house, took 'informal statements' from Walter and Selma Lewisohn and Viola Kraus. They were, in police terminology, 'possessed of reciprocal alibis' for longer than the period that turned out to be material: Walter said that he had been with or near Selma since the evening of the previous day, Selma said the same of him, each said the same of Viola, and she said the same of them. And so none of them was a suspect in the investigation. With that out of the way, but not until the fastidious Fox had polished the note-taker's notes of it, they spoke of their mutual friend Joseph Bowne Elwell's last night out.

ANY NUMBER CAN PLAY

The riddle of the slaying of Joseph Bowne Elwell might have been solved quickly had not a large number of individuals and several packs determined to find the solution; or even if some of the individuals and all of the leaders of the packs had been less keen to be the solver than to see the riddle solved. A prevalence of solipsism hindered anyone's chance of finding the answer. Too many cooks toiled, each in his own kitchen, each keeping some of the ingredients of his broth secret, lest any of those certain ingredients were just what a rival needed to make his broth exquisite, warranting the award to him of the Blue Ribbon. There was but one Blue Ribbon in this contest. It was vital to make sure that no one else received it, because success for another would mean failure for oneself. And that latter fate was too depressing to think about. Another's triumph, one's own defeat, had to be prevented at all costs. Costs in terms of Justice? Oh, those. Come to think of it, there *were* those, weren't there? Never mind.

From the start (and this was not unique to the Elwell case), the detectives of the local precinct went their investigative way, Captain Carey and his men went theirs – not at all concerned that the unspecializing detectives had got ideas above their station, were crazed with the notion that they, unaided by experts, could solve a murder case that was not of the ubiquitous thud-and-blunder sort: if it so happened that they stumbled upon the truth, and had the sense to recognize what they had stumbled upon, the homicide detectives would still be made to seem the victors — by Captain Carey, who would compose the final report on the case, and who could exact favours from bylined journalists.

The press was harmfully influential in several respects. Star muckrakers and sob-sisters, seconded to themselves-seconded Elwell-stories editors, vied with regular rivals and with crime reporters on their own papers and others for scoops. The no-holds-barred, billfolds-ajar scavenging for scoops must have produced tall tales; may have aided Elwell's killer by alerting him or her to leads that official investigators should already have followed, might soon be following. When scoopless, members of the Fourth Estate pin-stickingly guessed avenues that the official investigators would be exploring before long: it did not concern them that some of the official investigators, grateful for any suggestions and/or eager for pats from the press, turned the guesses into self-fulfilling prophesies — continued to do so even after dozens of suggested avenues had proved to be cul-de-sacs.

A stereotype of The American Reporter of the 1920s, the one that depicts him as a time-server using his bread-and-booze-winning tasks as practice in aid of a dream that he will one day settle down to writing The Great American Novel, seems largely supported by a study of what the papers said about the Elwell case: a numerical analysis of the romantic 'news' thrown up in the course of a month would show a volume at least equal to the size of an unedited novel by Thomas Wolfe. All of the fiction was accepted as fact by some, and some of it was accepted as fact by all. An 'if it's in the papers it must be true' belief was the spark for several of the errant actions of several of the official investigators. That the reactions of those grown men to press fictions were infected by the fictions goes some way towards explaining why those men now seem Natural caricatures of works of slight art such as 'Inspector Cramer', 'Mr Tutt', and 'Dr Thorndyke'.

The splurges of Elwelliana that, promised on placards, boosted the circulations of morning papers on Saturday, 12 June,[1] the day after the murder, were perceived by some who read all of them (not thereby becoming much wiser than if they had read just one) as harbingers of a bandwagon: an ooh-and-ah-provoking bandwagon with a long journey ahead. The journey would be long, whatever happened. If the riddle turned out to be impossible to solve, the investigation would last a long,

---

1. The editors of the following day's papers, the cumbersome Sunday ones, had a difficult decision to make: whether to give front-page precedence to Joseph Bowne Elwell or to Warren Gamaliel Harding, who on Saturday, by arrangement between leading villains of the Republican Party, meeting in a suite at the Blackstone Hotel, Chicago, (which they incidentally but legend-inspiringly filled with cigar-smoke), was nominated as the party's candidate for the Presidency of the United States of America. Harding expressed his incredulity at being nominated (which that year, the Democrats being unpopular, meant that he was destined for the White House) thus: 'We drew to a pair of deuces and filled.' None of the editors of the Sunday papers seems to have been struck by the poker-play link between the dead and the living cynosures; most chose not to opt, and presented a frontal double-bill of sensations.

publicity-attended time; an arrest and charge would be followed by legal proceedings, and there was no knowing how long they would occupy the courts and the front pages — an interminable time if the defendant was both guilty in the opinion of the trial jury and rich enough to retain lawyers to argue against the verdict, the sentence, or both, in at least one of the umpteen courts of appeal.

The earliest boarders of the bandwagon, and for most of its journey the turn-and-turn-about conductors of it, were two assistant district attorneys, John Joyce and John Dooling. Neither was gratified by the other's company *en route*. Joyce, the Assistant DA in charge of the Homicide Bureau, was the more entitled to be aboard. Dooling seems to have used his credential as *an* assistant DA as a pass; when denounced as an interloper, he sat tight till the District Attorney himself ordered him off — but later, ignoring Joyce's renewed protests, jumped on again.

The District Attorney, exhausted of ambition at the age of fifty-eight, was never among the passengers. His name was Edward Swann. A Democrat, he had been elected to his office in 1916, when he had resigned as a judge of the Court of General Sessions (though, as is the American way, he had retained the title of 'Judge'). He finically imbricated his grey hairs in a vain attempt to make them look sufficient, and wore pince-nez continuously — not, it seems, because he was lost without them but because their centre-piece hid its unsightly guttering of the bridge of his nose.

He looked strict, but cannot have been, else the feud between Joyce and Dooling would never have shown. That the latter was only ostensibly subservient to him is indicated by the fact that though Dooling alighted from the bandwagon at Swann's request on behalf of Joyce, he boarded again at the next stop.

Going by faded pictures of Joyce and Dooling, they looked much alike — of about the same height, stocky, pudgy-faced; but Joyce's hair was darker and unglossed — and of a similar age not far past forty. Their physical alikeness and their dislike of each other put one in mind of a scaled-down version of Tweedledum and Tweedledee — who, you will recall, 'Agreed to have a quarrel.'

Both of the assistant district attorneys were well aware that renown resulting from good deeds that were apparently unblemished by political ambition could be used towards the achievement of political renown. There were many extreme instances of that. Long ago, Ulysses S. Grant had been elected President by voters grateful for his generalship in the Civil War; and, more recently, Theodore Roosevelt's effective presidency of the Board of Police Commissioners of New York had been a springboard towards governership of the State, and that towards the Presidency. Till the bartering in the smoke-filled hotel-suite in Chicago, General Leonard Wood, joint-commander with Theodore Roosevelt of the Rough Riders during the Spanish-American War, was a front-runner for the Republican nomination for the Presidency.[1]

Joyce, a traveller on the Elwell bandwagon uninterruptedly from start to finish, was, so to say, and thus to adjoin metaphors, a machine-gunning self-advertiser, getting his name into many press accounts and ensuring that it peppered many of them. Dooling was a howitzer, less frequent of utterance than was Joyce but booming the utterances — as when, hardly settled on the bandwagon, before he had grounds for forming an opinion, let alone giving an opinionative statement, he announced:

> Whether . . . the killer . . . was a subordinate or friend, the evidence, I think, indicates that he gained admission because he had some routine business with Elwell, and that he murdered Elwell unexpectedly, while Elwell was sitting there reading his morning mail. I doubt if Elwell would have opened the door to a person whom he had reason to regard as an enemy. The possibility that someone came home with him and stayed with him until the shot was fired, or that someone with a key entered the house and awaited him, seems more unlikely.

Before Elwell was buried (on Tuesday, 15 June, with few reporters observing the ceremony, for the body had been smuggled from the Manhattan morgue to a funeral parlour in Ridgewood, and the time of the funeral as well as the fact that it was to be held at Ridgewood's Valleau Cemetery had been kept secret), the investigative schism between the detectives of the Homicide Bureau and those of the 28th Precinct had been noted by Inspector John Cray and mentioned by him to William Lahey,

---

1. *Plus ça change.* . . . Perhaps because career-politicians are almost invariably scurvy, American voters display a touching hope that success is versatile, a notion that strikes most Englishmen as being as quaint as that the England cricket team might win test-matches under the captaincy of someone with a shelf of cups won at county badminton tournaments. One thinks of Thomas Dewey, whose attempts to 'bust' gangs in New York in the late 1930s, first as a special prosecutor, then as District Attorney, were publicized to such an extent that he was chosen to govern the State; and who, having followed Theodore Roosevelt's route, stood for the Presidency in 1944, when he lost to Franklin Delano Roosevelt, and again in 1948, when most experts and all pollsters considered him the winner till the votes were counted in favour of Harry S. Truman. And of Dwight D. Eisenhower, whose success as a military commander led to his becoming President. And, of Richard M. Nixon, whose prosecution (some, myself not among them, now say persecution) of Alger Hiss was the main cause of his being picked as Vice-President under Eisenhower. A few of those who, twenty-two years later, in 1974, helped towards terminating Nixon's Presidency turned the attendant glory to political advantage.

the Second Deputy Police Commissioner, who, hoping to bridge the gap before he needed to pass worries about it farther up the hierarchy, called Captains Carey and Walsh to his office for a talking to; and while he was about it, spoke sternly to Acting Captain John Coughlin, the head of the Brooklyn detectives, who at the request of Inspector Cray had gathered information about Elwell's acquaintances in the borough but was unwilling to part with it. The substantive captains and the acting one promised to mend their respective ways. Coughlin, being insecure of rank, was as good as his word; but as soon as Carey and Walsh were out of the office, their incompatibility was clear again.

And quite as clear as their determination to go their own unsweet ways *vis-à-vis* each other was the determination of each of them to cold-shoulder the two interfering assistant district attorneys. No doubt neither Joyce nor Dooling would have co-operated with any interested parties other than reporters if the heads of the two police investigations had spoken revealingly to anyone other than their subordinates; but the separate and silent beavering of Carey and Walsh may, if a single reader is so charitable, be seen as an excuse for the similar subtlety of Joyce and Dooling.

One instance of how subterfuges by some investigaters caused rivals to waste their time is this: at the start, Joyce and Dooling were led to believe, or led themselves into believing, that the bullet that had killed Elwell was an army-issue .45, and (as was extensively reported in the press) they independently spent many hours, and their helpers days, in tracing ex-army acquaintances of Elwell's — only to learn, not from Carey or Walsh but from a newspaper, that, on the very first day, the cartridge found on the floor in the reception room had been sent for examination to William Jones, a former captain in the New York Police Department who was now a consultant on firearms, and that he had promptly reported that

the marking, 'Rem-U.M.C.,' on the cartridge is the mark of the Remington arms company. . . . If it were United States Army ammunition, it would have the initials of the arsenal and the date of manufacture on it.[1] There are three weapons in which it might have been fired, the Colts' revolver, the Smith &

---

1. 'Rem-U.M.C.' stood for Remington-Union Metallic Cartridge (Company). What had become of the number 17, or the digits 1 and 7, that Dr Charles Norris said that he had observed on the cartridge during his visit to the scene of the crime? Was the Medical Examiner mistaken, was William Jones sent a wrong cartridge, did he confuse the cartridge be had been sent with another on his work-bench, or did he notice the number of digits and fail to refer to it or them in his report? The last possibility is the most likely — made more so by the absence of a reference to the circle-sign (also observed by Norris) that the cartridge had been filled with smokeless powder.

Wesson revolver, and the automatic Colts' pistol. . . . The fact that the cartridge had been ejected . . . indicates that the weapon used was an automatic, which ejects the cartridge after every shot. Had the murderer used a revolver, it would have required a special action on his part to throw out the one shell. . . . There is no silencer which can be used on any of the three weapons. . . . A woman would have been unlikely to be in possession of such a weapon, but she could have fired it. Any woman that had shot one before could have used it.

[*Author: True, Jones's comments did not erase the possible military connection, but as the Colt .45 (Model 1911) automatic pistol was the standard handgun of the United States Army but not specific to that army, and as the cartridge was not army-issue, the connection was far less firm than either Joyce or Dooling had thought.*]

By the start of the second week of the investigation, the state-first, think-later performances of the two assistant district attorneys, which were in large measure due to one's desperation not to seem like an echo of the other, were causing them to make almost as many 'I never made any such statement' statements as original statements. Some of the correcting statements needed to be corrected: for instance, when Joyce complained that he had never voiced the opinion that the murderer was being shielded by a friend, he added that if he received any information about a shielder, he would give that person the Third Degree — and subsequently needed to state that he had never stated that he would consider the use of Third Degree methods of interrogation.

Perhaps that correction of a correction was believed by a few. However, stories about a shielder — or about many, a vast conspiracy of them — continued to appear. But when, those stories having been debased by their repetition, suggestions were made that the shielders were being shielded by the District Attorney, he, Edward Swann, decided that enough was enough. *He* made a statement, assuring the press and the public that there was no shielding going on so far as he and his subordinates were concerned, and adding:

A great many persons have written here that the statements in the press are so contradictory that they can make nothing of the case. The newspapers have complained that they have been receiving conflicting reports as to the progress made in the case.

Hereafter, all information will be given to the press myself, and in my absence by my chief assistant, Alfred J. Talley.

Since it is reasonable to suppose that Swann's edict was made known to the two men who had made it necessary, it is reasonable to conclude from their continuing chatter that each of them decided that as the other would not heed the edict, nor would he. For once, each was glad of the other's verbosity. Whereas solo statement-making might be construed as insubordinate, deserving of dismissal, two voices stating disharmoniously provided protection on the basis of Both for One, One for Both.

In the early days, Swann did get a few words in edgeways, but they were less satisfactory to the reporters than the issuances that the reporters had asked him to stifle. Though Joyce and Dooling contradicted themselves and each other, they spoke positively, opinionatively, helpfully towards the enlargement of headlines about the SLAIN TURFMAN/GAMBLER/SEDUCER/SOCIALITE, &c. Swann, on the other hand, was unsensationally negative: he queried pressmen's theories simply because they had no foundation, destroyed others by quoting hard, opposing facts, and hardly ever gave implicit support to any of the remainder by moving his features sufficiently to justify the use of phrases like 'a thoughtful expression' or by drooping his shoulders, which could be taken as a shrug — 'meaningful', 'non-committal', or 'expressing a wish to remain silent until investigations that are thought to be proceeding have been brought to a climax'.

Why, even Swann's references to offers of help from the public were negative — indicating that he wished that people would mind their own business. When the case was a week old, he delayed a press conference so as to talk in private to a woman visitor, and then snapped at the gathering of reporters:

> That was one of the absurd things that we have to investigate. Somebody sent us information that this lady knew all about the case and, in fact, that her husband had committed the murder. It turns out that they never heard of Elwell. About a thousand persons have given us similar information. We have

had stacks of anonymous letters, each naming somebody against whom the writer had a grudge. I guess nearly everybody with a grudge has tried to deliver the Elwell murderer to us. All sorts of people who never knew the man have been named.

Unless someone intelligent among the DA's staff was given a chaff-sorting task, the excessive number of worthless tips would almost certainly have caused any that were worth-while to be disregarded. That assertion is based on a maxim of forensic science: If you don't expect to find *anything*, don't expect to find *something*. The task had to be assigned to one person only, for if two or more took a hand, it was unlikely that any concurrence or association of tips would be spotted, thus allowing the possibility of finding a sum greater than its parts.

That the communications were treated at all methodically seems to be ruled out by subsequent amused remarks from Swann's right-hand man, Alfred Talley, that were divulged, equally amusedly, by reporters for the *Times*:

> The District Attorney's mail has been fat with occult tips. The crime has evidently made as great a sensation in pure ether as in the muggy atmosphere of New York. . . . More than a score of persons stand accused by name on ouija-board evidence. With impartial ferocity the little instrument has levelled its ghostly accusation against men and women in equal numbers. . . . In spite of their more than mortal knowledge, the ouijas apparently have followed the news closely. . . . Several have described the manner of the crime in great detail, sometimes giving independent conceptions of the tragedy, but usually confirming the supposition that the newspapers have a large psychic circulation, and occasionally being curiously misled by inaccurate statements which have been published. . . .
>
> Some letters, which bore evidence that the writers were crazy, were consigned to the 'nut' file, which is kept for its possible future value in dealing with lunatics. . . .
>
> The keys to the Elwell home seem to be the favourite topic for deduction by the letter-writing sleuths. . . . Among the many reasons offered by the correspondents for the murder of Elwell was the writers' belief that the racing man owed large sums that he

refused to pay; then there are letters which declare he was killed because he sought to collect large sums owed to him. . . .

Women in various cities are given as old-time acquaintances of Elwell in some of the letters, and trips as far west as Chicago and as far south as Florida were advocated by the authors as likely to disclose the motive for the crime and the murderer. One man stated that if the District Attorney would offer a reward of $10,000 the murderer would be led into the Criminal Court Building. Another man, writing from New Jersey, enclosed just a tintype, vintage of Coney Island 1892, with the legend across it, 'This is the criminal'. Still another communicant forwarded a pair of dice, stated that he knew Elwell well, and expressed his belief that the dice had something to do with the case. . . .

One writer . . . confessed that he had murdered Elwell and added the information that the automatic pistol would be found at the bottom of the Hudson River.

Another writer, a man with an office in the financial district, revealed that the Elwell murder had become a topic of general discussion at weddings in this city these days. He said he had heard a man at a wedding say that Elwell made a practice of turning his affairs with married women to profit, and that at one time Elwell was heard to tell a fashionably dressed young woman that she could 'lose the money at bridge'. Elwell was then seen to put a roll of bills into his pocket, reported the downtown letter writer.

In another issue of the *Times*, another of its reporters — straight-faced, this one — imparted the views of criminologists:

Violent criminals are divided into three classes: defectives, insane persons and mental superiors — mental superiors who, overwhelmed with the sense of wrong which they believe the law cannot adequately remedy, inflict the supreme punishment by their own hand. The police, as the records of prisons and asylums show, have been more or less successful in dealing with the members of the first two categories. It is natural that this should be so; but it is also natural that the police should not be so successful in dealing with the third category — they are handicapped by the latter's mental superiority. . . .

The motive of the defective would have been robbery. The evidence shows that there was no robbery or attempted robbery. The evidence that the shot was fired by a madman is equally contrary. There were no signs of a struggle in the room or the house. . . .[1] There was nothing to show that an attempt had been made to divert suspicion, as might have been indulged in by a defective or a madman.

Leaving his readers to wonder at the mental superiority of murderous mental superiors who made no attempt to divert suspicion, the reporter moved on to uncriminological matters that we are already aware of.

On Wednesday, 16 June, another of the *Times* Brigade ordered to gather 'all the news that was fit to print' about the Elwell case reported on a claustrophobic time he had had the day before, under the heading **25,000 JAM ELWELL BLOCK**. The number does not seem to have been a misprint, for, as you will see, it also appeared in the report; but one is dubious of the reporter's arithmetic: even if there was an 0 too many, that would still have crammed very large crowds into quite a small area.

About 25,000 persons yesterday visited the block in West Seventieth Street between Broadway and West End Avenue, where the Elwell house is located. Several traffic patrolmen were on duty at both ends of the block to regulate the motor cars attracted to the neighbourhood of the murder.

The detectives have been consistently annoyed with all sorts of cranks going to the house to volunteer their services in solving the mystery. . . . A woman of 60, who told the detectives she had come all the way

---

1. Author: I skip at this point because that damned wet cigarette is mentioned yet again. Only in passing. One wouldn't mind it if the criminologists had used its wetness in aid of a suspicion that it was discarded by a defective rather than a detective.

from Chicago because she was interested in the case, advised them to pin their faith in the ouija board and employ it until the mystery was solved. . . .

One man, a doctor, 94 years old, who refused to give his name, spends most of each day in front of the house in company with newspapermen.

Murder cases have a way of enlisting persons with Bunyanesque or Happy-Family-like names, the role-appropriateness of which would never be allowed of the names of characters in crime novels. One thinks of Mr Sherlock, the serendipitous Nemesis in the first Brighton Trunk Case; of Mr Death, the holder of the vital clue in the Müller case; of Chief Superintendent Proven Sharpe, the solver of several English West Country cases; of —

The three association-names are sufficient as provers of the point; a long list would only be handy for a game of Trivial Pursuit for keen readers of murder stories. But such a list would be deficient without the name of the elderly doctor who refused to give it to the reporter for the *Times*. He was a Cook (Roland of that ilk) — and of the too many extra-investigative cooks in the Elwell case, he meddled most influentially.

Considering his refrain, it is understandable why he preferred to remain anonymous. Supposing that he was not an egomaniac, even any of those would have shown a certain shyness if they had had the temerity to say what he said, which was this:

Dr Norris ought to be sacked for having failed to do the most important thing that should have been done at the autopsy, *viz.* the photographing of Elwell's eyeballs — for it was a well-known fact that dead retinas retained photographic images of the last thing they jointly saw. Dr Norris needn't have taken a photograph of the photographs if Elwell had been shot from behind; but as Elwell had been shot by someone in his full view, a pair of pictures of the murderer had been available for anyone with a camera suited to taking snaps of dead eyeballs to photograph, having remembered to load the camera with ultra-sensitive film that, when developed by an untra-sensitive developer, would reveal what the retinas had retained. There might still be time to remedy Dr Norris's sin of omission. The body should be exhumed — at dead of night would be best, since there was no telling whether or not eyeballs grown accustomed to the darkness within a coffin had their images wiped out by unexpected light.

All but one of the reporters who did stints in West Seventieth Street wished that the oracular Dr Cook would go away — or, better still, bequeath his eyeballs to researchers at Bellevue, and instantly drop dead. The reporter who had no such wish worked for the *Times*. Presumably he was not the crowd-counting one. Whichever of them he was, he seems to have visited his newspaper's morgue, looked in the drawer marked E for Eyeballs, and there found a cutting that suggested that someone in the *Sûreté*, unrelated to Jules Verne, had, if the translator had got it right, commented on the *possibility* of what Dr Cook was broadcasting as ophthalmic fact to visitors to West Seventieth Street, however many of them there were. Consequently, the *Times* published an article, 'How Paris Would Treat the Elwell Case', that contained implicit criticism of Dr Norris for having neglected to photograph, stare into, or even lift the lids of Elwell's all-revealing eyes.[1]

---

1. The retina-retention notion is said to have been conceived by a nineteenth-century laboratory worker who saw what he thought was a likeness of the flame of his bunsen-burner on the retina of a frog that he had just killed on behalf of science.

The notion is widely assumed to have impressed either Frederick Browne or William Kennedy, whichever of those villains it was who on 27 September 1927, in a quiet road between Romford and Ongar, north-east of London, fired four bullets into Police Constable George Gutteridge — two of them through his eyes. The eyes are — or, at any rate, used to be — favoured secondary targets of gunmen employed by Mafiosi to 'wipe out' people deemed to be offensive; but that may have had a *pour encourager les autres* inspiration as opposed to a superstitious self-protective one.

The day after the article appeared, Dooling was placed in an awkward position by yet another of the *Times* reporters, who, catching him in the presence but not the company of detectives, asked him to comment on the article. Not wishing to speak ill of the produce of a journalist — particularly not of anything by a journalist employed by the *Times* — Dooling temporized, muttering uncomplimentarily about the French police but raising his voice to say that the account of their methods had interested him 'very much'. So grown in confidence as to be willing to admit that he didn't know everything, he said that he knew nothing about the retina-retention notion.

A detective butted in: 'That is a pure invention of fiction — an absurdity of short-story writers.'

Shocked by such heresy against the press, Dooling sought to distance himself from it. 'Well, I am going to find out about the theory,' he announced. 'I will speak to expert photographers and medical men on that subject.' Turning to Captain Carey, he asked if Elwell's eyes had been photographed —

'and the Captain only smiled.'

Dr Norris, when quizzed by reporters, put Carey's smile into angry words, saying that even if the notion held water, which it didn't, it was irrelevant to the Elwell case: Elwell had not died for some time after being shot, and, while lingering, may have opened his eyes, and must have *had* them opened — by the ambulance surgeon or by a hospital nurse or intern, or by all of them; and perhaps others. So if there had been any 'last image' on his retinas, it would not have been of his murderer but of one or more ministering angels.

Surprisingly, no one appears to have misread or taken advantage of the reporting of Dr Norris's remarks. There were no follow-up stories reminiscent of some spawned by details of Jack the Ripper's rippings, suggesting that Elwell was the victim of a person with medical know-how. One rather wishes that, as befell Dr Forbes Winslow, the obtrusive intruder into the Ripper case, Dr Roland Cook had found himself suspected of being the perpetrator of what he meddled in. He would have been none the worse for, and might have been quenched by, a grilling.

THE MEMBERS OF THE PARTY

◆ ——————— ◆

Three of four things that the investigators found intriguing in the first statements of Walter and Selma Lewisohn and Viola Kraus (and, a day after they had made those statements, of Octavio Figueroa) were disassociated from the staters. In Viola's case, one of the disassociations was of very recent origin, having come about as soon as accurate clocks had struck midnight on Wednesday, 9 June. And that was what made it intriguing.

1. Thursday, 10 June, was a Red Letter Day for Viola that — so she stated — had quite slipped her mind as being such till its evening, when, while dining at the Ritz-Carlton with her sister and brother-in-law, an old friend, and a new, foreign acquaintance, she had been made aware of the amused presence of Victor von Schlegell, sitting at a nearby table with a woman in black, and had then, only then, thought what date it was, and realized that his amusement was due to the fact that her divorce from him had become absolute that morning. A most odd coincidence, their coming together (well, no — not together: close enough for him to smile at her and for her to scowl at him) so soon after their official parting.

2. A less remarkable coincidence was that the last public function attended by Joseph Bowne Elwell, that being the *Midnight Frolic* in the Aerial Gardens, had also been attended by Elizabeth Washburn, *née* Clarkson, whom he had known for six or seven years but had not seen since her marriage — to a man who (somehow or other, Viola had learned of this) had insisted on the return of a wedding present from Elwell.

3. After the *Frolic* — at about a quarter to two on the morning of Elwell's death — he had excused himself from sharing a cab with the rest of the party; had been loitering outside the New Amsterdam

Theatre when the cab, commodious enough for five passengers, had driven away with four. (Though none of them, in their statements, explained, or suggested an explanation, for Elwell's decision not to accompany them, Viola's admission that she and Elwell had 'had words' — an admission that was probably, and understandably, made on the basis that honesty was the best policy in regard to a matter that might be mentioned by others, giving rise to suspicions if she had not done so — seemed a likely explanation.)

Each of those investigator-intriguing points will have been recapitulative for the attentive reader. That is not so of the fourth, which appeared only in Viola's statement, and was immediately seen as being unambiguously important in that it showed that Elwell was at home, awake or awoken, six hours before Mrs Larsen found him dying:

4. Viola stated that at about half-past two in the morning, half an hour or so after her return to the Lewisohns' Manhattan residence, she had telephoned Elwell. Her explanation for the call was never made public — unless, as seems preposterous considering the unearthly hour, it was that she wanted to remind him that he, she and the Lewisohns were to spend a long weekend on the latters' estate in New Jersey. That reminder was the only part of the telephone conversation, as recounted by Viola, that was revealed by the investigators — though they did let it be known that 'she judged from Elwell's conversation at the time that he was perfectly normal, not nervous in the least'.[1]

Viola — so she had said when asked before she left the house, in the company of her sister and brother-in-law[2] and the lawyer Lyttleton Fox, soon after four o'clock on the first day of the investigation — had no idea

---

1. Author: I have given Viola the benefit of the doubt that she referred to the telephone call in her first statement. Weeks later, Edward Swann, while admitting that he had never spoken to her, said that he 'understood' that she had not mentioned the call till she was interviewed 'for the third or fourth time' by an assistant district attorney. What he should have said, it seems, is that she had not mentioned the call to Joyce or Dooling in her first two or three interviews by one or other of them. Certainly, police investigators knew of the call at an early stage.
   As will appear, much confusion arose as to the times, even the dates, of certain calls made to or from 244 West Seventieth Street prior to the discovery of the crime — and as to the intended or actual recipients of some of the outgoing calls.

2. Whether the Lewisohns and Viola were dressed for the country doesn't seem to have been subsequently mentioned by any of the reporters, more than when they had arrived, whom they had to push through, Walter's chauffeur acting as spear-head, to get to the car. Press photographs, supposedly of the exeunt, are too crowded with supernumeraries — reporters, detectives, and voluntary spectators — to give an answer to the question.

where her newly-ex husband was living. But she recalled that he was employed by the United & Globe Rubber Company and was a member of the Engineers' Club.

As to Victor von Schlegell's residence, the detectives were not stumped for long. One of them thought to look in the telephone book, and there found the address: an apartment in the Knickerbocker Studios, 22 East Sixty-Second Street. Either the address-finding detective or another went to the Knickerbocker Studios, and soon telephoned back to report that Von Schlegell was not at home; that, according to the janitor, he had been absent since before ten o'clock that morning; that, again according to the janitor, he kept his car at the Willett Garage, which was on West Fifty-Eighth Street, even closer to Fifth Avenue than were the Knicker-bocker Studios. The detective, already as excited as the one taking his call was beginning to be, said that he was going to the garage and would telephone again once he had made inquiries there.

His excitement had increased by the time that he did so — for he had learned from Aloysius Mullaney, the manager of the garage, of hectic happenings there and in the vicinity that morning. Going by Mullaney's subsequent statement, the happenings were as follows:

Arriving at the garage at 8.30 a.m., Mullaney was told by the floorman, William Brainbridge, that someone — whether a man or a woman, Brainbridge couldn't be sure — had telephoned within the past half-hour, asking for Mr Von Schlegell's car to be got ready immediately as he urgently needed to drive to Atlantic City. Mullaney: 'I had not got any message from him the night before — Thursday night — about his car. The car would not start, and I asked the chauffeur [the man who parked customers' vehicles in the garage and brought them to the entrance when they were needed] to go down and see what he could do with it. Later on, I found out what the trouble was and they got the car running, and I telephoned, about ten or eleven o'clock, to Mr Von Schlegell. Before that, he had come to the garage about nine o'clock. His car was one flight down, and I hollered up the elevator shaft, and he said: "Why the hell haven't you got the car ready?" He stayed and watched the men working on it about half an hour and then left. He did not say where he was going. When the car was ready, I telephoned to a number I had in my pocket. I was told by a woman to drive it round to the Knickerbocker Studios. We got it started, but it laid down again. After we finally got the car started, I was going in it round the corner of Madison Avenue when a gentleman hollered out of a taxi-cab: "Hey, Al!" I turned round. Mr Edson [a working colleague of Von Schlegell's — and, one gathers from both Aloysius Mullaney's recognition of Edson and Edson's hollered shortening of 'Aloysius' to 'Al', a patron of the Willett Garage] was in the cab with Mr Von Schlegell when he hollered. They were going south and I was going north. I signalled to him and came up after him and they stopped and Mr Von Schlegell got out of the taxi and I pulled alongside the curb. I put the suitcases from the taxi in the car. . . . Mr Von Schlegell had on a Panama hat and a blue suit. . . . Mr Edson had on a soft hat, but I do not remember what other clothes he was wearing.'

The fact that Mullaney's statement did not go on to explain what became of Edson may be a good ground for believing that he did not give that information to the first detective who asked him to think back — and that the detective, too excited by what Mullaney had said to notice what he hadn't, did not ask him to remedy the omission. On the other hand, there is a reasonable ground for believing that Mullaney did tell the detective what became of Edson — and that, a few days later, when he was belatedly asked to make a formal statement, the statement-taker persuaded him to drop Edson from the narrative the minute that gentleman had been adorned with a soft hat. The ground for that belief is this: In the period between the detective's visit to the garage and the taking of the formal statement, there was some distinctly odd police-work, and the police would not afterwards have wanted anything on the record that made any of the oddities appear odder still.

On the Friday night, the detective who had hurried to the Knicker-bocker Studios and eventually made a telephone call from there to his colleagues before hurrying to the Willett Garage, whence he eventually made another telephone call, then hurried back to the Knickerbocker Studios and, after having a second talk with the janitor, made a third telephone call. Having done that, and though footsore by now, he hurried round the corner to the Knickerbocker *Chambers*, an apartment-house at 47 East Sixty-First Street; the rear wall of the Chambers was diagonally across from the rear wall of the Studios. A talk with the janitor of the Chambers so revitalized the detective that, rather than merely hurrying back to the Studios, he raced to them. Arrived for the third time, he made a fourth telephone call.

From the third and fourth calls, the detectives at 244 West Seventieth Street (now designated as Murder Headquarters) gathered the following:

Since soon after Christmas, Victor von Schlegell had frequently, and increasingly, entertained a young woman in his apartment; and, again according to the Studios' janitor, Von Schlegell and his lady-friend had often left the Studios together, both dressed to the nines, and had often returned together from the on-the-town excursions. The Studios' janitor was no more inquisitive than others of his occupation: neither Von

Elly Hope Anderson

Schlegell nor his lady-friend had practised subterfuge towards keeping their joint sojourns in the apartment or their comings and goings secret. On the contrary — whenever the lady was in the apartment at breakfast-time, Von Schlegell had used the 'blower' to inform the Studios' breakfast-making maid that he required a tray for two; and some time ago he had written the lady's name and address on one of his visiting-cards and given it to the janitor, saying that the details could be passed on to any respectable-looking person who asked to see him when, at a time when he was unlikely to be at his office, he was not at home. (Von Schlegell had given a similarly-detailed card to Aloysius Mullaney.) The name on the card was that of Elly Hope Anderson: the address was that of an apartment in the Knickerbocker Chambers.

The janitor recalled that, only the evening before, at about eight o'clock on that Thursday evening, Von Schlegell and Miss Anderson had sauntered arm-in-arm from the building, both formally attired — she in a gown of black chiffon.

Black chiffon?

Yes, the janitor confirmed: Miss Anderson's gown was certainly black, and if it wasn't of chiffon, then he didn't know what chiffon was.

Black chiffon:

A sure sign, what with the tallying of the janitor's description of Elly Hope Anderson's face and figure with the unanimous descriptions given by the Lewisohns and Viola Kraus of the face and figure of Von Schlegell's companion at the Ritz-Carlton ('pretty' . . . 'of Norse type' . . . 'early twenties' . . . 'slim, and blonde'), that Elly Hope Anderson and Von Schlegell's companion were one and the same.

Where was she now?

Well, not in the fully-furnished apartment on the top floor of the Knickerbocker Chambers (living-room, bedroom, bathroom: rent, $1,000 per annum) that she had not fully utilized.

Now it was the turn of the *Chambers'* janitor to help the police with their inquiries. Miss Anderson, he said, had departed that very afternoon — in great haste, leaving many of her personal possessions behind (which she was perfectly entitled to do, since she had paid a year's rent, none of which was returnable, before moving into the apartment last December):

> When I saw her this afternoon, she told me that she was returning to her home in Minneapolis, and asked me to forward any letters I received for her. She is the daughter of a wealthy manufacturer of electrical instruments in Minneapolis. While she has been here, she has studied classical music with Madam Sembrick [sic].[1] She brought a piano to the apartment — it is still there — and spent most of her time practising classical music. She also has a very beautiful contralto voice, and dresses in the latest fashion.
>
> I knew Miss Anderson was a friend of Mr Von Schlegell. She told me that she met him when he was a student at the University of Minnesota. She drove up to the door one day in a fine big automobile, and I said to her: 'That's a fine big automobile you have, Miss Anderson,' and she said: 'That's not mine. That belongs to Mr Von Schlegell.'

1. Marcella Sembrich. Born in Poland in 1858, she was a musical infant prodigy, at first under her real name of Marcelina Kochanska. ('Sembrich', her mother's maiden-name, was adopted because it was easy to pronounce; as the Chambers' janitor demonstrated, it was not secure against misspelling.) After giving violin and piano recitals, she decided — perhaps on the advice of Franz Liszt, but if so, not as a reflection upon her instrumentalism — to follow a career as an operatic soprano, and made her début as such in Athens in 1877. She spent the two following years at Dresden, and then appeared as Lucia at Covent Garden, so pleasingly to London opera-goers that she was invited to return for the next season, which turned out to be the first of five consecutive seasons for her; during those years, she also sang in France, Russia, Spain — and America, her first appearance at the Metropolitan Opera being in 1883, the year of that theatre's opening, when she once more triumphed as Lucia (and on the last night of the season displayed her versatility by playing Chopin on the piano and Bériot on the violin as well as singing Rossini). She was a member of the Metropolitan company in all but one of the years from 1898 to 1909, when she retired from the opera stage, and gave concert performances in far-flung parts of the civilized world till 1917. Long before then, she had become an American citizen. She taught singing in Manhattan — both privately and at the Juilliard School — and Philadelphia, chiefly at the Curtis Institute of Music, till shortly before her death in 1935.

I remember that on Thursday, the day before Elwell was killed, Miss Anderson came home in the early evening, and I met her at the door. She was dressed in a white dress and a red cape, and said she had an engagement to meet Mr Von Schlegell that night to have dinner at the Ritz-Carlton. She said she thought he wouldn't like her to wear that dress to dinner, so she went up to her apartment, and in about an hour she came down dressed in black.

Elly Hope Anderson's apparently sudden decision to leave Manhattan (for Minneapolis: a destination that didn't interest the investigators for some considerable time) made Von Schlegell's non-availability seem, to some of the investigators, even more suspicious. They piled one *What If?* upon another: *What If*, contrary to the impression Von Schlegell had given, he was broken-hearted by his loss of Viola? *What If*, seeing her with Elwell at the Ritz-Carlton, he had pretended indifference while fretting that their companionship was deep — that Viola's morose muttering at Elwell, just as if they were married, was a sign that they intended to be? *What If* the invisible fretting had become a far worse vexation, thought by Von Schlegell to be relievable only by the despatch of Elwell? *What If*, having murdered Elwell, he had decided to go into hiding? Fitting Miss Elly into the progression of *What Ifs* took some ingenuity — but *What If* she, so madly and yet unselfishly in love with Von Schlegell that helping towards his unvexing was of greater account to her than the fact that such help left him with the hope of regaining her rival, had taken a hand in the murder and then, subsequent to her loved one's flight from justice, taken a flight of her own?

Putting her flight aside for future reference, Captain Walsh sent some of his men galloping off in three directions that struck him as being sensibly in aid of tracing the male fugitive. But not at once. He waited till the morning after Von Schlegell's fugitiveness had been inferred.

That was a Saturday morning — but as, in those days, most offices were open five and a half days a week, and some for six, a member of Walsh's squad went to the Equitable Building and ascended to Suite 3002, confident that he would speak to an employee of the United & Globe Rubber Company. His unexpectation of finding Von Schlegell there was not denied by whoever he spoke to. That person, probably a receptionist, probably unaware that the detective was one, told him that Mr Von Schlegell was not in the office that day. If he asked whether Mr Von Schlegell has been in the office the previous day, he received an expected answer: no, or just for a while in the morning. He certainly didn't enquire of Mr Von Schlegell's whereabouts; didn't ask whether Mr Von Schlegell was expected in the office in the foreseeable future. And didn't request a few words with Mr Von Schlegell's colleague, Mr Edson. His mission

The Equitable Building

accomplished to his entire satisfaction, he telephoned Captain Walsh to tell him so. The captain told him that, just to be on the safe side, he was to be surveillant of the office till it was closed. First thing on Monday morning, the detective and others of the 28th Precinct, or those others alone, renewed the surveillance; and by noon were under the surveillance of newspapermen.

Also on the Saturday morning, a detective took the first shift in the watching of the Engineers' Club. And more than one went to the Knickerbocker Studios and, the pass-key having been enveigled from the janitor, searched Von Schlegell's apartment — without finding a single clue. One of those detectives remained at the Studios, the first shift in the watching there.

The most charitable surmise one can make of Captain Walsh's ignoring of Aloysius Mullaney's stated recollection of what his floorman had told him at 8.30 on the Friday morning — that Von Schlegell urgently needed his car for a trip to Atlantic City — is that he reasoned that no fugitive from justice was likely to reveal the location of his intended bolt-hole to a blue-collar worker of his slight acquaintance: wherever Von Schlegell was heading, one could be pretty sure that it wasn't Atlantic City.[1]

1. Twelve years before, Superintendent John Ord, leader of the investigation into the murder of Marion Gilchrist at her home in West Princes Street, Glasgow, had made a similar if-he-said-he-was-going-there, he-must-be-somewhere-else assumption regarding *his* 'fugitive from justice', who was generally known as Oscar Slater.

Captain Walsh must have been disgruntled by a telephone call from his man at the Knickerbocker Studios at nine o'clock on Monday night, soon after Victor von Schlegell arrived home and complained to the still astonished apprehender that he was feeling tired following a complicated journey from Atlantic City — to be precise, from Young's Pier, poking out over the Atlantic from Atlantic City, which was the venue of a convention of the Master Car Builders that he had attended over the weekend, from Friday afternoon. The alertness of the night-shift detective in the lobby of the Engineers' Club was called into question by Von Schlegell's casual added comment that he had got back to Manhattan soon after six, and had dined at his club before making his way home. He was fagged out, he repeated to the detective, and so would be grateful if the detective could leave whatever was wanted of him till he had had a good night's sleep.

The detective may have thought that a reasonable request — but not the telephoned Captain Walsh, who ordered him to deliver Von Schlegell to 244 West Seventieth Street with all possible speed.

The delivery was effected by cab. During the ride through Central Park, Von Schlegell moaned retrospectively of the besetting of his endeavours to get to Atlantic City three days before, of how the last straw on the Friday had complicated his journey back to Manhattan. The detective, not feeling kindly, did not advise him to save his moaning till it was asked for by a statement-taker. And so he heard the following, parts of which were at variance with parts of what another detective had heard from Aloysius Mullaney:

On the morning of Thursday, 10 June, Von Schlegell was asked by Andrew Broughton, his boss at United & Globe, to attend the convention of the Master Car Builders — an ironical gathering so far as his troubled getting to it was concerned. As there was something the matter with the ignition of his car, he told a workman at the Willett Garage to look at it. That was on the Thursday. The following morning, between eight and eleven, he was given the causes for irritation later confessed to by Mullaney, and then sought out Mr Edson (finding him wearing a golfing outfit, about to leave for a country club), explained his predicament, and arranged to borrow a car of his. He and Mr Edson drove in that car to the Knickerbocker Studios, where he picked up his weekend bag, and were driving back to Mr Edson's home when the latter observed Mullaney in his, Von Schlegell's, car, as a consequence of which he set off in that car towards Atlantic City. The car broke down near Perth Amboy, New Jersey. He had it towed to a repair shop, boarded a train to Red Bank, and there hired a cab to take him the rest of the way. Today, after a weekend with convening Master Car Builders, he had taken a train from Atlantic

City to Perth Amboy, collected his car, and driven back to Manhattan. He told the detective that, until their meeting, he hadn't the faintest idea that the police wanted to talk to him with regard to the Elwell murder — which he had read about on Saturday morning. The newspaper account, while mentioning him, had not indicated either that the police were keen to question him or that they didn't know where he was. Had no one thought to ask at his office as to his whereabouts? Why, almost anyone there could have told the police where to find him. And, come to think of it, he had told at least three Willett employees that he needed to drive to Atlantic City. Had the police not visited the garage? And if so, had Aloysius Mullaney not spoken of Mr Edson — who, if approached by the police, would have at once directed them to the convention on Young's Pier?

Von Schlegell's questions had received no answers from the detective when both men alighted from the cab and entered the house. So many of the loitering reporters subsequently said that Von Schlegell, after walking through the vestibule, 'glanced at the murder room' that one wonders whether any of them actually saw him do so — a suspicion that is strengthened by the comment of an exceptional reporter: 'On his arrival at the house, Von Schlegell [was] mistaken for one of the army of detectives who had been running down hundreds of clues and rumours without throwing any light on the motive or circumstances of the murder.'

He had kept the investigators waiting: now they repaid the inconvenience in kind. He would be interviewed in due course, he was told. Till he was needed, he was to stay in the guest bedroom at the top of the house, his apprehender keeping him silent company, watching to ensure that he didn't handle anything (since the room where the crime was committed was the only one in the house that had yet been dusted for fingerprints).

Unbeknown to Von Schlegell, while he languished in the guest bedroom, the den, directly below, was occupied by his ex-wife, her sister and brother-in-law, Assistant District Attorney John Joyce, and (though Joyce described the occasion as 'informal') Walter Lewisohn's attorney, Lyttleton Fox. Any informal questions that Joyce asked were intended to augment or clarify the statements made by the questionees three days before.

The Lewisohns, Viola and Fox departed from the house at midnight, a detective having telephoned Walter's chauffeur to bring the car around. Joyce then took an hour's break before having Von Schlegell, even blearier-eyed than he had been on arrival, escorted into the den.

He answered Joyce's questions, and spoke without prompting of other matters that seemed to him relevant, for three hours. As well as repeating his moans to his apprehender, he gave his recollections of occurrences on Thursday night: the quaintly coincidental proximating of himself with his just-ex wife at the Ritz-Carlton; his greeting of and friendly remarks to Elwell (all reciprocated, he said — contrary to Walter Lewisohn's statement that his 'Hello, Joe' was 'completely ignored' by Elwell); his unusually early descent, soon after ten, from the rooftop restaurant — unusually early because both he and his companion (Joyce's ears must have pricked up at that word) wanted a good night's sleep, he in preparation for the journey to and activities in Atlantic City, she in preparation for a far longer journey, back to her home in Minneapolis.

Did he really need to identify his companion? Oh, very well. The lady's name was Elly Hope Anderson. But would Mr Joyce be so kind as to keep that from the press?

Having received assurance, he spoke of Miss Anderson, unaware that not all of the ground he covered was, to the investigators, virgin territory. The details given by Von Schlegell that increased the height, though not necessarily the depth, of the investigators' stock of knowledge were these: *He and Miss Anderson had strolled from the Ritz-Carlton to the Knickerbocker Studios, had entered his apartment there. The good night's sleep they had both enjoyed was preceded by, made sounder by, a short while of enjoyment which, however long it lasted, occupied part of the time they spent in his bed — from which they arose shortly after seven o'clock on Friday morning. At about ten past that hour, he ordered breakfast for himself and Miss Anderson, and that was served at eight. He, having partaken of the meal, telephoned the Willett Garage to enquire whether his car was repaired and ready for collection.*

Miss Anderson's intention to go to Minneapolis that day was of longer standing than his to go to Atlantic City. It had not been decided whether their reunion would be in Minneapolis or Manhattan. But that they would meet again was, d.v., assured, for they planned to be married.

Some time after half-past four on Tuesday morning, Joyce excused himself from Von Schlegell's presence and went downstairs to talk to Captain Walsh. Supposing that he said what he should have done, he said that two persons had to be spoken to: Andrew Broughton, president of the United & Globe Rubber Company, and Elly Hope Anderson. If Broughton confirmed that his vice-president's trip to Atlantic City was arranged almost a full day before Elwell was murdered, then the trip could hardly be termed a flight from justice; and since it was the apparent flight from justice that had made Von Schlegell a prime suspect, Broughton's confirmation would virtually eradicate the suspicion. And if Elly Hope Anderson admitted, however demurely, that the whole of her last night in Manhattan, through till breakfast-time, was spent in Von Schlegell's

VICTOR VON SCHLEGELL

FIND VON SCHLEGELL PISTOL

He Is "Groggy" After Five-Hour Gruelling Examination but Answers Questions Frankly.

ANOTHER WOMAN IN CASE

Taxi Driver Says He Took Her to Elwell Home Shortly After the Shooting

Mrs. Viola Von Schlegell-Kraus and her former husband, Victor Von Schlegell, from whom she obtained a final degree of divorce the day before Joseph Bowne Elwell was murdered, again were questioned yesterday and last night by John T. Dooling, Assistant District Attorney.

The Von Schlegell inquisition in the District Attorney's office lasted more than five hours in the afternoon. Then they went to the Von Schlegell apartment.

Mr. Swann said that after leaving the Von Schlegell apartment, Mr. Dooling and the others interviewed the maid who took breakfast to the tenants of the Knickerbocker Chambers. The woman said Von Schlegell called her by telephone between 7 and 8 o'clock on the morning of the murder and ordered breakfast for two in his apartment at 8:15.

The woman said she admitted herself with a pass key and left the breakfast without seeing any one in the apartment. According to Detective Cunliffe, she said she returned later and found the breakfast untouched.

Miss Kraus, a close friend of Elwell, was questioned concerning her relations with the slain turfman in the evening at the home of Walter Lewisohn, her brother-in-law, 154 East ... Street, and in the presence ... She had telephoned to ... on Friday after the ... later the same ... Walter company, he would have an alibi even firmer than his ex-wife's, for neither of the Lewisohns had been as close to her during the period in which Elwell was murdered as he claimed to have been to Elly Hope Anderson.

Soon after five on Tuesday morning, Joyce told Von Schlegell that he was free to leave — on the understanding that he would not go out of Manhattan without informing Captain Walsh of his precise destination and getting the captain's permission to go there. Seeing the crowd of reporters in the street, Von Schlegell asked for, and was granted, police protection till he had boarded a cab on the stand outside the Sherman Square Hotel. And, just before leaving, he reminded Joyce of his assurance.

Joyce kept his word. But the press, lacking the name of Von Schlegell's companion at the Ritz-Carlton, unanimously entitled her The Woman in Black — which made her seem very mysterious indeed. Elly Hope Anderson, whose identity was eventually revealed, would have been better off if she had been referred to by her name from the start. She never escaped from the epithet, for it was so accepted by the time it became redundant that reporters then felt obliged to refer to her as 'Elly Hope Anderson, the Woman in Black' or, ringing the changes in a way that did much to revive her mysteriousness, as 'The Woman in Black, whose real name is generally believed to be Elly Hope Anderson'.

Von Schlegell did not get much work done in the four days following his awkward return from Atlantic City. When he was at his office, which wasn't often, the lobby was littered with reporters, their importunateness unavailing: his secretary, temporarily sentinel, was rehearsed in what to say, and said it till she was hoarse — 'Mr Von Schlegell says that he has nothing to say and that you should see Assistant District Attorney Joyce for any comment concerning him.'

Though the two important parts of his statement had promptly been corroborated, one by Andrew Broughton, the other by Elly Hope Anderson (during questioning by a Minneapolis detective), he was interviewed by Joyce, in *his* office, at least four times, on one of those occasions for over five hours. The presence of Lyttleton Fox during that long interview led reporters to suggest that Walter Lewisohn was lending Von Schlegell a hand; but since the firm of O'Brien, Boardman, Parker & Fox was based in the Equitable Building, on the floor below the United & Globe suite, it seems as likely that Von Schlegell, feeling that he needed legal protection, requested it from a lawyer who was nearby, who may even have done work for his company. Reporters guessed that Joyce's 'determination to get at the truth' from Von Schlegell was emphasized to the latter by the presence at all of the interviews of specially burly detectives, and headline-writers insisted that he was ON THE ELWELL GRILL.

A Detective Cunniffe was quoted in the press as saying that the maid at the Knickerbocker Studios was 'now convinced' *either* that when she had delivered Von Schlegell's order of breakfast for two 'at a time [8.10] when Elwell may yet have been unharmed', the apartment was empty, or that she had found the contents of the tray untouched upon her return at some time after nine. The story attracted the attention of Assistant District Attorney Dooling. As it was new to him, and as he was unaware of a Detective Cunniffe among the police investigators, he concluded that Cunniffe was a special officer, meant to be an 'undercover man', who had spoken out of turn by revealing information that Walsh or Carey or both had meant to keep secret. And so he arranged for the maid and the detective to be brought to him. Soon tearful, the maid insisted that she had neither of the alternative convictions that had been attributed to her: never had had either of them: had never before set eyes on that detective — meaning Cunniffe, who, having to raise his voice so as to be heard above her bawling, said that he had never before set eyes on *her*, had never said anything about her to the press, and, just to set the record entirely straight, was named Cunnliffe, not Cunniffe.

With a friend like one of his, Von Schlegell could have done without enemies. The friend telephoned Edward Swann and, speaking anonymously, revealed that Von Schlegell had told him that he had an automatic pistol tucked away in his apartment — that he daren't touch it, lest the age of fingerprints could be reckoned — that he was frightened to mention it to anyone he was not quite sure he could trust. An unlikely tale, Swann must have thought, considering that Von Schlegell's apartment had been searched during his absence in, as it turned out, Atlantic City. But he asked Captain Walsh to have the apartment searched again. The officer Walsh assigned to the task was the misquoted Detective Cunnliffe. Without needing to tax his powers of observation, Cunnliffe established the truth of what Von Schlegell's untrue friend had said. On a shelf in a closet, in plain view once the door of the closet was opened, was a Colt automatic pistol. Any excitement that Cunnliffe felt was soon quelled by his initially-unmanual examination of his find, which showed not only that the weapon was as dusty as its very dusty resting-place but that it was of .38 calibre, a whole .07 less than the weapon that had been used to murder Joseph Bowne Elwell.

For a reason that is hard to make out (perhaps because someone on the DA's staff wondered whether the apartment contained another handgun, hidden rather than out of sight of searchers who didn't think to open closet doors), an hour or so after Cunnliffe had removed the .38 automatic, Von Schlegell was called to the DA's office and asked if he owned a firearm of any sort. He at once said that he had a .38 automatic, and offered to show it to anyone who was interested. Both Dooling and another assistant district attorney, a man named Unger, said that they would be much obliged, and followed Von Schlegell as he led the way. (The *Times*: 'In the corridor outside of Dooling's office there were several loud bangs, as flashlight powders exploded. Von Schlegell did not appear to be in the least concerned and went calmly on with the others.') Arrived at the apartment, Von Schlegell went straight to the closet — and was shocked by what he didn't see. Both assistant district attorneys restrained their mirth while one of them explained the jape to Von Schlegell — who, since he was still clearly suffering from shock, was allowed to stay in the apartment, recovering, till the following morning.

Whichever paper he read when he woke up contained an account of a press conference at which Dooling was badgered by reporters who, keen to keep the 'Von Schlegell angle' alive, wanted a straight yes-or-no to the question of whether the Sullivan Law, New York State's gun-control statute, was to be upheld in the case of a person found in unauthorized possession of a firearm. Eventually, Dooling said no.

Thus ended the Von Schlegell angle.[1]

William Mayhew Washburn's possession of a Colt automatic pistol — of the 'right' calibre: .45 — was one of two divergences from ordinariness that allowed investigators and reporters who spoke of angles to speak of a 'Washburn angle'. But only the most obsessionally obstinate of the angle-minded extended their curiosity regarding William and Elizabeth Washburn, or one or other of that married pair, beyond a day or so.

You will recall that, like Victor von Schlegell at the Ritz-Carlton, Elizabeth had exchanged greetings with Joseph Bowne Elwell in the Aerial Gardens, just before, during, or directly after the *Frolic* performed around the midnight of Thursday, 10 June. You will recall, too, that Elizabeth and Elwell had been acquainted for some six years; that William Washburn, whom she had married in October, was not with her at the *Frolic*, and that, after their honeymoon, he had insisted upon refunding to Elwell $200 that the latter had sent as a wedding present.

Was it possible that Elizabeth, returned home from the *Frolic*, had

---

1. Two years later, Von Schlegell and Elly Hope Anderson were covertly married by a Justice of the Peace at Greenwich, Connecticut — covertly, it is safe to assume, because they feared that if reporters gained foreknowledge of the ceremony, it would be turned into rather a rowdy occasion, and the following day's papers would carry stories about The Woman in Black who had become The Bride in Pink or some such pastel colour.

spoken to William of her sighting of Elwell, and that William, suspicious of Elwell and so suspecting that she had seen more of him than she had said, had lain awake for a while, tormentedly tossing and turning, and then arisen, suspicion twisted into fact by his tired mind, and, with tiredness now the excuse for rashness, rushed to the residence of the man who, to him undoubtedly, had made him cuckold, and put an end to him? That concocted sequence could be assisted towards credibility by comparison of William Washburn to Harry Kendall Thaw, who had figuratively tossed and turned for four years prior to relieving his anguish at his wife's premarital mishandling by Stanford White by murdering the mishandler.

Some time after Dooling had been ordered by his superior, Swann, to let go of the Elwell case, he had a word with William Washburn — who told him unhesitatingly that he had kept his army-issued automatic as a *souvenir de guerre*. Dooling asked if he might see the memento. Assenting, Washburn explained that it meant so little to him that he had left it at his mother's home when he, just married, had moved from there. His mother was spending the summer at the Massachusetts seaside resort of Manchester; her house, 52 East Seventy-Ninth Street, was boarded up. But he had a key. Suddenly a mite apprehensive, he said that though he would be only too happy to admit Dooling to the house, he would like their movements within it to be observed by a non-partisan third-party. The third-party he chose was Harold Content: an excellent choice, for Mr Content, once an Assistant United States District Attorney, was an old friend of the Washburn family and had been a friend of Elwell's for a less considerable time. The three men entered the house and, once accustomed to its shadowiness, made darker to their eyes by the unclouded sunlight that dazzled the quiet street, took a serpentine path between furnishings hump-backed by dust-sheets to a particular piece of furniture: a chiffonier so vast, so tall, that it needed a dust-sheet special to its extent. As if inaugurating the thing, Washburn wrested its covering to each side of it, then stepped away, well away, and told Dooling to delve in its compartments. No record of the expedition mentions how many of the dozens of them Dooling delved in till the Colt .45 automatic pistol was revealed; nor whether a box of its ammunition was revealed there and then or through Dooling's delving in some other nook or cranny of the complicated chiffonier; nor whether the box was full.

Subsequent examination of the finds by an expert on ballistics showed, anti-climactically, that Washburn's souvenir had not been used for many months — probably not since the war and, more to the point of the examination, certainly not as recently as Elwell's murder — and that the cartridges of the bullets in the box, unlike the one that had been found on the floor of the reception room, had marked signs of having been issued from a military arsenal.

That evidence proved only that Washburn's souvenir (which, incidentally, was not perceived by the press as a further indication that the Sullivan Law was more honoured in the breach than the observance) was not the Elwell murder-weapon. The evidence did not prove that Washburn was innocent: maybe he had another gun — *the* gun — tucked away somewhere.

Evidence of a more positive sort was needed.

That was provided — to the entire satisfaction of all, excluding the most dedicated adherents to the 'Washburn angle' — by two of his domestic servants. Unless both of them were as good at telling lies as was Jane Cox (the servant in the Bravo household at Balham, South London, who in 1876 saved her mistress Florence from the tribulation of being tried for the poisoning to death of her husband Charles), what they said proved *almost* positively that William Washburn was at home, in no fit state to venture from it, during the period in which Elwell was murdered. And unless Washburn was a better actor than John Wilkes Booth had been, the testimony of the two servants proved *quite* positively that that was so. They said that, with all due respect to their master, he was extravagantly intoxicated when he was delivered home (from wherever he had been) at about one o'clock on the morning of Friday, 11 June; was not merely asleep but unconscious by the time their mistress returned from the *Frolic* an hour later; was still more dead than alive at eight o'clock. If, in such a state, he had been capable of crawling to West Seventieth Street, capable of killing once he got there, he would surely, for the sake of his poor head, have chosen a way of murdering from among those many that were accomplishable in dead silence.

Late in the afternoon of Saturday, 12 June, by which time Walter and Selma Lewisohn, Viola Kraus, and Octavio Figueroa had all of them said that all four of them had departed in one cab from outside the New Amsterdam Theatre at about a quarter to two on Friday morning, the investigators, their minds concentrated on the unanimously-stated *1.45 a.m.*, took the other unanimously-stated detail for granted:

Of the five members of the party at the *Frolic*, four had afterwards got into a cab that would take three of them to a house on East Sixty-Third Street and the fourth to the Ritz-Carlton, the hotel where he was staying — and when the cab had drawn away, the fifth member of the party, Joseph Bowne Elwell, was standing outside the theatre.

Severally, the investigators sighed gratitude for a couple of incontrovertible facts in a case that didn't have nearly enough of them.

But then Philip Bender, having read of the incontrovertible facts in a newspaper that a Saturday passenger had left in his cab, came forward with the intention of controverting one of them.

All at once, the investigators were united — though, since they weren't speaking to one another, they didn't know it. You may be assured that they, without exception, wished that someone, anyone, other than Philip Bender had answered the call of a New Amsterdam doorman for a cab at 1.45 on Friday morning. A few of those who could 'pull clout' in regard to the licensing of Manhattan cab-drivers may have thought of using that power towards what was, to them, the good end of making Philip Bender shut up.

Though everyone official that he spoke to was clearly underwhelmed by his recollection that there were three, not four, passengers in his cab when he pulled away from the New Amsterdam, en route to, first, the Lewisohns' residence, second, the Ritz-Carlton, he persevered with the broadcasting of the memory, insisted that his arithmetic was right.

So loathe were the investigators to give him the least encouragement that it was not till a newspaper published three days after his first appearance asked why no written statement had been taken from him that one was. Since the statement seems to have been mislaid before the ink of Bender's signature had dried upon it, we must depend on the press for his account:

> Bender . . . said that he was sure from the description of the party and from the location of their residences that he was the man who had driven them home. . . . He asserted that he had driven only two men and one woman.
> 'I remember distinctly,' he said, 'that I started to turn down the front seats, but that somebody stopped me, saying that it was not necessary; that they could all sit in the back. The one woman and two men took their seats there.'
> When Bender was urged to think it over again, he exclaimed emphatically:
> 'I'll bet my wagon that there were only three in the car.'

One woman — Selma Lewisohn or Viola Kraus — and two men: Walter Lewisohn and Octavio Figueroa. Of the surviving members of the Ritz-Carlton/Frolic party, the Argentine publisher was clearly the person to confront Bender: after all, so far as was known he had never met Elwell before the Thursday evening: chauvinism seemed the only ground for distrust of him.

On the morning of Wednesday, 16 June, Bender arrived at 244 West Seventieth Street to make the statement that, so said the *Times*, 'the investigators did not appear anxious to get'. And a few minutes later, so said the *News* on the following day, using the tense that subsequently appealed to Arthur Carey,

> Octavio Figueroa . . . rushes up. Before one is hardly conscious of his presence he has darted into the house. . . . Immaculately dressed, his very dark skin appears even darker because of his light straw hat, spotless linen and stylish blue suit. Elusive, secretive, refusing to speak to any but detectives, he is the personification of evasion.
>
> Click! The cameras have been 'shot' as the foreigner comes out of the house. But, quicker than the shutters can close, he has thrown up his hand to hide his face and turned his back to the photographers. He moves, not with the graceful glide of the panther but with the swiftness of an eel.
>
> He is the man of mystery.

Subsequently, perhaps because Figueroa feared that being 'the personification of evasion', let alone 'the man of mystery', might land him in American hot water, even in an American prison on a charge of murder, he tried to change his image. Talking to reporters invited to his room at the Ritz-Carlton, he said that the police had introduced him to Philip Bender:

> I could not remember the man, but I most certainly did remember that *four* persons were in the cab from the theatre. The other three alighted at the Lewisohn residence, where I said good-night to them, and the chauffeur then drove me to my hotel.
>
> Bender told me that he was not sure whether there were three or four persons in the cab. He was able to remember something which I could not recall, however. He remembered that I gave him a 40-cent tip and complimented him on his taxi-cab.
>
> I am not trying to shield anyone.

Either Figueroa invented Bender's uncertainty or Bender lied when, following publication of the Argentine's comments, he said that he had never told anyone that he was at all uncertain of the number of people he had driven from the New Amsterdam: *three* was what he had stated — *three* was what he stuck to.

The day after he said that, he was scheduled to appear at the District Attorney's office for further questioning. But whoever had wanted to question him decided, at the last minute, that he *didn't* want to. When Bender turned up, he was told to go away.

Since anonymity was so unusual of any of the DA's men, it seems reasonable to guess that the attorney who changed his mind apropos of Bender was the same modest one who, at about the same time, told a *Times* reporter that though certain members of the party still had some explaining to do, all the party-going incidents were looked upon by the investigators as 'merely thrilling by-play, contemporaneous action which led up to the tragedy, but apparently having no logical connection with it'.

FINDING THE LADIES

The longer Joseph Bowne Elwell was no more, the more of a ladies' man he became. His body lay mouldering in a grave, but his sexual-drive drove on, making him a Casanova-shading legend in his after-lifetime.

The *Times* did not help innovatively towards creating the legend: not at first, at any rate — not while there was a lingering of *rigor mortis* — nor even while John D. Van Emburg, a mortician of Ridgewood, was poring over advanced textbooks of his trade in a fastidious quest for tips on how to plug the entrance-hole of a .45 bullet. The *Times*'s first report, headed

J.B. ELWELL, WHIST

EXPERT AND RACE-

HORSE OWNER, SLAIN,

was decently reticent in regard to the victim's attraction to and for the opposite sex. On Tuesday, the day of the funeral, the paper was wordier of the case than its rivals but aloof from their muck-raking — seeking to uphold its renown as an organ that, advertisements apart, contained nothing but the truth:[1]

> The only photographs which [Elwell]
> preserved were snapshots, lacking in sen-
> timental value. Many were groups of twenty
> or thirty, taken at Palm Beach, at country
> clubs, at golf courses, and at other fashion-
> able places frequented by Elwell. There
> were no autographed pictures of women

---

1. As Rex Stout would have Archie Goodwin say in *Gambit* (New York, 1962): 'When the last trumpet sounds the *Times* will want to check with Gabriel himself, and for the next edition will try to get it confirmed by even Higher Authority.'

> and no acquaintances were distinguished
> above the others by having a fine photo-
> graph of herself in his collection.
> Elwell was conscientious in burning his
> letters. There were no archives of intrigue
> among the papers found in his cabinet and
> drawers. . . . The only document extant
> which might suggest an adventure arrived
> on the day of his death. It was written on
> the stationery of the Hotel Biltmore, and
> simply said the writer had telephoned un-
> successfully to him on Thursday, and
> wanted to let him know she was in town.

But the voice of the *Times* was a fairly genteel one sighing in a wilderness of whoopers. Of whoopers who, as we know, called an address-book a Love List; who, when paper-clipped scribblings of other names and addresses came to light, called *them* a Love List as well; who, when a record of fees owed by female bridge-pupils was found, called it a Pension List.

The Pension List provides a good illustration of how the investigators, confused by one another, were further confused by the press. When the record of owings was found, none of the investigators was struck by the thought that one of the owers may have taken more lessons than she could afford and, being too honest to fiddle her housekeeping account, had felt that she had no alternative but to dispose of her creditor — and so the record was put aside, put out of mind, while items that deserved consideration as possible clues were so considered; meantime, the press decided that the record was a Pension List; before long, the Pension List assumed a double-life of its own — perceived by some papers as a list of women who were in Elwell's debt, by others as a list of women who were blackmailing him: in its latter manifestation, the Pension List was offered to investigators who were quite unaware that it was a perverted version of the hardly considerable record of owings, and soon afterwards the *Times* reported that

> information has reached detectives that the
> slain turfman had a 'pension list' of married
> women, to whom he supplied money from
> time to time. The story, as reported to the
> detectives, was that the women were the
> wives of well-to-do men, but compelled
> Elwell to give them money under threats of
> exposing their relations with him to their
> husbands.

The detectives place little credence in the report. Their investigation of Elwell's activities revealed that he was not the kind to give away money, even under threat. From his many friends the detectives learned that Elwell's motive in life was to obtain, not to give money away. He lived lavishly to maintain his peculiar standing among people whom he met in a social way, and frequently boasted of his ability to make large sums of money easily.

One theory advanced in connection with the 'pension list' story was that Elwell was shot to death by the husband of one of the women. The detectives have been unable to find any basis for that phase of the story.

The theory outlined in that last paragraph was a particularization of one of John Dooling's first guesses — that 'some father, husband or brother committed the crime'. The guess seems to have flowered from remarks made in Dooling's presence by William Barnes and Edwin Rhodes soon after they both learned that they were no longer employed by Elwell. The remarks, and Dooling's instant reply to a question suggested by them, were reported as follows:

William Barnes said he knew fifty women who were intimate with Elwell. The chauffeur, Rhodes, said that he knew much of his own knowledge, but that he had received most of his information regarding the women in Elwell's circle from Annie Kane, a former housekeeper, who was superseded by Mrs Marie Larsen last October.

Annie Kane, according to the chauffeur, told him of all sorts of intrigues of Elwell with married and unmarried women. On his own behalf the chauffeur told what he knew of chance conquests which Elwell had made from his automobile. Elwell would hail women at random, according to Rhodes, and, if rebuffed, would explain that it was a mistake in identity, which explanation would sometimes lead to a conversation with their riding away side by side. . . . Probably the element of doubt, the wonder of what lay behind each new face, held an irresistible attraction for the gambler. He would follow these frothy butterflies from

> one cabaret to another, said Rhodes, and
> often would take these strangers home with
> him.
> 'Have you found that Elwell had many
> enemies?' John T. Dooling was asked.
> 'He had several, all right,' Dooling re-
> plied.

Directly after Rhodes's comments were reported, he wished that he had never made them — or rather, that the reports of them had not been conjoined with reports of the question to Dooling and his answer. The juxtaposition led many newspaper readers to believe that he, Rhodes, was one of Elwell's 'several' enemies: therefore, high on the list of murder-suspects. A small percentage of the believers went to the trouble of imparting their belief to the investigators, some pointing out that — supposing that Rhodes did not have a set of keys to his employer's residence, which was to them unlikely — he was among the select few whom Elwell, never mind his disarray, would have admitted to the house. One of the believers referred to Rhodes's pretty young wife Katherine: from what Rhodes had said of Elwell's insatiable desire for pretty young women, it was hardly likely that the pretty young Kate had escaped Elwell's lascivious notice — and, oh, by the way, she had a grey dress, which meant, of course, that she was the lunchtime companion of Elwell's on Tuesday, 8 June, who had just been described by Mrs Larsen as 'a little, short, fat, dark-haired, pretty girl of about twenty-four, who wore a grey dress that was trimmed with fur at the bottom'.[1]

As a consequence of the last-mentioned believer's call, detectives visited the Rhodes' furnished apartment on West Sixty-First Street. Since Edwin was absent, gassing with reporters, Katherine was extremely unnerved by the visit. Soon after the detectives' departure, Edwin and his train of reporters appeared, Katherine had hysterics, and then, still not quite herself, complained that she had been 'mercilessly questioned' by some of the visitors while the rest ransacked the apartment 'in search of a grey dress, a pistol, and other things, none of which were found'.

> 'I never had a grey dress in my life,' she
> said. 'They will never find anything against
> Eddie. I never spoke to Elwell myself,
> though I met him once when he was in
> Lexington about a month ago. He met me
> only as the wife of Eddie, and simply lifted
> his hat.'

1. See page 59.

She said her husband had got up at about
seven o'clock on the morning of the murder
and left without waiting for breakfast. He
went to the garage and was working on
Elwell's car in the morning. The first information which he had about the murder,
he said, was about noon, when he hurried to
the house.[1] 'I have never seen Mrs Larsen in
my life,' said Mrs Rhodes. 'The detectives
are trying to put the blame on Eddie
because they cannot clear up the case.'
Mrs Rhodes's big blue eyes, set wide
apart, filled with tears, and she nervously
patted her curly light brown hair, which falls
low on her forehead.

Readers of that report may not have found in it any reason for crossing
Edwin Rhodes's name from the list of suspects, but the colour-conscious
among them must have concluded that Katherine — lacking a grey dress,
and with light brown as opposed to dark hair — was not The Woman in
Grey. That conclusion was soon confirmed by John Joyce, who announced
that the actual Woman in Grey, whose proper name he refused to reveal,
had come forward 'of her own volition' and proved that 'she was in no way
associated with the crime'. The press either didn't try to identify her or
tried but without success.

The 'young woman of fair complexion' who had lunched with Elwell at
his home on Monday, 7 June[2] — the day before his lunch with The
Woman in Grey — was never traced. If the police were ever keen to trace
her, the keenness must have been soon blunted by Mrs Larsen's
unsatisfactoriness as an eye-witness. At first, she said that she didn't recall
any woman having lunch with Elwell on the Monday; then, after Joseph
Wagstaff had stated that he had driven 'a young woman of fair
complexion' from the house at 2.20 that afternoon, she spoke of 'a little,
short, fat girl' — but when reminded that that description was part of her
description of The Woman in Grey, spoke of a young woman with blonde
hair. It is possible that if Mrs Larsen had not tried to specify the
blondeness, the young woman would have come forward. But as the best,
or worst, that Mrs Larsen could manage was 'mud-gutter blonde', the

1. Presumably, his continuous presence at the Chatsworth Garage from about half-past
seven till noon on the day of the murder was confirmed by employees there. But how was it
that he did not learn of the crime till noon? Did George Gernant, the garage-mechanic who
learnt of it before nine (see page 77), take the rest of the morning off?

2. See page 59.

young woman, whoever she was, and however unconceited, would have been desperate not to admit, least of all to herself, that her tresses were of that gruesome hue.

Mrs Larsen.

On the first evening of the investigation, a detective told a reporter that, strictly between themselves, it was his view and that of every other detective who had had dealings with the housekeeper during the day that she was 'just plain stupid'.

But by the second evening, the detectives' view of the housekeeper had changed. Indeed, by then some of them were most suspicious of Mrs Larsen. None suspected that she had murdered her master; but those unconscientious ones who hoped — despite Dr Norris's firm conclusion, belatedly concurred with by Dr Otto Schultze — that The Elwell Murder Case could be tucked away as The Elwell Suicide, were eagerly suspicious that Mrs Larsen had done some housekeeping on the Friday morning in what she considered the worthy cause of character-disinfection. Perhaps some of the disinfecting had, wittingly or unwittingly on her part, had the effect of removing or disguising suicide-suggestive clues.[1]

The Norris/Schultze-ignoring detectives believed that they had grounds — one in particular — for suspecting that Mrs Larsen had tampered a simple case of suicide into a hard one of murder. They couldn't disprove her assertion that, as Elwell's housekeeper, she had kept herself so much to herself that she had rarely seen and never taken much notice of any of his female visitors; but, knowing that nosiness was almost always an offshoot from stupidity, they felt that she couldn't have it both ways — she couldn't be stupid *and* uninquisitive, for that was a contradiction in terms, like speaking of an unobservant detective. It had been akin to prising clams from shells, getting her to describe The Woman in Grey and The

---

1. No one seems to have latched on to Mrs Larsen's ardent Swedish Lutheranism as an explanation for why she might have dreaded, on Elwell's behalf, that he would be found guilty of suicide. To her, suicide was a mortal sin — 'a transgression of the Fifth Commandment, for no person is the absolute owner of his body and life in the sight of God' (*Lutheran Cyclopaedia*, St. Louis, Missouri; no date).

That at least one high-ranking, cost-unconscious detective suspected that Mrs Larsen had hidden the gun — and still harboured the suspicion when the investigation was in its sixth day — is indicated by the fact that, on Wednesday, 16 June, plumbers tore away the fittings and tiles in the washroom on the ground floor, next to the reception room, in a vain search for the weapon. Whoever hired the plumbers cannot have entertained the notion that someone, having shot Elwell in the head, might have popped into the washroom to relieve himself or herself of the gun before leaving the scene of the crime. Of the people in the house following Mrs Larsen's arrival and prior to the arrival of detectives, only she could have intentionally altered Elwell's immediate surroundings.

'Artist's Conception of high-life web that Elwell spun and was finally caught in.'

Mud-Gutter Blonde: uncertainty was one thing, unwillingness quite another, and the detectives were pretty sure that her unhelpfulness could be put down to her unwillingness to be helpful.

The main ground for looking askance at Mrs Larsen was the discovery — not during the first search of the house, but during the second or third — of a negligee of pink silk.

Two things made that slight garment, one of a number of female nighties that had or would come to light, seem largely significant — seem a ground for suspecting that Mrs Larsen had housekept in Elwell's house when he no longer cared whether she did or not. First: it was deposited, as if hidden, in a grey cardboard box which, in turn, was deposited, as if hidden, in a closet in Elwell's bedroom. Second: the portion of it that when it was worn had provided some cover for the wearer's left nipple had been snipped off — for no other reason, apparently, than because that portion had been adorned with the monogram, plain initial or initials, or first name of the person who had bought it or for whom it had been bought. The become-anonymous negligee pricked the press's fancy more than the rest of the finds put together. Wanting to tell it apart from the everynight *lingerie*, the reporters, with one ragged voice (the *Times* men making an echo), called it a KIMONO. They didn't care that it *wasn't* a kimono. It lacked a sash, was unoriental, and bore no resemblance to a dressing-gown — but none of those deficiencies stood in the way of its transformation into a kimono: *the* kimono. Need it be said that the erstwhile wearer of the kimono, her identity snipped off, was called The Kimono Girl?

Shortly after the discovery of the marred negligee, a.k.a. kimono, a detective cast his mind back to the first morning, and recalled a glimpse of Mrs Larsen conversing excitedly with an equally excited young woman on the stairs leading up from the ground floor. Depending on whether the detective was one of Captain Walsh's men or a member of Captain Carey's squad, he enquired among detectives from either the 28th Precinct or the Homicide Bureau whether anyone had observed what he had just remembered observing.

Overhearing those enquiries, John Dooling associated the detective's recollection with the suspicions about Mrs Larsen, and decided that it would be a good idea to grill her. Without mentioning his intention to any investigators outside the tight circle of his own helpers, he made arrangements for The Grilling of Marie Larsen to be presented in a conference room at the District Attorney's office — an all-ticket affair, the audience composed entirely of ladies and gentlemen of the press.

Before his female co-star was led in, he said a few introductory words — and announced that he had 'assumed direction of the Elwell murder investigation'.

(Next morning, when John Joyce read a notice of the performance, the top-of-the-page reference to Dooling the Director caused him to be endangered by apoplexy. It was the first of Joyce's last straws so far as his supposed colleague was concerned. In his anxiety to regain supremacy, he magnified a hope as fact, telling reporters that they could 'look for a break today', and then shouted at them: 'I have been on this case from the beginning — *and in charge of this investigation.* If Dooling steps in, I'll step out.' Told of Joyce's outburst, Dooling, calm as a stagnant pond, murmured modestly that neither he nor 'the other Assistant District Attorney' was directing the investigation: 'Judge Swann has charge of the case.' Told of the shemozzle between Joyce and Dooling, Edward Swann attributed the former's 'upset state' to 'long hours of hard work and overwrought nerves', but said nothing for publication about the latter — whom he subsequently, but without effect, told to mind his own business.)

Excerpts from The Grilling of Marie Larsen:[1]

(*Beginning with a cool, wearied air to answer unimportant questions and to plead ignorance to important ones,* MRS LARSEN *gradually begins to give frightened glances and to make partial revelations, and finally to become hysterical and tell a great deal, in fear and trembling, under the relentless examination of* MR DOOLING.)

MR DOOLING: Were there not some women's clothes in the house?

MRS LARSEN: No — only a pink silk gown, a cap and slippers.

MR DOOLING: To whom did they belong?

MRS LARSEN: I do not know.

(*After flushing and evading,* MRS LARSEN *says that what she meant is that she never saw a female acquaintance of Elwell's wearing night apparel. She admits that she was frequently aware of the presence of a particular woman; and further admits that she now assumes that the discovered garments belonged to that woman.*)

MR DOOLING: You hid them, didn't you, Mrs Larsen, in order to prevent a woman's name from being dragged into the case?

MRS LARSEN: Yes.

MR DOOLING: Now, Mrs Larsen, what else did you hide?

MRS LARSEN: Oh, my God, my God, I hid nothing else!

MR DOOLING: Did this woman ask you to hide the clothes?

MRS LARSEN: No.

MR DOOLING: How did you come to hide them without being asked?

MRS LARSEN: I thought it would not be nice for them to be found there.

(MR DOOLING *asks* MRS LARSEN *if she has seen the pistol with which Elwell was killed. She exclaims in alarm and answers in the negative.*)

MR DOOLING: When did you last see this woman?

MRS LARSEN: About two weeks before Mr Elwell was killed.

(MR DOOLING *expresses dubiousness regarding that answer, and* MRS LARSEN *eventually breaks down, admitting that she saw the woman who owned the garments a few hours after the murder. The woman, she says, arrived at the house before newspaper accounts of the murder had been printed, and got her information, apparently, by telephone or messenger.*)

MRS LARSEN (*continuing*): She came up all excited and said, 'Oh, what accident, Mrs Larsen?'

MR DOOLING: I see. She knew your name, though you didn't know hers?

MRS LARSEN: Yes.

MR DOOLING: What did she do then?

MRS LARSEN: She ran upstairs, but the detectives were on that floor.

MR DOOLING: What story did she tell them?

MRS LARSEN: I don't know.

MR DOOLING: Did you cut the name or initials from that silk garment?

MRS LARSEN: No! No! That had been cut off a long time before. It was that way before I came to work for Mr Elwell.

MR DOOLING: How did you come to see it?

MRS LARSEN: I saw it in the box where it was kept.

---

1. Author: I have taken the liberty of turning reporters' comments into stage directions.

(MRS LARSEN *insists that she was not bribed or requested to hide the garment.*)

MRS LARSEN (*reiterating*): All the woman said to me that day was, 'Mrs Larsen, what accident?'

MR DOOLING: Did you hide the thing before or after the woman came?

MRS LARSEN: It was — I think — Oh, how can I remember? There was so much going on.

(MR DOOLING *decides to cut short the examination in the presence of spectators.*)

MR DOOLING (*to the spectators*): I think, perhaps, if I talk to Mrs Larsen alone she will tell me a good many things that she does not like to tell me now.

MRS LARSEN: *nods her head.*

(*Exeunt spectators.*)

If Mrs Larsen did tell more, the press never got to hear the disclosures. But soon after the second, secret act of The Grilling, Dooling announced that the negligee-owner, she who had made a fleeting appearance at the house within hours of the discovery of the crime, had been identified. She would be referred to as 'Miss Wilson' — rather a come-down, that, from The Kimono Girl.

The Miss Wilson disguise didn't stay opaque for long — not after an investigator revealed that 'the woman in question' had spoken to Elwell on the telephone at half-past two on the morning of his murder. None of the newspapers broke her cover; but even the most dim-witted of their readers deduced that, unless Elwell had taken two telephone calls from different women at about 2.30 a.m. on the Friday, Miss Wilson, formerly The Kimono Girl, was Viola Kraus.

She had been interviewed, in the presence only of the interviewer and Lyttleton Fox, by the time that the Miss Wilson disguise was inadequate. And she, with a little help from her lawyer-friend, had coped admirably, fooling the interviewer – not to mention those who subsequently saw his notes — into believing that she was, albeit retardedly, a veritable paragon of honesty. She had shown herself (or rather, had not shown herself) to be mistress of the art of issue-confusion.

The greatest of her several triumphs lay in getting nearly everyone to accept that her brief encounter with Mrs Larsen on the staircase happened hours later than the time of its occurrence. Unless certain detectives were incapable of connecting one fact with another, among those who were not taken in were Captain Carey, the detective who answered the telephone call from Walter Lewisohn shortly after one o'clock in the first afternoon of the investigation, and the detective or detectives who, within a quarter of an hour of the telephone call, ushered Mr and Mrs Lewisohn, Viola Kraus and Lyttleton Fox up to Elwell's den. One can only assume that those men of the law, and others who spotted Viola's deliberate mistakes, decided, for some reason or another, not to let on.

According to Viola,

> Mr Elwell was to have gone with Mrs Lewisohn and myself to her home at Elwood Park, New Jersey, to play golf Friday afternoon and Saturday. It was to have been a small house-party, and we intended to start around two o'clock Friday afternoon in the motor. The night before, just before we left him at the *Midnight Frolic*, he asked us to call him up and tell him when he should be ready, so on Friday, around noon, I telephoned his house to say we would all call by for him at about half-past two.
>
> A man's voice answered the telephone, and when I asked for Mr Elwell he asked me if I was a friend of his, which, of course, I said I was. Then the voice said very solemnly over the wire: 'If you are a friend of Mr Elwell's, you'll come here at once.'
>
> I was frightened, puzzled, and I said: 'What's the matter?'
>
> 'Mr Elwell is very, very sick, and he needs your help right away. He wants you to come at once. Will you come?'
>
> 'Do you want me to bring a doctor?' I asked.
>
> 'Never mind the doctor; just come here yourself as soon as you can,' the voice said.

My sister was then at our mother's house. I telephoned Selma at once and told her of the request, and she said she would meet me at Elwell's house right away.

I reached the house in Seventieth Street around one or two o'clock. The result was that we first encountered the reporters and photographers and then the police.

The detectives asked me all sorts of questions. I was completely overwhelmed by the whole thing. Mrs Lewisohn came in just a few minutes later, and they questioned her in the same terrible and embarrassing way. If it had not been for my telephone call to the house, I shouldn't have gone there, and then we wouldn't have been subjected to this fearfully unpleasant notoriety.

I don't suppose I had been at Elwell's house twice before in my life. . . . I always thought Mr Elwell a nice fellow, but he did not have the least attraction for me sentimentally. . . . There are any number of fairly nice people who knew and liked Mr Elwell just as we did. We often met him at their houses, but fortunately for them their names have not come out, and I am glad for their sakes that this is the case. We never heard an unkind word said about him, and everybody seemed glad to have him around. He was never what you would call an intimate friend of ours, but distinctly a friendly acquaintance.

Excepting some bits of padding, or bolstering, none of Viola's tale can be accepted. The fact that it *was* generally accepted (not the fact that it was never publicly disputed) lends support to the adage that the most successful liars are those who tell the most audacious lies.

More than a month after Viola had given her brilliant display of hoodwinking, the New York *American* published a cable-dispatch from a correspondent in Ireland who had been told by Annie Kane, Elwell's housekeeper prior to her return to her emerald-green homeland, that Miss Wilson (the *American* was glad of that name for its protection against a libel-suit) had once threatened the life of the man who had since been murdered. Not surprisingly, Viola denied that she had done any such thing — and took the opportunity to deny some of the host of less hurtful canards that had come to her notice:

> She further stated [having stated that Annie Kane was a shocking liar] that she had not been deserted by Elwell, and did not fear that she would be deserted by Elwell; that she was until recently a married woman, and that he had never proposed marriage to her, and the subject had never been suggested or discussed; that she had not had any controversy or disagreement with any other woman regarding Mr Elwell, or any other man.

So there.

By no means all of the female section of the 'fairly nice people' referred to by Viola as being fortunate to have escaped a fate like her own escaped that fate for long. And some women — some of whom were not even *fairly nice* — positively invited the befalling of that fate.

Item. One of the snapshots that Elwell had not bothered to buy an album for was of a woman who, according to the detective who chanced upon the picture, was 'of striking appearance and strong physique'. She was wearing a bathing costume; but as, in those days, women who bathed alfresco wore negligibly less when doing so than when they were not, the detective's description led reporters to believe that, whoever the bathing beauty was, she would be quite a sight no matter what her attire. That belief was soon confirmed. Either someone recognized the woman or, as seems more likely, the snap held a handwritten clue to her identity. She was Mrs Amelia Hardy. Since she was Polish-born, her first name was probably of her own choosing; but less probably so than was the name by which she was known to close friends, which was Molly. She was divorced from an American. The fact that she had a ten-year-old daughter, named Gloria, indicates that she had been divorced for at least a decade and nine months. At the invitation of an investigator, she came to the 'murder house' on the first Sunday. And her sister came, too. The sister was Countess Sonia de Szinswaska: also a divorcee; as beautiful and as tall as Amelia, but less well developed. The sisters remained in the house for five hours, and during that time reporters on the sidewalk 'occasionally' heard 'a woman's voice raised to a high pitch issuing from within'. When they at last emerged, 'they pulled their hat-brims over their faces to baffle photographers, in which they were successful'. John Joyce subsequently explained:

> The Countess and her sister were questioned because they were at one time good friends of Mr Elwell.
> The Countess, who is a Pole, said that she first met Mr Elwell at Carlsbad in 1913, but that she had not seen him for more than a year. She said that she knew Mr Elwell pretty well, but had never visited the house while he was residing there, although her sister had.
> Mrs Hardy said that she, like her sister, had not seen Mr Elwell for more than a year. She said that the last time she had seen Mr Elwell was in 1918, when he was about to travel to Palm Beach.
> The two sisters said that they had been told that Mr Elwell, a member of the American Protective League, was responsible for the detention of the Countess as a suspected spy during the war, but that they knew no reason why he should have done such a thing and that he had not only denied it but had made representations to Washington which aided in giving her liberty after two months.

On the Friday following the inquisition at the house, the sisters spent almost as long at the DA's office. On that occasion, the reporters without heard no high-pitched voice issuing from within. Emerging, Amelia and Sonia at once parted — the former, saying nothing that the following reporters' papers would dare print, to return to the apartment she shared with her daughter and sister at 200 West Fifty-Seventh Street, and the latter to soothe her larynx with lemon-tea in a restaurant near the Criminal Court Building. Reporters hovered while the Countess sipped, and then had their uncharacteristically quiet patience rewarded — not merely by the sight of 'a calculating look coming into her big brown eyes' but by an extempore discourse on 'the difference between Continental and American outlooks in a murder mystery', parts of which were so controversial that a verbatim rendering is called for:

> Americans entertain a sort of childish curiosity in relation to a man's private life. They are inquisitive and greedy for intimate news. Over here, the newspapers are too chivalrous with a woman in a mystery. They defend her. It is not so on the Continent. There, where humanity is older and wiser, we say, 'Cherchez la femme.' I frankly believe the woman is always to blame. I wonder who the woman is in this case? Joe Elwell was no worse than most men: the only difference is that his affairs are being exposed — he has been found out.

Excepting a suspicion that the Countess subscribed to the proverb, 'Revenge is a dish to be eaten cold' — or that Amelia Hardy did, at least once in a sisterly way — there seems no reason for suspecting that either of the physically admirable sisters caused Joseph Bowne Elwell to rue his membership of the American Protective League during the brief time it took for a bullet to explode from a gun and burrow through his skull.

Item. The Countess was not the only titled lady to be involved in the case. There was also the Princess Dalla Patra Hassan el Kammel. No one could blame waggish reporters for saying things like 'the Princess Kammel gave us the hump' — indeed, pun-loving readers would have blamed the reporters if they had not said such things. The Princess and her entourage spent but a short time at the DA's office, just long enough for her to make Joyce comprehend that her sole connection with Elwell was as a pupil of bridge. The only further copy that reporters were able to gather was that she was probably, not certainly, a niece of a dead khedive of Egypt, which was her native land. It wasn't that she was reticent: the trouble was that since not a single reporter had majored in Arabic, none of them could make out more than a few words of what she said. If the Princess proved anything, it was that the game of bridge, first played by the British but not the Egyptians in Egypt, transcended language-barriers.

Item. On the first Monday, a buxom lass dressed all in white spent half an hour outside the house, chatting with reporters, then five minutes inside, and then another half-hour outside, renewing acquaintance with the reporters, who, barring a few crusty ones, were glad of the renewal. During the totalled hour, she explained that she was a masseuse, pronouncing the second syllable as a rhyme of *goose*, and that, round about Christmas, having been recommended to Elwell 'by one of his lady-friends', she had treated him four times for 'poor circulation resulting from influenza'. Preaching to the converted, she assured the reporters that the laying on of her hands was 'pleasurably therapeutic'. In the course of getting her massage across to the media, she made sure that everyone knew her name and the address from which she supplied a 'twenty-four-hour service, seven days a week'. Mrs June Gard, of 119 West Seventy-Sixth Street, cannot ever afterwards have needed to advertise.

Item. At his morning press conference on Wednesday, 16 June, Joyce let it be known that he had been told that 'Elwell is supposed to have been an acquaintance of Mrs Ruby N. Davies, whose husband, Lieutenant La Verne A. Davies, recently sued a prominent Philadelphian for alienation of her affections. Detectives have been sent to question Mrs Davies, and we are trying to get in touch with the lieutenant.' The assembled reporters seem to have been too busy scribbling that inch of copy to wonder what on earth the suing of a prominent Philadelphian had to do with the slaying of a famous New Yorker. But by lunchtime a representative of the *News* was untidying the entrance to the Davies' house at 39 East Sixty-First Street:

> Mrs Davies steps out of a new limousine. . . . She has a neat figure, which would instantly attract the attention of the male of the species. She is about five feet four inches tall, rather plump, and she wears a 'natty' dress of blue, with a hat of henna straw. Her hair is wavy and chestnut brown, but it is only when you gaze into her wondrous dark blue eyes that you realize her great beauty. She reminds one of Anita Stewart [a star of stage and, latterly, screen], and about her is an appealing wistfulness.
>
> 'I never knew Mr Elwell personally,' she declares. 'He was pointed out to me at Saratoga, but I know none of his friends or relatives.
>
> 'All this trouble, I am sure, has come through spite work. The only times I have seen my husband during the last two or three years was when he has annoyed me. The last time I saw him was about twenty days ago at the Biltmore Hotel.
>
> 'I have filed suit for divorce. I never lived with him as his wife,' she declares proudly.
>
> And as a reason or excuse for her matrimonial venture she announces:

> 'I married in April 1916, in a fit of despondency.'
> With Mrs Davies, at the time of her arrival, is a tall, slim man, of sallow complexion, with a tiny black moustache. As he gets out of the car he takes off a Panama hat and throws it into the tonneau of the machine, replacing the hat with a cloth cap.

That is the last we hear of the wistful Ruby, who seems to have had undeserved Elwellian notoriety thrust upon her more efficiently by an assistant district attorney who was desperate for something to say at a press conference than by a misinformer who simply relished the opportunity of getting Ruby's linen — dirtied, but not by Elwell — washed in public. Surprisingly, considering the sinister-sounding word-picture of the man with a hat for all occasions, we hear no more of him either. And as for the lieutenant (who, one gathers, lived with Ruby till she, prompted by despondency, married him; and who she clearly believed was the spiteful person who had communicated with Joyce), either Joyce's efforts to get in touch with him were unsuccessful or, though successful, fruitless of information that was the slightest help to the investigation that the efforts were supposed to be in aid of.

On the tenth day of that investigation, a Christian Sabbath, there was a full house for the evening service at the Calvary Baptist Church on West Fifty-Seventh Street, close to the Carnegie concert hall, resultant from the spreading abroad of the tidings that the Reverend Doctor John Roach Straton, who was thought by some to be God's Ambassador on Earth, was going to preach on the Elwell case, using the text from *Proverbs*, 31, 10: 'Who can find a virtuous woman? for her price is far above rubies.' (If Mrs Davies received a handbill advertising the event, she must have prayed, though not at the Calvary Baptist Church, that that last word would not be misprinted anywhere as 'Ruby's'.)

The Reverend Doctor Straton not only wandered from the publicized nub of the sermon but also said things about the Elwell case that cast a new, unDivine light upon it. Clearly, he didn't give a ———— for Earthly Truths.

> Tonight, as we stand in the shadow of the Elwell tragedy, which has stunned the city, I wish to press home to every mind and heart the lessons to be drawn from it. The Elwell tragedy has in it every element of degeneration and social decay that this age knows. The most acute and menacing malady is the abnormal over-development of sex-consciousness. It is the most important and dangerous problem that confronts New York.

Sexitis caused the death of Joseph Bowne Elwell.
What were the scenes in the last night? A gay dinner at a fashionable hotel. Fancy food and high prices. Dancing — not with his own wife but with other women, one of them a divorcee. Then to the *Midnight Frolic*. Then, with perverted taste still unsatisfied, going in the early morning hours to a cabaret, there joined by other boon companions, male and female, and more 'daring' dancing still. Then out upon the streets to buy a sporting paper from a boy who ought to have been home in bed. Then whirled to his residence in a racing automobile, so that the poetic consistency of the whole thing might be sustained to the end.[1] Then, with daybreak almost at hand, not to bed, but, as though to give a complete illustration of an utterly abnormal life and the perversion of nature at every point, turning night into day. Then reading the racing news as he sat at ease in his own home — gloating, perhaps, with the gambler's glee over news of his own winnings.

Then! Yes, *then!* What next?

The Death Angel! The stealthy step of the slayer! The noiseless presence of one who had come to kill!

Who? Someone robbed in gambling? Some poor fool crazed with jealousy? Some jilted jade seeking vengeance? Some poor girl, led astray and then cast aside for a fresher flower? Some father who had heard the sobbed-out story of shame from his little daughter's lips? Some brother coming like Nemesis to avenge betrayed trust and outraged innocence?

Which one of those, we do not know. We only know that there was the crack of a revolver (held, possibly, in the little hand of a little woman), and a lump of lead went crashing through a brain filled with lust and horse-racing records and details of gambling — and the haunting shadow of a great fear, because of a wasted life and a record of evil deeds.

So he was found, sitting bolt-upright in a chair, a bullet-hole through his

---

1. The Reverend Doctor Straton's poetic consistency was sustained by five-day-old newspaper reports that at 3.45 on the morning of the murder 'a low, greenish-blue racing automobile, evidently very powerful', had 'screeched to a halt outside Elwell's house', Elwell had alighted and gone into the house, and, 'with a series of explosions', the car had sped away towards Sherman Square. The incident was said to have been described by John Isdale, First Mate of the British freighter *Ariano*, who had been spending a few days with relatives who lived at 236 West Seventieth Street. In fact, it had been described by Isdale's Uncle Max — he going roughly by what his nephew had told him before leaving for Philadelphia, where the *Ariano* was berthed.

The Reverend Doctor Straton, who was an honourable man, cannot have seen the succession of follow-up reports, based on interviews with John Isdale at Pier 38, South Philadelphia, each of which diminished Uncle Max's hearsay: the merchant mariner *had* heard a car pull up somewhere along the block at 3.45 on the morning of the murder — or at that time on the previous morning; he *had* looked through his bedroom window (but couldn't be sure whether or not he had got up to do so) and had seen a car driving away; he had not been able to tell the colour of the car; all that he remembered of the vehicle was that it was 'small'; he had not seen Elwell or anyone else entering No. 244; and yes, it *was* possible that he had been rudely awoken, not on the Friday morning, but at 3.30 a.m. the previous day — when a woman creating a disturbance on the block had been carried off in a police car.

head, a letter about his race-horses still held in his lifeless hand, the sporting newspaper he had just been reading lying on the floor by his side. Just across the hallway, the boudoir of his lady-friends — with the dainty toilet articles, powders and paint, and gold-tipped cigarettes in the drawer. Those things were around him, but Death was now in the household, and his spirit had gone out into Eternity to meet God!

Sexitis has so ravaged New York that even Paris is astonished! The city is a modern Babylon, except that its roof-gardens rise far higher than the hanging gardens towered. The people of this city are money-mad and pleasure-crazed. America is on a joy-ride when we should all be at a prayer-meeting.

During the sermon, no one in the congregation said or did anything that might have interrupted the flow of a lesser mortal — or rather, immortal — than the Reverend Doctor Straton; but when his bowing motion as he closed the Good Book indicated that he was done, the souls most carried away by his Words said the first thing that entered their heads, *viz.* 'Hallelujah!' If there was anyone present who was versed in the Old

Testament *Psalms* and who had read accounts of the Elwell case with a critical eye, he or she should have risen and enquired, with reference to the reverend ranter: 'Who is this that darkeneth counsel by words without knowledge?'

But no one did anything of the sort.

You will have noted the Straton throwaway line with reference to the Widow Elwell. If Elwell had danced with *her* on the Ritz-Carlton roof, rather than with Other Women, one of them a divorcee, the cautionary tale of his life and death would have been a mite less cautionary. Why, according to the Straton method of inductive reasoning, if he had danced undaringly with Helen, that little candle of wholesomeness would have illumined for him the naughtiness of his ways, making him all of a sudden repentant of his sins and desperate for an early night, abed with a good woman whose very presence would have deterred anyone from murdering him — a bonus that would have deprived Straton of a thundering good subject for a sermon.

Soon after condemning her departed husband as, among other regretable things, a 'piker' and a 'chicken-chaser', Helen changed her tune, or muted it, in the cause of buttering up her parents-in-law, the sole beneficiaries of their son's will. Thinking more of Richard Derby's future than of her own, she was keen to get a decent slice of the estate without having to go to the expense of hiring a probate lawyer.

Oddly, the fact that she and Richard Derby were legally entitled to a small share of the estate, no matter what the testator had wished, seems never to have been construed as a possible motive for the murder. Though the reporters, or their sub-editors, were adept at accusing people of the crime without actually making accusations, not a whiff of innuendo sullied the Widow Elwell. If she was ever officially suspected, the suspicion was at the very start of the case, and then fleeting. One must accept Captain Carey's word that 'Mrs Elwell's movements on the morning of the murder [were] carefully checked. It was impossible for her to have been anywhere near the house at the time of the shooting.' The investigators took care not to inconvenience her, allowing her to tell them when she was free to answer questions about Elwell's distant past; she postponed at least two appointments at the DA's office because of last-minute rearrangements of her bridge-tutoring schedule, and insisted on being collected from and returned to her apartment by limousine.

She was with the mourners at the funeral, and had done her best to appear *of* them by wearing black from head to toe: a heavy crepe veil saved her from having to dissemble sorrow, and a black ostrich-feather fan saved her from stifling. Richard Derby, summoned from Andover, accompanied her. His tears were unforced. Earlier that day, Elwell's will — found, with other documents, in a box in the Columbia Trust Company's vault — had been filed in the Manhattan Surrogate's office. If Helen had not known the terms of the will prior to her husband's death, she knew them now.

Two days later (again wearing all of the outfit of black, a colour that didn't suit her: that, without even a white hankie to relieve it, gave her the resemblance of a wrecked umbrella), she visited 244 West Seventieth Street for the first and, so far as is known, only time. And in the evening she was at home to a representative of the *Times*.

Had the reporter suffered from hay-fever, he would have needed to phone his office for someone to replace him. Helen had received more floral tributes than her dead husband. The 'neatly furnished sitting-room' was crowded with the symbols of a sympathy that she didn't merit; their many fragrances mingled to make a breathtaking wall-to-wall quilt.

Separately perfumed, Helen sat in a large armchair in the centre of the room. She was not wearing her veil. Every so often, a slight gust of sultry air entered through the half-open window, ruffling her kerchief of black lace, rearranging the pattern of the quilt. Richard Derby obeyed her earlier-issued order that he was to be seen but not heard. The reporter, moist on an upright chair, noted her every phrase.

None of them that outlined incidents that occurred before her widowhood complement what we already know. Some of the remainder, and Helen's visual additions to them, help towards an understanding of her:

> Mrs Elwell smiled to her son and told how happy she was to become on intimate terms again with his grandparents, uncle and aunt. She told how his grandfather patted him on the back at the cemetery Tuesday and of the invitation he had received from his aunt to spend some time with her. She was delighted, she said, that her late husband's family were treating her and Richard so kindly after four years of complete estrangement. As soon as she separated from Mr Elwell, she said, the friendship with his relatives ceased, as she was unwilling that tales be brought from one to the other. Richard had not seen his father's parents for so long a time, his mother said, that he didn't know them, and was greatly surprised to find they were so 'nice and friendly'.

'You can't imagine what a queer sort of feeling overcame me this afternoon when I walked through the Elwell house and saw the paintings and Chinese porcelains which I had bought,' said Mrs Elwell. 'There was no artistic taste displayed at all; and I don't see how the furnishings can be described as "luxurious". Those that he had were placed in a very unartistic manner.[1] But as I looked from one picture to the other or from one valuable porcelain to the other, knowing that they were once in my own home, a feeling came over me that is indescribable. I won't say that they were all mine, but the majority were, and at a few hundred dollars each, amounted to quite a sum.'

Mrs Elwell, when asked if she had any theory to offer concerning the murder of her husband, replied in the negative. Since she had not seen him in four years, she did not know of his actions or of his friends, she said. She is not reading many of the newspaper accounts of the police investigation, she said, as some are putting in too much 'colour' and also printing interviews with her which she never gave.

Patting Richard on the head, she exclaimed: 'Isn't he a darling son?'

Looking at the fifteen-year-old boy, well built and towering far above his mother, the reporter agreed that he was a fine fellow, and the interview ended.

Helen the stake-claimer received encouragement in one respect, though not in another, from answers given to reporters by Elwell's brother Walter at about the time she was diligently making passing remarks in aid of her cause to the man from the *Times*. In reply to the question, 'Is there any document of Elwell's which makes provision for his son?', Walter said:

1. Providing a postscript to the published interview, Edward Swann supported Helen's pooh-poohing of reports that the house was luxuriously or tastefully furnished. However, *chacun son goût* does not explain his entire dislike of the contents — and his entire dislike cannot have been to Helen's liking. What he said was this: 'The house was furnished poorly and in very bad taste. The different hangings and pieces bore no relation to each other in size, period or general description. It looked to me like a jumble of second-hand stuff, thrown together without the least judgement. There was nothing of value in it. There were no antiques, and no two reproductions seemed to represent the same period or school. Huge pieces of furniture and scrawny ones were all mixed together.'

'No, but it was my brother's wish, and a verbal agreement was made to that effect. The boy will be provided for always.' In reply to the question, 'How about Mrs Elwell, the widow?', Walter said: 'I don't know about her,' and walked away, all smiles but firm in his pretence that he was deaf to variations on the question from reporters who believed that he did know about Mrs Elwell.

Some three weeks later, she received a missive, posted in Ulster, that caused her heart to lurch with the lovely hope that Richard Derby might inherit *all* of his father's worldly assets. The buff-coloured envelope held three sheets of fairly white paper, two of which, ruled vertically as well as horizontally, were decorated at the top by drawings of standard lamps, those drawings either side of the printed words, ' "ROYAL STANDARD" "PURE OIL" "WHITE MAY"/FINEST OIL LAMPS/Bought of Augustine Kane,/Grocer, Carrickloughan, Camlough.' The important parts of the handwritten message were as follows:

> Dear Madam,
>   My name is Annie Kane have been a housekeeper for Mr Elwell for nearly three years. . . . The reason I am writing you this letter is because I had a paper from New York and in it I see where yourself and son are cut off in Mr Elwell's will and this will it states was drawn up in 1915, but I saw a will drawn up in 1917 or 18, in which it stated that everything went to his son Richard but nothing to his wife, H.D. Elwell. He also stated in will his reasons for making a small bequest to his Father Mother and sisters was that he had already provided for them substancially [sic]. . . . Myself and the girl I had working with me[1] read the will a couple of times and knowing a little of his business, we both were pleased to see that he had made provision for his son. When I read the paper I wished I was in New York if I could be of any assistance to you. Hoping this information may be of some use to you, and if I can be of any assistance to you at any time will be pleased to do what I can for you.
>   I remain
>   Respectfully
>   ANNIE KANE

Helen's lovely hope was soon dashed. Her lawyer visited Elwell's, Frederick Ingraham, and came away sadly confident that what Annie Kane and her temporary helper had seen was a cyclostyle copy of a *draft* of a will that, at some time during the war, Elwell had asked his lawyer to prepare but which had never become the basis of a legal document.

Ever after, Helen suspected that a new will *had* been prepared: that Elwell had signed it: that he had signed it in the presence of witnesses who had themselves signed it but who, for some suspicious reason, said nothing

---

1. Temporarily; probably during a move.

after his death in aid of disproving the validity of the will made in 1915. Her suspicion is understandable. What is inexplicable is the reason why Elwell toyed with the idea of making a new will. Many possible reasons spring to mind; but as there are certainly many more that don't, it would be silly to elect a favourite.

On Friday, 18 June, 'Investigator' of the *News* noted that 'the circle [of suspects] is growing narrower':

> Tracing his way along the persistent scarlet thread of passion shot through the warp and woof of the life fabric of Joseph Bowne Elwell, District Attorney Swann seeks the deeper stain of murder.[1]
> Woman after woman is revealed.
> Now it is a woman of society who knows the man merely as a teacher of bridge whist. She merely sought to learn to play the game a little better than her acquaintances of some fashionable coterie;
> Now a woman whose path has led through many entanglements, perhaps separation or divorce, perhaps alienation suits;
> Again a woman whose interests are divided between the stage and revelry at later hours;
> But it is always a woman.
> It is never a woman who could be called unsophisticated in the ways of the world.

On Monday, 21 June, Edward Swann told the press:

> We do not intend to have any woman brought into the case unnecessarily. We have nothing to make public about women who are innocent or women whose indiscretions have no apparent connection with the crime.

Item. Subsequent to the DA's laudable announcement, The Woman in Black and The Woman in Grey were joined by The Woman in *White* — that colour bestowed upon the woman as a disguise, not because the investigative bestower was a devotee of Wilkie Collins, nor because the

---

1. Had 'Investigator' read Conan Doyle's *A Study in Scarlet* and been specially impressed by one sentence, that being: ' "There's the scarlet thread of murder running through the colourless skein of life, and our duty is to unravel it, and isolate it, and expose every inch of it." '?

woman was sartorially attached to it, but simply because it was the natural successor to black and grey. The Woman in White was eventually revealed in her true colours as Josephine Lewis Peet Wilmerding, a leading light of Manhattan's high society. She had been 'socially prominent' before her marriage to the even more socially prominent Cuthbert Mortimer Wilmerding in 1914, had continued to be so during the marriage, and had remained so following her divorce from Mr Wilmerding in 1917.

She was 'fingered' by that arch Irish reminiscer, Annie Kane — who, in addition to alleging that 'Miss Wilson' (Viola Kraus) had once threatened Elwell's life, alleged that The Woman in White had once threatened Miss Wilson's life during a heated quarrel between them over 'ownership' of Elwell.

Throwing off the white shroud as soon as it was seen through, Josephine Wilmerding told Dooling to tell the press what she had told him, Joyce, Talley and Swann. Dooling seems to have decided that Josephine's social prominence entitled her to a retelling that must have taken hours to write and which took him nearly an hour to read aloud. It can be condensed to half a dozen paragraphs:

> She denies categorically all the charges and insinuations by Annie Kane. She denies ever having seen Annie Kane, and would not know her if she came into the room at this minute.
>
> She says that she first met Mr Elwell in February 1918 at Palm Beach, where she was then living with her aunt and uncle, that Elwell entertained there a great deal and that she recalls that among his visitors down there was a gentleman named William Pendleton, who she thinks had been a visitor or a guest at Elwell's for about a month. She says that the very best people at Palm Beach were entertained by Elwell. Parties of twenty-five or more would go out on his boat.
>
> She returned north in about the month of March 1918, and understood that Mr Elwell remained in the south until June; that his lateness in leaving was occasioned by his building operations or the sale of some real estate. She says that, after he came up here in June, she saw him a couple of times at different places, in New York hotels, etc., and met him at public functions. She says that she and her sister went to his home one evening and spent a little time looking at the furnishings. She knows nothing of any of the garments found in the house.
>
> Later in the summer of 1918, Mr Elwell was a guest at her grandmother's home at Narragansett Pier, Rhode Island, for the weekend. The last time she saw Mr Elwell was about the month of January 1919, when she was recovering from an operation for appendicitis. She was then in a private sanitarium in this city and he made a visit lasting about two minutes.
>
> She says that at one time he referred to his activities in the American Protective League, and indicated that in the course of his activities he might have antagonized somebody.

She met Mrs Viola von Schlegell last winter at the Ritz. She recalls only talking to her once. There was no feeling in the matter. She says that she never had any quarrel or controversy with 'Miss Wilson' or anybody else about Elwell; that at first she thought he was a very pleasant, agreeable person, and took him a little more seriously than she did later. Subsequently she rather satisfied herself that he was very gallant to every lady. From that time on, she did not take him seriously.

Of course, Viola Kraus had to comment on Annie Kane's allegation that she — or rather, 'Miss Wilson' — had quarrelled with Josephine — or rather, The Woman in White — and that the latter had threatened to kill her. She denied any knowledge of the incident.

Either the press, confused by the reminiscences issuing from Augustine Kane's grocery shop in Carrickloughan, falsely attributed a further allegation to the former housekeeper, or she really did allege that 'Miss Wilson' had once threatened to kill *her*. It was as well for Annie Kane, who seems not merely to have kissed the Blarney Stone but to have bitten off more than she could chew of it, that no one paid much attention to stories suggesting that she was lucky to be alive to tell her tales: otherwise, she might have become The Woman in the Pinny and been extradited from Armagh to New York, there to explain why a lady-friend of Elwell's had taken such a dislike to her.

'Investigator' of the *News*:

> We turn to the sporting page.
> After a pageant of beautiful women, the refreshing air of the race-track revives our interest in the Elwell murder mystery.
> One tires of mere beauty. One would not attend the *Ziegfeld Follies* seven days in succession. One may even have a surfeit of pink kimonos. . . .
> Wherefore we turn to the sporting page.
> We find Elwell's colours in the first race at Latonia.
> 'Right Over Might' wins the first at fair odds.
> It is Elwell's horse —
> 'Right Over Might.'
> What a name to dwell upon!

Item. A sifting through a pile of seemingly inconsequential mail in Elwell's den revealed a note posted on 1 June 1920 at Versailles, Kentucky. It was

from Anne Russell Griffy.[1] She thanked Elwell for a bouquet he had sent
her while she was being treated for tonsillitis in a Lexington hospital. Her
gratitude was not expressed effusively; her thanks for the kind thought
were not preceded or followed by lines that anyone could read between.
Even so, Captain Carey despatched one of his men, Detective Sergeant
Harry Oswald, to Lexington, telling him to ascertain whether Miss Griffy
had had her tonsils or something else removed at the hospital; and, in any
case, to ascertain whether or not any of Miss Griffy's menfolk might have
blamed her need for hospital treatment upon Elwell. So as to help towards
justification of Oswald's travel expenses, he was to kill two other birds in
Kentucky, one being to try to solve the sixteen-year-old mystery of why an
unknown woman had taken a pot-shot at Elwell outside the Galt House
hotel,[2] and the other to ask among the horse-racing fraternity of enemies
of Elwell within their midst.

When Oswald boarded a train to Lexington, so did a dozen or so
reporters, one of whom would write:

> The scene changes. . . .
> We get a glimpse of the gorgeous
> pageant of horse-racing in Kentucky, so
> famous for its chivalrous men, its beautiful
> women, its thoroughbred horses, its blue
> grass.
> Instead of the white lights and night
> revelry of Broadway we see the dash of
> high-bred horses, the gay throng of prettily
> gowned women.
> Instead of the science of the card table we
> turn to the trickery of the betting ring.
> Instead of the painted lips of a city's
> triflers we note the sun-bronzed cheeks of
> graceful outdoor girls of the Blue-grass.
> We visualize a distinguished Kentuckian
> and his charming daughter.
> The inference is plain, of course.

But the inference turned out to be no more than that. None of Oswald's
errands was productive, and he returned to Manhattan clueless. While he
— and his fellow travellers — journeyed home, Anne Russell Griffy
screamed at a Lexington reporter:

1. See page 55.

2. See page 28.

My father's name is Porter Griffy. He is a resident of Woodford County. My brother's name is Norton Griffy, and he resides at Akron, Ohio. Neither my father nor my brother knew Elwell or had any knowledge of my acquaintance with him.

After a few more screamed words, she burst into tears, and the reporter, fearing that Porter or Norton might be as protective of her as had once been suspected, apologized for having discommoded her and hastened away.

Next morning, in Manhattan, a 'high-ranking detective' let it be known that

newspapers have been given misinformation, and false clews have been followed purposely. Little faith was ever placed in the Lexington, Kentucky, story. The 'camouflage' information has been given to throw the murderess off her guard and lead her to betray herself.

Miss Griffy and others of the flock of decoy-ducks must have had their feathers ruffled anew by that blithe statement.

Item. One of the three unopened letters lying on the floor by the dying man's feet was from — or appeared to be from — a woman. Written on the stationery of the Biltmore Hotel, the letter expressed regret that the writer had been unable to get in touch with Elwell on Thursday, 10 June, and requested him to make an appointment for a meeting 'at any convenient time up until Sunday'.

What was the signature? 'Clara', the reporters were told. And so they knew that, whatever the signature was, it didn't look anything like 'Clara'.

Detectives searched the Biltmore Hotel for 'Clara', but found no sign of that person.

Three and a half years went by. Then a Pole, certainly not of Countess Sonia de Szinswaska's circle, entered the Elwell case. His name was Rafael Schermann. His entrance was considered by the *Times* to merit coverage on the front page. He was described as a psycho-graphologist, and was said to have 'solved many crime mysteries for the police of Vienna, where he lived for five years before coming to New York'. When asked by the police commissioner of the latter city whether he could solve any local crime mysteries, he said, 'Of course,' and offered to give a demonstration of psycho-graphology, just for a nominal fee, in his suite at the Waldorf-Astoria. Unfortunately, the commissioner was just off to Bermuda; but he arranged for proxies to test Schermann's uncanny powers.

The psycho-graphologist was handed the 'Clara' letter. Having fondled it, and gone into a small trance over it, he enquired: 'Have you ever found this lady?'

'No,' confessed one of the commissioner's proxies.

'No wonder,' cried Rafael Schermann, and kept his audience in suspense for a while before saying:

'That is no lady. That is a gentleman.'

LAST MOVEMENTS AND SWANN SONG

The Elwell case must have prompted telephone subscribers on the Columbus exchange to look askance at their bills.

Columbus was not a 'direct-dialling' exchange. All being well, when an ear-piece was lifted from its hook, the tilting up of the hook caused a blink on the switchboard, and the alerted operator came on the line and then tried to make the requested connection; if the attempt was successful, the operator noted the subscriber's number, the number called, when the call began and when it ended.

The data-collection procedure was all very well in theory; but that it was fallible in practice was indicated on the sixth day of the Elwell investigation (Wednesday, 16 June), when a detective, pondering on Viola Kraus's statement that she had made a telephone call to Elwell at 2.30 on the morning of his murder, suddenly had the bright idea of asking the superintendent of the Columbus exchange, on West Fifty-Eighth Street, whether or not any calls had been made *from* Columbus 9689, Elwell's number, in the early hours of that morning — and was assured that there had been *three*:

at 4.39, to William Pendleton's number in Far Rockaway;

at 6.09, to Walter Elwell's number in Ridgewood;

at 6.16, to a number in Garden City, Long Island, that was listed as that of a man named S.A. Varling.

The detective telephoned, first, Elwell's former partner in the Beach Racing Stables, second, Elwell's brother, and third, the mysterious Mr Varling — and in each case was told that the information given by the exchange superintendent was cock-eyed. Each of the men asserted that he had received no telephone call from anyone at any time during the first eight hours or so of the Friday. Mr Varling told the detective that he had never even heard of Joseph Bowne Elwell before the latter's death.

And so the detective got back to the superintendent, and soon afterwards was told that, yes, a closer look at the records showed that the information given earlier was not quite accurate:

For one thing, the Garden City number had been called on a Friday morning in *May* — and not from Columbus 9689.

For another, the calls to Far Rockaway and Ridgewood had been made, respectively, at 4.39 and 6.09 *p.m.* on Friday, 11 June.

For another, there had been no calls whatsoever from Columbus 9689 on the morning of that Friday till shortly after 8.30 (when Patrolman Singer had telephoned his station).

By the time the superintendent made those amendments, press reports were agog with conjecture: 'the murderer was in the house for hours threatening Elwell' . . . 'Elwell was telephoning to friends either to get them to give some evidence in his favour which would avert the assassin's wrath or to raise a sum of money demanded by a blackmailer'.

Hearing of the all-important third amendment, John Joyce telephoned the superintendent, asking if he was absolutely sure of it. Positive, said the superintendent. John Dooling telephoned the superintendent, asking the same question and getting the same answer. On this occasion quicker on the uptake than Joyce, Dooling informed reporters that 'there were no calls at all from or to[1] the Elwell residence on the morning of the murder before the hour when the murder was discovered. I have been in touch with the telephone company as late as twenty minutes ago.' As soon as Dooling had had his say, Joyce gathered the reporters around him and announced: 'It is positive that there were no calls from or to[2] the Elwell house early on the morning of the murder.'

No sooner had the two similar statements appeared in print than Dooling stated that he was 'in communication with' a Columbus operator named Margaret Entler, who 'distinctly remembers that she tried to put through a call from Columbus 9689 at approximately 2.30 on Friday morning, but without success'.

---

1. 'Or to' appears, at first sight, to have been a guess by Dooling, an instance of his tendency to protest too much. Although Columbus operators helped operators on other exchanges to connect calls to Columbus numbers, they kept no record of non-Columbus calls to any of the 19,473 'subscriber stations' on the Columbus exchange (which had been opened in 1892, and which served an area that, roughly speaking, stretched north from West Forty-Ninth Street to West Seventy-Fifth Street, and east from the Hudson River to the western side of Central Park).

2. Either Joyce had got wind of his rival's statement, and was determined that his should not be comparatively deficient, or the superintendent, over-keen to make amends for his initial inaccuracies, had exaggerated his knowledge to both of the assistant district attorneys.

Confusing the reporters — and, before long, their readers — still more, the day after Dooling made the statement about Margaret Entler's recollection, Edward Swann stated that Margaret Entler 'remembers distinctly that in the early morning of Friday, June 11, a call came in from Columbus 9689. The ticket in possession of the telephone company is dated 11 June, 1920, but does not give the hour. The recollection of an official of the telephone company is, however, that the call came in between 12.30 and one o'clock in the morning. The young lady operator is not at her boarding-house on East Eighty-First Street, but the boarding-house keeper informed me that she is spending a two weeks' vacation at Rutherford, New Jersey. I have directed that a detective be sent to Rutherford in an effort to find this girl and fix more definitely the exact time of the message.'

Reporters pointed out to Swann that, only the day before, Dooling had told them that Miss Entler distinctly remembered a 'no-answer' call around 2.30 — and that if a call was made from Columbus 9689 between 12.30 and one o'clock, the caller must have been someone other than Elwell, for he was then enjoying the *Midnight Frolic* in the Aerial Gardens. 'The District Attorney's confidence in his announcement of the hour remained unshaken' — and such firmness gave reporters the confidence to write of the 'hidden hours' during which 'the unknown assassin lurked in the turfman's grey-stone dwelling', awaiting the intended victim's return.

The detective sent to Rutherford to find Margaret Entler failed in his mission; but Miss Entler, reading in a paper that she was wanted, returned the ten miles to Manhattan and presented herself at the District Attorney's office. She stated her recollection of not just one but two attempts to get a number for a caller on Columbus 9689 — neither attempt at a time that coincided with either of those already given. The first attempt, she said, began at about 1.45, and was given up after nine minutes; the second began at about 2.04, and was also given up after nine minutes. She couldn't remember whether the twice-unsuccessful caller was male or female, 'but the voice was a natural one, without agitation or excitement'. The number the caller had wanted was Far Rockaway 1841.

That was William Pendleton's number.

Pendleton was invited to the District Attorney's office. Parts of the statement he made were rendered to the press as follows:

> He says that the telephone instrument in his bedroom is on a little table between his bed and Mrs Pendleton's bed. There is also an extension to the maid's room. He says that the telephone did not ring in his house at any time in the early morning of the day in question; that it could not have rung without awakening Mrs Pendleton or himself; he knew of no reason why Elwell should

have telephoned him so early in the morning. . . . He says that he returned home at midnight the night before, put his car into his garage at that time, went to bed, and rose at 8.30 a.m. and drove Mrs Pendleton to the station at Far Rockaway to catch the 10.26 train.

He says he now realizes that his earlier statement that he had not seen Elwell for eight months was incorrect, since he now recalls casual meetings with him.

He has thought the matter over and allowed his mind to go back for many months regarding conversations with Elwell and with his friends, and he cannot suggest to the District Attorney the name of any person who may have killed Elwell, or any cause that motivated his killing.

Though both Pendleton's wife and their maid, Margaret Makin, corroborated his account of the curious incident of the telephone bell that had not rung in the night-time, the investigators — and the press — remained suspicious. The suspicion was strengthened by Mrs Marie Larsen's assertion that, just before Christmas, Elwell had left a set of keys under the front-door mat so that Pendleton could let himself in 'on a matter of business' while he, Elwell, was absent.[1] And by Pendleton's assertion, when contradicting Mrs Larsen, that he had 'not seen Elwell for eight months or more', which was seen to be a lie as soon as he made it: the investigators had already heard from several lunchers in the clubhouse at the Belmont Park race-track on the day before the murder that Elwell and Pendleton had also lunched there, though not sharing a table.[2]

With extreme carefulness of innuendo, reporters wondered whether Pendleton (referred to by most of them as 'the anonymous suspect') had not been roused from slumber by a total of eighteen minutes of ringing for the simple reason that he was wide awake and miles away from home at the time. Perhaps it was Pendleton who had tried to *make* the calls to Far Rockaway 1841. Perhaps his wife and their maid, both cognisant of his intention to murder Elwell, and both having agreed to give him an at-home alibi, had, at the first ring, flown into each other's arms, and so remained, mutually determined not to answer a call that might be from someone wanting to speak to him, till after the final ring of the second attempt to get through. Of course, that imagined tableau of the two terrified alibiers raised the rather difficult question of why on earth Pendleton, a lethal-minded trespasser in Elwell's house, had wanted to get

1. See page 93.

2. Some other lunchers in the clubhouse may have had their memories of the presence of Elwell *and Pendleton* jogged by a chatty obituary of Elwell in *The Thoroughbred Record* of 19 June, which, in speaking of the Beach Racing Stables, made several references to Pendleton, and concluded, 'Mr Elwell . . . was at the Belmont course on Thursday afternoon lunching in the clubhouse and seemed in the best of health and spirits'. (The obituarist also noted that 'it was Mr Elwell's intention to bring [his] stable East in the near future'.)

in touch with one or other or both of the women he had so recently, purposefully, left in Far Rockaway. Perhaps he had all of a sudden remembered that he hadn't put a note out for the milkman, or had left a wet cigarette burning, or had forgotten to turn off a downstairs light. Or something of the sort. All would be revealed.

On the very day (Saturday, 27 June) when 'the anonymous suspect' made his first, sly appearance in print (the topmost headline of six, 56 words in all, above the *Times*'s report read: ALL ELWELL CLUES CENTRE ON A MAN; ARREST EXPECTED), 'the anonymous suspect' *disappeared!*

Well, if *that* didn't prove that he was the murderer, what did the word 'proof' *mean?* That question, or one like it, was put to Dooling — who, peculiarly restrained, said only that he was 'puzzled at the man's disappearance'. Joyce couldn't be found (a strange fact, that, but not strange enough to make any of the reporters speak of *his* disappearance). Swann was 'away in the country, and could not be found'. Talley said that 'the suspect was likely to be taken into custody as soon as found'. None of the visible detectives, neither Carey's nor Walsh's, would say anything; and neither Carey nor Walsh could be found.

The stories that appeared next morning (the topmost headline of six, only 49 words in all, above the *Times*'s report read: ELWELL SUSPECT DISAPPEARS) had the effect of making the suspect *re*appear.

Still slightly breathless from the hurriedness of his return, William Pendleton held a press conference in a shed in the grounds of the Rockaway Hunt Club.

He had come from Saratoga Springs, he said. He had gone there, with friends, to arrange the rental of a house for himself, his wife, and their maid throughout the impending Saratoga race-meeting. He spoke of 'crossed wires' in the District Attorney's office, saying that he had called on Edward Swann at the Manhattan Club the night before his departure and informed him that he would be in Saratoga for a short time. It was a mystery to him why members of the DA's staff had spent a day and a half searching for a man whose whereabouts were known to the DA; an even bigger mystery was why the DA, returned from the country that morning, had let the search continue. He also said, among other things:

> While in Saratoga, I saw a newspaper, and from what I read between the lines I judged that they were shooting at me. . . . I thought I would come back.
>
> If the whole thing were not so serious, it would be the damnedest joke I ever saw. Of course, it *is* serious, but the whole thing is a fiasco.
>
> When I came back to the club today, they all came over to me and asked, 'What is all this we read about you?'
>
> I am completely flabbergasted. Everything that I have said has been

published and republished time and again. I have been questioned by Mr Swann, Mr Talley and Mr Dooling. I have answered all the questions I have been able to. If they ask me any more questions, I think I'll go crazy.

Next day, Edward Swann was visited by Pendleton's lawyer, and afterwards announced:

> There is no 'suspect' in the Elwell murder case. That statement in the newspapers is a grave injustice to the man referred to by them, against whom we have no legal evidence that would justify an arrest or even the detention of any person as a material witness. Such statements may make interesting newspaper copy, but they are contrary to the facts and misleading to the public. I want it understood that no one but myself or, during my absence, Mr Talley is to give out news to the press. Information from any other persons is to be disregarded.

He refused to admit that Talley had given out the news that 'the suspect was likely to be taken into custody as soon as found'.

It appeared that William Pendleton was, to use horse-racing parlance, scratched from the frame of runners in the Elwell's Murderer Stakes. But that appearance was deceptive. A week after Swann's castigation of the press for doing Pendleton 'a grave injustice', and his pious comment about the need for 'legal evidence', he forgot all about the need for legal evidence when calling a press conference at which he did Pendleton a far graver injustice than any done by the newspapers.

While Dooling did a poor imitation of modesty in the background, Swann spouted his assistant's 'important contradictions of every important part of William Pendleton's statement'. The *most* important contradictions were of (1) Pendleton's assertion that he had driven his wife to the railway station on the Friday morning (which, said Swann, was contradicted by Henry Hensler, a taxi-driver of Far Rockaway, who was certain that *he* had driven Mrs Pendleton to the station) and of (2) Pendleton's assertion that he had returned home at midnight on the Thursday, put his car in his garage, gone to bed, and stayed there till 8.30 a.m. That assertion, said Swann, was contradicted by John Doyle, a worker at the Atlas Garage at 9 East Fifty-Second Street, who was certain that 'at two o'clock on the morning of the murder, Oliver W. Bird, Jr., and George W. Bird, Jr., friends of Pendleton, appeared at the Atlas Garage with the Pendleton car, and were then driven home in it by Doyle; that while driving back to the Atlas Garage, Doyle was seen by George B. Post, Jr., who shouted at him, 'That is Penny's car,' and boarded it and was dropped at the Knickerbocker Club; and that the Pendleton car thereafter remained in the Atlas Garage until 8 a.m., when somebody who has not been identified took it away.'

Swann — quite forgetting his seven-day-old edict that only he or Talley were to talk to the press — stood admiringly by while Dooling talked to the press:

'The fact that Mr [Oliver] Bird did drive the car to the garage on the morning of June 11 is proved not only by the garage employee Doyle, but by the garage records and by the independent testimony of George B. Post, Jr. Mr Bird was somewhat vague in his recollection. He remembered the incident, but disagreed with the garage employee as to the date.' Dooling added, meaningfully: 'Mr Bird, you know, was on that drive to Saratoga Springs, along with Mr Pendleton and others, several days ago. The Pendletons and the Birds are very good friends.'

Next day, Swann was obliged to contradict the contradictions of Pendleton's statement. With no blush of contrition, he said that he had publicized the apparent contradictions of Pendleton's statement because 'they were impeding the investigation, and it was necessary to call attention to them in order to have them explained'. The explanations of them were as follows:

(1) Because of Henry Hensler's routine calls at the Pendleton residence, he made a mistake: although he may have called at the house on the morning of June 11, he did not drive Mrs Pendleton to the railway station.

(2) George B. Post, Jr., and Mr and Mrs Oliver W. Bird, Jr., fixed the date of June 8 as the morning in which Mr Pendleton's car was in this city. Mr Post has stated:

'I remember distinctly the night, or early morning, that I was taken into Mr Pendleton's car. I recall that I played bridge at the Knickerbocker Club, Fifth

ASSISTANT DISTRICT ATTORNEY JOHN T DOOLING QUESTIONS WM H PENDLETON

Avenue and Sixty-Second Street (Telephone Schyler 7300) earlier in the evening. I have referred to my account with the Knickerbocker Club, and I find that I was there on Monday and Tuesday, June 7 and 8. My account shows that I was not at the club on the night of June 10 or the morning of June 11. For this reason I feel positive that the date of my riding to the club in Mr Pendleton's car was the early morning of June 8. I was never in the car except that one time.'

The above statement, verified by the records of the Knickerbocker Club, shows that John Doyle, Atlas Garage, was mistaken as to the date upon which he drove Mr Post in Mr Pendleton's car.

A reporter for the *Times* enquired of Swann: 'Then the assumption that Mr Pendleton was in the Elwell residence at 1.45 on the morning of June 11, and that he tried to call his own home, falls to the ground?'

'Yes, certainly,' Swann snapped. 'I am not doubting anyone and I am whitewashing no one. The facts seem to shift one way and another from day to day.'

Another reporter reminded Swann of something he had said only the day before, that being: 'There are six million people in this city. Can you conceive of any one of the six million seeking to telephone to Far Rockaway 1841 with the exception of Pendleton himself?'

Without commenting on the reminder, Swann flounced from the room, bumping against Dooling as he did so. It was noticeable that he did not apologise.

Left to their own assumptional devices, most of the reporters concluded that Margaret Entler's memory was as frail as her superintendent's ability to read his operators' notes: that if she was right in saying that she had tried unsuccessfully to connect Columbus 9689 with Far Rockaway 1841, she was wrong in saying that the attempts were made on the Friday morning. She — like John Doyle, the demi-Atlas of East Fifty-Second Street — could do with some tuition on how to read a calendar.

(Readers of this book who have read of the Wallace murder case, which occurred in Liverpool, England, in 1931, will by now have had several slight attacks of *déjà vu*. In that case, too, the evidence of a telephone operator who said that she was sure that she had rung a number without getting a reply was opposed by people at the receiving end who said that they were sure that the phone had not rung. There was also important evidence concerning locks and keys, the time of a milk-delivery, and a missing murder-weapon. And the investigators in Liverpool in 1931 were quite as inept as those in Manhattan in 1920.[1])

1. See, for instance, *The Killing of Julia Wallace* by Jonathan Goodman; London, 1969 and 1976; New York, 1976.

While the Pendleton show was still running, yet another troupe of investigators began contributing to the Elwell motley. They were Federal Prohibition Enforcement Agents — 'dry agents', for short. Their leader's name was James Shevlin. The name of the special counsel assigned to Mr Shevlin was August Hasenflug.

It seems odd that the dry agents took no visible interest in the Elwell case till it was approaching three weeks of age. Another oddity is that, during that time, the newspapers made only passing reference to the fact that Elwell was the treasurer of the Studio Club. What makes the latter oddity odder still is that an incident at Elwell's house on the first Thursday of the investigation gave cause for suspicion against the club's president, H.H. Porter, whose ability to take part in the high-stake gambling at the club was due to the high salary and higher fringe-benefits he enjoyed as president of the American Water Works, the offices of which were at 60 Broad Street, in the heart of the financial district at the southern tip of the island. The incident was noted in the *News* as follows:

> [H.H. Porter] is seen at the Elwell home. He arrives in a taxi-cab and, dodging reporters and photographers, darts into the house in search of Assistant District Attorney Joyce. In Joyce's absence, [Porter] refuses to talk to detectives and rushes out. He covers his face with a handkerchief. His vision is obscured and he stumbles when entering the cab.

Perhaps, round about that time, so many people were covering their faces, with the unintended result that they couldn't see where they were going, that Mr Porter's doing likewise was not considered at all quaint — no more peculiar than his dodging, darting and rushing.

In any event, apart from Mr Porter's trip to, and in escaping from, Elwell's home, neither he nor any of his activities gave rise to press comment for a surprisingly long while. And the club over which he presided was given only slight publicity during the same period.

On Tuesday, 29 June, rumours were reported as the 'news' that

> Elwell was engaged in illicit whiskey transactions mounting into large figures immediately before his death. . . . He had raised, or had been entrusted with raising, $12,700 for the purchase of whiskey, during the week of the murder . . . and the whiskey had been actually delivered into the hands of an organization to which he belonged. A

cheque for this amount, drawn by Elwell and said to have been deposited on the day before his death, was hastily withdrawn on the day of his death. . . .

The alleged 'bootlegging' transactions were said to have been revealed by a German wholesale liquor dealer, who said that, because of the withdrawal of the cheque, he had never been paid for the whiskey. The dealer was quoted as saying that the transaction had been negotiated for Elwell by a man who had at one time been in Elwell's employ. This man pointed out the danger of discovery and arrest if an examination of Elwell's bank account led to the uncovering of wholesale trading in violation of the Volstead Act. . . .

The whiskey dealer, it was stated, only wanted $6,700, that being the actual price of the whiskey, the other $6,000 being graft levied by Elwell, or his representative, or both of them, against the principals for whom the whiskey was purchased.

The theory advanced from this is that Elwell's inability to raise the money necessary to cover the cheque led to a quarrel between the turfman and either one of his associates or an associate of the liquor dealer; that Elwell's frantic efforts to telephone his friends [sic] early on the morning he was killed were made in an attempt to raise this money; that the assassin called upon him the morning of the murder in an effort to effect a settlement; that a heated quarrel ensued; that Elwell perhaps sought to stave off payment because of the illicit nature of the deal and that the shooting followed.

'. . . an organization to which [Elwell] belonged': the Studio Club?

'. . . a man who had at one time been in Elwell's employ': William Barnes, the steward of the Studio Club?

Both possible answers were soon unrivalled. Meanwhile, $12,700 dwindled to $4,000; it was learned that Elwell had not made out a cheque for more than a thousand dollars during the last month of his life (and, obviously therefore, no such cheque had been hastily withdrawn on the day of his death); one German liquor dealer became two, who were promptly supplanted by an Italian called Toni; the two official spokesmen for the DA's office, the DA himself and Alfred Talley, stated, respectively, that a bootlegging motive had never occurred to anyone in the DA's office and that a bootlegging motive had been suspected by the DA since the early days of the investigation.

William Barnes, given the choice of being interviewed by Alfred Talley or by James Shevlin, elected, presumably on the basis of 'better the devil you know', to talk to Talley; and did so for more than two hours. He had a reason for perturbation other than the suspicion that he had infringed the dry laws: newspaper stories that a crooked roulette wheel had been found at 244 West Seventieth Street (instantly denied by every investigator asked to confirm them) had been transformed into a rumour that Barnes 'had a hold on Elwell because he knew the circumstances under which Elwell had cheated a man out of $50,000 at cards'. At attempt by Dooling to scotch the rumour by saying, 'The person reported to have been cheated is a well-known man who could not possibly be suspected in connection with the murder,' had only made it worse for Barnes, for the ingenious inference had been drawn that, though the well-known man may not have murdered Elwell, he *had* been cheated by Elwell, who had, in turn, been blackmailed by Barnes, who possessed proof of the cheating.

And so Barnes, with two suspicions hanging over him, was prepared to sacrifice anybody in the cause of allaying the bootlegging one. *Anybody* — irrespective of great favours done to him, long friendships, or family ties. As soon as Barnes had scuttled out through the tradesmen's entrance, Talley informed the crowd of reporters and dry agents sweltering in the lobby that 'William Barnes, questioned in regard to the bootlegging story, says he thinks it is his brother who is meant'.

Later in the day, James Shevlin announced that there was no evidence that Elwell had been involved in bootlegging or that anyone associated with the Studio Club had been or was.

Next morning, Shevlin, speaking in the Custom House at the foot of Broadway, announced that there *was* evidence that Elwell 'was in the bootlegging business on a considerable scale', and that 'one cellar to which the liquor was supplied is that of an organization of which many prominent business and sporting men are members'.

Newspaper readers, by now as skilled at the decipherment of inference as Elwell had been at the fathoming of the meaning of others' bids at the bridge-table, knew at once that the organization referred to by Shevlin was the Studio Club. And so none of them was surprised by subsequent news items reporting that the club had been raided, a veritable reservoir of booze drained from the cellar, and the steward charged with violations of

The Custom House

the Prohibition laws.

What *was* surprising was the news that dry agents, acting on information supplied by William Barnes, had — no, not raided, but 'received admittance to' — 405 Park Avenue, the home of H.H. Porter, president of the Studio Club (just a block south) and of the American Water Works, and confiscated 48 quarts of whiskey. Even more surprising than that was the news, printed not long afterwards, that the titular mainspring of America's water had actually been *prosecuted* for illegal possession of whiskey — had actually been convicted (chiefly on the evidence of William Barnes, who had admitted vendition of the liquor) and fined $250. A week later, the admitted vendor was fined $200 — that sum taking into account other admitted sales to other members of the club. When the jovial judge asked whether the fine would be paid by Mr Porter, Barnes's equally jovial lawyer chortled that his client hoped so.

While justice was being seen to be done in regard to the bootlegging Barnes and one of his vendees, investigators continued to burrow for information that might prove that Elwell's death was due to his dealings in ardent spirits.

The dry agents really did start off with the hope that they could co-operate with the DA and his men; but when, after a few days, the hope remained unrealized, they set up a 'closed shop' of their own. Preparing the ground for an announcement of the separateness, Shevlin told reporters that the Studio Club had been one of many illicit oases in the city, then complained that Swann was being 'obstructive', and then, without pausing for breath, spoke of 'the ready availability of liquor in exclusive gentlemen's clubs' — a juxtaposition that seemed to indicate that he believed that Swann's club, the Manhattan, was an illicit oasis, and that the DA liked a drink as much as the next member.

The opportunity to make the announcement came on Friday, 2 July. Two of Shevlin's 'Elwell agents', William Lord and Daniel Mangin, arrived at the DA's office at 10 a.m., having been told to do so by Talley, who had intimated that Dooling 'possessed important information in connection with the alleged Elwell bootlegging plot', and waited, without seeing hide or hair of either of the assistant district attorneys, till 3 p.m. — whereupon Lord exclaimed for the benefit of reporters: 'I'm not going to waste any more time with the District Attorney's office. We have conferred with them several times without obtaining any important results, and I'm tired of coming up here to be filled up with hot air. I'm weary of being kidded by Talley and Dooling, who are unduly delaying investigation of the "whiskey ring" feature of the murder mystery.' Lord and Mangin had hardly got back to the Custom House before a spokesman for Shevlin announced 'pursuance of the investigation along our own lines, independent of the District Attorney's office'.

That independent investigation proved unfruitful; Dooling's 'important information in connection with the alleged Elwell bootlegging plot' must have turned out to be unimportant, for it was never referred to again; if Carey or Walsh came upon bootleg-relevant information, no one else got to know of it.

The *Times*, 24 June: 'While District Attorney Swann and his assistants have been examining witnesses at the Criminal Court Building, Police Captains Carey and Thomas F. Walsh have been conducting separate inquiries into the activities of certain persons whose names have been mentioned in the case. . . . The detectives are confident they will solve the mystery. . . . They have been remarkably successful in concealing their movements in the investigation. . . . All day long detectives trooped in and out of Captain Carey's Homicide Bureau with every outward appearance of having completed or being about to start on an important mission. Captain Carey was busy most of the day answering telephone calls from detectives assigned to the case in different parts of the city.'

The *Times*, 26 June: 'The mass of detail in connection with the case has been so great, it became apparent yesterday, that one set of investigators has been in possession of information which others have been seeking for days.'

On 27 June, a Sunday, a detective unaffiliated with either Carey or Walsh revealed that 'new experiments have just been completed at Police Headquarters. A number of shots were fired from a Colt .45 automatic pistol at graduated distances into white paper. The cartridges were loaded with smokeless powder, with which the bullet which killed Elwell was fired. The experiments prove that suicide is not a scientific possibility.' Soon afterwards, someone in the DA's office told reporters that it didn't matter that the reincarnated suicide theory had been shot down — because 'we believe we are on the track of the murderer'.

Edward Swann, speaking on 28 June: 'After eighteen days, neither my office nor the police have anybody we can point at with suspicion. We have got a thousand and one collateral details, but on the main issue the evidence is entirely devoid of any fact that would justify us in accusing any man or woman. If it was a murder, the murderer has kept his own counsel.' Asked to explain 'If it was a murder', he said: 'Well, it might be suicide. But for the absence of the gun, I would say so.' Asked why Elwell might have committed suicide, he said: 'Well, I don't know. He was broke, wasn't he?' Asked what evidence there was that Elwell was broke, he said: 'We can't find sufficient evidence for someone else to have killed him,' and hastily withdrew.

From 29 June till 9 July, a Friday, Swann ran the gamut of emotions between dreadful pessimism and euphoric optimism. On the following day, the *Times* published an editorial, its tone more sorrowful than angry:

A SEARCHER
IN NEED OF A GUIDE

There is ungraciousness always, and usually something worse, in finding fault with a man who, confronted with a hard job, has tackled it energetically and is doing it the best he can. When, however, the best is rather obviously open to improvement and mistakes have been made for which excuses are much needed, then criticism, if it be in moderation and considerate, is not unpardonable, even though the man at whom it is directed has presumably the most commendable of intentions.

Therefore, admitting that the Elwell mystery is more than dark and that a District Attorney is not under obligation to be a detective of genius, one still is justified in complaining of the seeming recklessness with which Mr Swann turns the fire of public suspicion first here, then there, and of the frequency with which he gives out 'official information' one day, only to declare it, a day or two later, entirely worthless.

Newspapers have against Mr Swann the grievance that rarely has anybody, oftener than he in this case, given to the people who say, 'You can't believe anything you see in the papers!' an opportunity to repeat their favourite criticism. In this ill service he has surpassed even the prophets of the Weather Bureau. And to no end as yet apparent he has brought painful embarrassment on a number of people whose indiscretions and follies, whatever else they may have been, did not rise to the commission of murder.

And the Elwell mystery grows darker day by day!

Swann was away for the weekend, 'unavailable for comment'. When he returned, he refused even to admit that he had read what the *Times* had said about him.

John Joyce (sounding as if he honestly meant it): 'I'll do no more talking about the murder of Elwell.'

John Dooling (sounding as if he hoped to God that no one would answer truthfully): 'Do we look discouraged?'

On Tuesday the thirteenth, Isidore Polozker, an Assistant United States District Attorney of Detroit, Michigan, received a telephone call from a man with a foreign accent who declined to disclose his identity. During the call, which lasted a quarter of an hour, the man said that the investigators of the Elwell murder 'ought to leave other people alone: they had nothing to do with the crime', and went on to claim entire credit, saying that he, once a soldier, had sought the hand of a Bohemian countess in the capitals of Europe; his love unrequited, he had abandoned his native land for America; so had the countess; he had shot Elwell for having removed the last vestige of his hope of marrying into the aristocracy — and would surrender 'when he got round to it'.

Mr Polozker told the press about the telephone call, and reporters told Swann about it. Trying to stay calm, he exclaimed: 'It is either a hoax, in my opinion, or is the vapourings of a disordered mind! At no time have I received any information that Elwell was on intimate terms with any countess.'

A reporter pointed out that, way back, there had been a lot of investigating of a Polish countess called Sonia de Szinswaska; another recalled that the first meeting between the Countess de Szinswaska and Elwell was at Carlsbad, which was in Bohemia — so maybe Mr Swann would like to comment on the suggestion that Sonia wasn't a Polish countess but a Bohemian one: *the* Bohemian one: the motive for The Slaying of Joseph Bowne Elwell.

Swann's eyes watered behind his pince-nez. 'A comment . . .?' he muttered — and then repeated those words, his voice high-pitched this time. Making an incoherent sound suggestive of plaintiveness, he staggered out of sight.

The Elwell murder case, which started with a bang heard only by the culprit and the victim, ended with a whimper.

THE THREAD'S END

The mystery is not a police puzzle, but a
psychological puzzle. The ravelled ball must be
unravelled by finding the thread's end in Elwell's
own mysterious self.

Anon., 'The Man of Many Masks';
The New York *Times*, 20 June 1920

Joseph Bowne Elwell was slain by, or in obedience to the order of,
Walter Lewisohn.

That is my firm belief.

Let me explain what I think happened, and why I think it happened. I
shall leave some of the reasons for my belief till the end.

The saying, 'No one suddenly becomes a murderer', is less credible than
a saying that I have just made up: *No one suddenly becomes a madman.*

Two men: Walter Lewisohn and Joseph Bowne Elwell.

Almost without doubt, by the start of June 1920 Lewisohn was mentally
unstable. That instability may have been exacerbated by his love for the
beautiful dancer, Leonora Hughes. Or his passion for her — uninhibited,
perhaps because he, fabulously rich since birth, had always been able to
afford to do without inhibitions; ruthless to the extent that he did not try
to hide his passion for Leonora from his wife — may have been but a
symptom of his instability. Whichever, he was desperate to own Leonora:
desperate that no other man should.

Without the slightest doubt, long before the start of June 1920 Elwell
was notorious as a philanderer. Even male friends and acquaintances who
stood up for him, suggesting that his notoriety was out of proportion to the
volume of his quests for women with virtues as easy as his own, let alone of
his actual conquests, were forced to allow that he was 'certainly no

Joseph'.[1] It was assumed by many that if Elwell's 'chicken-chasing' hadn't been generally successful, he would have given up the chase long ago. Lewisohn was one of the many. He knew of his sister-in-law Viola's attachment to Elwell (though he may not have known that the strength of her attachment was signified by the presence of a nightgown identifiable as hers in Elwell's house); and he knew of other women who either had accepted his friend's invitations to tête-à-têtes or looked forward to being asked. If Lewisohn ever prayed, he prayed that his Leonora had never been sullied by the lecher; that she never would be; that she would be his, and his alone, for ever.

In the last week of May 1920, a few days before Elwell's return to Manhattan, he wrote only the second letter to his wife since their separation in January 1916. He asked for a divorce.

He spent the weekend of 5 and 6 June with the Lewisohns and Viola at the Lewisohns' house in New Jersey. None of his three companions subsequently stated that he had mentioned that he was seeking a divorce; none was asked if he had. If, as is likely, he did speak of his intention, the fact that Viola would, by the end of the week, be free to remarry cannot have been thought irrelevant to his disclosure by Viola herself or by either of the Lewisohns. The near-concurrence of Elwell's disclosure and Viola's divorce may have led Walter Lewisohn to draw two false conclusions — one, that Elwell was not his rival for Leonora, giving him a feeling of wonderful relief; the other, that the sexually-indiscriminate Elwell planned to marry Viola, filling him with horror that his sister-in-law, whom he idolised, might jump from the frying-pan of her marriage to Victor von Schlegell into a dreadful fire. If Lewisohn, his confused mind further confused by the relieving and horrifying implications of what Elwell had said, decided that Viola had to be protected at all costs, then the inexplicable detachment of a wheel from Elwell's car when he was heading home from the Lewisohns' country place is not inexplicable at all.

Why was Leonora not a member of Lewisohn's party at the Ritz-Carlton? Why, considering that he was a stickler for social niceties, did he permit a 3/2 imbalance between the male members of the party and the female ones? The coincidence of Victor von Schlegell's proximity to Viola seems to have so intrigued the investigators that those questions, and others about the party, were never asked. And Leonora was omitted from *les femmes* brought into the case in response to the instruction *cherchez*. One cannot help thinking that some of the unasked questions did occur to

1. An expression, common at the time, that seems to have died. It stemmed from the story of Joseph and Potiphar's wife in chapter 39 of *Genesis*.

some of the investigators but were not asked for fear that the rich and powerful Mr Lewisohn would consider them impertinent; Dooling may not have been speaking of Lewisohn when, in regard to the Barnes-blackmailing-Elwell story, he said, 'The person reported to have been cheated is a well-known man who could not possibly be suspected in connection with the murder,' but the comment does suggest that men as well-known as Lewisohn were, metaphorically, more likely to get away with murder than were those perceived to be their inferiors.

In the five days between the weekend in the country and the party at the Ritz-Carlton that, so everyone said, was *not* a celebration of Viola's divorce from Von Schlegell, she and Lewisohn may have discussed whether or not she should marry Elwell. If so, he would have been perplexed as to what advice he should give: her marriage to Elwell would mean that Elwell could not use the lure of a promise of marriage so as to enveigle Leonora into a sexual relationship — but the thought of 'Mrs Viola Elwell', of Elwell's being kin to the Lewisohn Family, caused a sickening swaying of the mind.

Viola may have decided against marrying Elwell — but that certainly doesn't mean that she would not have wanted him to propose marriage. So far as her self-esteem was concerned, the ideal time for that proposal was on the day when her divorce became absolute: in the evening of that day, at the Ritz-Carlton. Subsequently, it was suggested that her muted peevishness with Elwell, starting at the Ritz and continuing or resuming in the Aerial Gardens, was caused by post-marital tension — that that ailment, afflicting her throughout the day, had been worsened by her sighting of her ex-husband with The Woman in Black. I don't believe that.

It would be interesting to know what she wrote on Elwell's shirt-cuff while they were sitting side by side at the Ritz. Next day, the scribbling on the cuff was noted by detectives. But none could make out the words. If Viola was asked to expound them, and did, her answer was never imparted to the press.

I think she was made peevish by Elwell — by his telling her that *her* divorce was immaterial to his decision to seek divorce from Helen. That would have constituted a nasty let-down at any time; but it would have been especially depressing, deflating, on the very day of her divorce — and if, looking forward to a proposal, she had given kindly thought to the question of how she could let Elwell down lightly. Being a man, I cannot help saying that Viola, just like a woman, would have forgotten her own intended rebuff, considered that *she* had been rebuffed, and yearned for the chance of accepting a marriage-proposal from Elwell.

Was she still hoping to make him change his mind at 2.30 a.m. on

Leonora Hughes

Friday, when she telephoned him?

By then, Selma Lewisohn knew the cause of her sister's disconsolation. And Walter Lewisohn thought he knew the cause. If Viola had explained to Selma, and Selma to Walter, the explanation he heard may have varied from the original. Whatever he heard, it had increased his awful foreboding: he thought he had heard what he had most dreaded hearing: now he *knew* Elwell's intention.

There was no doubt in Lewisohn's crazed mind.

No doubt that Elwell planned to entice Leonora away from him.

No doubt that a murder had to be arranged.

Arranged? Yes; though Lewisohn was one of the few people whom Elwell would have let into his house at a strange time and without first donning his toupee and inserting his dentures, it is probable that Lewisohn arranged for the slaying to be consummated on his behalf. He knew who to get in touch with. And he knew a man who, if there *were* keys to the house other than those held by Elwell and Mrs Larsen, was the most likely person to possess them — a man who, if he did have the keys, could be persuaded to let them be misused.

He, Walter Lewisohn, could sleep soundly, untroubled by nightmares and perhaps occasionally soothed by dreams of Leonora, while, in a house on the far side of Central Park, a deadly rival was being made innocuous.

The most likely person to have had a spare set of keys to the front doors of 244 West Seventieth Street was the owner of that house. His name, you will recall, was Bernard Sandler. He was a lawyer: not of the top flight. His office was at 150 Broadway, close to the southern tip of Manhattan; he lived, with his wife Bertha, in an apartment at 1771 Madison Avenue, half a dozen blocks north-east of Central Park, in the district called Harlem. He was acquainted with Walter Lewisohn. It was by virtue of Lewisohn's introduction of him to Elwell that the latter had become his tenant.

He must, following his tenant's sudden death, have made a statement to one or other of the investigators. And he must, in that statement, have said that he did not have keys to the new locks that had been fitted to the front doors of his house after it was broken into. Though there was no certainty as to how many sets of keys there were; no certainty as to who was responsible for having the new locks fitted; no certainty as to the identity of the locksmith — Sandler's statement must have been accepted as gospel-truth. So far as I have seen, Sandler's name was absent from the total of hundreds of columns of newsprint devoted to What the Investigators Said: more surprising, none of the press theorists about the locks and keys brought Sandler's name into their discussions.

Some time after the summer of 1920, Bernard Sandler, the run-of-the-mill lawyer, was retained by the Lewisohns as a legal representative in addition to the prestigious Lyttleton Fox. He was still so retained in May 1924, when he told a *Times* reporter that he was thinking of asking for a re-investigation of the Elwell case. He hoped, he said, 'that Miss Viola Kraus could be cleared absolutely'.

Viola was then living in Paris. If she heard of Sandler's expressed hope, she must have been rather upset with him for having seemed to contradict Edward Swann's statement in July 1920 that, 'after questioning and re-questioning, it is clearly established that she knows nothing about the case'.

Having thought aloud of asking for a re-investigation, Sandler decided not to. His talk with the *Times* reporter is of interest only in that it proves that he was still retained by the Lewisohns in May 1924: he spoke of 'my client, Mrs Walter Lewisohn'. There is no indication of how much longer he was retained; nor of any legal task he performed on behalf of any member of the family that gives a clue to how he earned whatever regular honorarium he was paid.

When, in June 1920, Viola was asked to comment on the recollection wrested from Mrs Larsen that she, Viola (referred to by the press at that time as 'Miss Wilson'), had paid a fleeting visit to the house a few hours after the discovery of the shooting, she told such a pack of lies that one needs to be quite good at arithmetic to be able to count them. Not all of the lies can have escaped the notice of all of the investigators — yet none of the noticing investigators intimated in public that Viola's statement, rather than being nothing but the truth, bore only slight resemblances of it. One must suppose that the reticence is an example of investigators' squirrelling of facts that were at all likely to conjoin with facts squirrelled by competitors.

A sample of Viola's lies:

She said that she paid only one visit to the house — 'around one or two o'clock' in the afternoon — in the few hours following the start of the case. In fact, she visited the house twice: at some time during the morning, having phoned the house and been told by a detective that Elwell had 'had an accident', she rushed to the house, encountered Mrs Larsen on the stairs ('Oh, what accident, Mrs Larsen?'), and rushed out again; shortly before 1.30 p.m., as a consequence of Walter Lewisohn's telephone call to the house less than a quarter of an hour before, she returned in the company of Walter and Selma Lewisohn and their lawyer Lyttleton Fox. She pretended that *her* telephone call in the morning was the call made by *Lewisohn* shortly after 1 p.m.

She claimed that, alarmed by what the detective had told her over the telephone, she telephoned Selma, who 'was then at our mother's house', and that Selma 'said she would meet me at Elwell's house right away. . . . I reached the house in Seventieth Street around one or two o'clock. The result was that we first encountered the reporters and photographers and then the police.'

Expert liars will admire that quotation for the way in which it starts off with Viola and Selma in different places, arranging to meet at Elwell's house, and finishes up with the implication that they arrived at the house together. Actually, of course, they *travelled* to the house together — in a chauffeur-driven car that held two other passengers, Lyttleton Fox and Walter Lewisohn, the latter the instigator of the trip following *his* telephone conversation with a detective shortly after 1 p.m. To be fair to Viola, she may not have wished to imply that she and Selma, just the two of them, arrived at the house together — certainly not if she was thinking ahead to what she *had* to say next so as to turn two visits into one: 'The detectives asked me all sorts of questions. I was completely overwhelmed by the whole thing. Mrs Lewisohn came in just a few minutes later, and they questioned her in the same terrible and embarrassing way. If it hadn't been for my telephone call to the house, I shouldn't have gone there, and then we wouldn't have been subjected to this fearfully unpleasant notoriety.' Again, expert liars must gasp with admiration: in the space of four sentences, containing the vital throw-away lines, 'Mrs Lewisohn came in just a few minutes later' and 'If it hadn't been for my telephone call', Viola encompassed her morning visit within her accompanied afternoon one.

Unless it is believed that Viola, following her first visit to the house, said nothing of what she had learned there to the Lewisohns, then Walter Lewisohn was aware that Elwell was dead when he telephoned the house shortly after 1 p.m., ostensibly mystified by the fact that Elwell had not turned up for a one-o'clock appointment.

Unless it is believed that Lyttleton Fox just happened to be with Lewisohn shortly after 1 p.m., having called upon him to discuss matters involving civil law or simply for a social chat, then he — as well as Lewisohn, as well as Viola, and presumably as well as Selma — was already aware that Elwell was dead: he had been ordered to be on hand to provide legal advice and help to his clients in regard to their association with a murder victim.

Why did Viola *need* to pretend that she did not visit the house in the morning? What stopped her from admitting the visit, explaining that she did not linger because (as was probably true) Mrs Larsen's answer to her question gave her such a shock that she didn't know what to do — but knew that the one thing she did not want to do was to talk about Elwell to detectives investigating his murder? When she gave the lie-filled statement, she was already the subject of 'fearfully unpleasant notoriety': the truth would not have made the notoriety worse.

I can think of no more likely an explanation for her lies than that if she had told the truth, her sister's husband would have been asked why he had telephoned to enquire about the unpunctuality of a man whom he knew to be dead. That would have put Walter Lewisohn in a very awkward spot. His response — fluster or a lie more patent than any of Viola's — might have caused an investigator to conclude that, despite Mr Lewisohn's being such a well-known man, he should be intensively questioned rather than 'informally interviewed'. Intensive questioning might have brought several truths to light, one being that Walter Lewisohn was insane.

By 1922, his irrationality was apparent to many people who knew him, either socially or through dealings with him as a director of Lewisohn Brothers (Bankers) of 11 Broadway. A few of his business acquaintances wondered whether his abnormal behaviour was attributable to worries, apparently not shared by his brother Frederick, over the loss of part of the immense profit his firm had gained from collaboration with a stock-manipulator named Jesse Livermore in a scheme to inflate the price of stock in the Seneca Copper Company, of which both of the Lewisohn brothers were directors. On the advice of doctors and psychiatrists that he needed to relax in warm surroundings well away from Manhattan, he was sent to Palm Beach in the company of male nurses. Unable to relax, he escaped from the nurses and returned home; soon after the nurses had caught up with him, he and they set off for Sulphur Springs, Texas; again having returned home, he was taken by replacement nurses to a dude-ranch in Wyoming. By May 1923, he was back in Manhattan. He was more irrational than ever.

On Tuesday, 22 May, he was visited by two men, strangers to him, who said that Leonora Hughes was seriously ill in Greenwich, Connecticut, and wanted him by her side. He accompanied the men to the Blythewood Sanitarium for the Insane at Greenwich, and was confined there. He asked after Leonora, and was told that she, having recovered, had gone elsewhere.

The only loose fitting in his comfortable cell was a dummy telephone. During most of the wakeful hours of the rest of his life, he conducted a one-sided conversation into the telephone with an imagined Leonora. The

Walter Lewisohn

Leonora Hughes

noises in his head were altogether pleasing ones. He heard what he wanted to hear: Leonora loved him. Most of the time when he was not talking to her, he used up reams of paper in writing what he thought were love-letters, sealed their envelopes with kisses, and entrusted them to white-coated attendants, who, once they were off duty, threw the letters into a garbage-bin.

In July there were two periods, neither longer than half an hour, when the mist in his mind was cleared just enough for him to glimpse reality. He scribbled requests to be released, and paid an attendant or persuaded a visitor to send them to the District Attorney of Westchester County, in which the sanitarium was situated. As the DA, a man named Arthur Rowland, was in the peculiar position of not being admitted to practise before the Connecticut courts, he passed the notes to a lawyer who was. According to Rowland, 'The first message was quite short and direct. The second message was longer and did not read like the previous one. . . . The name of a popular dancer was mentioned, and I concluded then that Mr Lewisohn was not of sound mind.' The deputed lawyer, Jeremiah Toomey, set in motion an application for a writ of habeas corpus, and on 18 September, after several delays, the matter was brought before a Common Pleas Court. The judge, Toomey, and counsel representing the sanitarium and the Lewisohn family visited Walter Lewisohn, and Toomey then announced that, at the judge's suggestion, he had withdrawn the application:

> The judge declared that the mental condition of Mr Lewisohn did not make it safe to release him from the institution. Counsel for the institution also served on me a letter signed by Lewisohn in which he stated that he did not want me to go on with the proceeding. . . . Lewisohn told me that he had been enamoured of Leonora Hughes, the dancer, and that his family had threatened to have him committed to an asylum.

In May 1924 — on the application of Frederick Lewisohn — a Commissioner in Lunacy, sitting with a sheriff's jury, considered testimony intended to prove that Walter Lewisohn was incurably insane. Dr Menas Gregory, a psychiatrist at Bellevue Hospital, Manhattan, stated his opinion that Lewisohn had chronic delusional insanity and that there was no hope that his mind would clear.

An accountant had estimated that Lewisohn owned property worth $1,262,957 and had liabilities of $178,660. Considering that the accountant had reckoned that the value of all of the treasures in all of Lewisohn's residences was a mere $10,000, that his stocks were worth only $68,000 (far less than the selling price of his seat in the New York Stock Exchange), and that his double-fronted house on East Sixty-Third Street would fetch no more than $80,000,[1] it is safe to say that he was not actually down to his last million.

The Commissioner in Lunacy concurred with the jury's decision, arrived at without much discussion, that Walter Lewisohn was insane and unlikely ever to be otherwise.

Lewisohn was never released from the Blythewood Sanitarium. No information can be had as to whether, as the years went by, he tired of the telephone toy; gave up writing what he thought were love-letters; forgot about Leonora, or at least, having fondled away her photograph, forgot what she had looked like; or ever mumbled what sounded like another name — that of a man who, long, long ago, may also have loved Leonora: who, owing to a suspicion of his love for her, had been slain.

---

1. In April 1927, the residence was sold for $160,000 to Judge Samuel Seabury (who, three years later, headed an investigation into New York City's maladministration, one of the conclusions of which was that the police department was riddled with corruption).

Lewisohn passed away peacefully in his sleep on Thursday, 11 August 1938, just over eighteen years after the unpeaceful passing of Joseph Bowne Elwell, his friend till a week or so before they were members of a party that began on the roof of the Ritz-Carlton and continued on the roof of the New Amsterdam Theatre, the venue of a *Midnight Frolic*.[1]

1. If my belief about Walter Lewisohn is correct, there are parallels between the murder of Elwell and that of John Mudie in London in 1946. Thomas Ley, a well-to-do madman who had emigrated to England from New South Wales, where he had once been Minister of Justice, was curiously jealous of his mistress, Mrs Maggie Brook, who was also from Australia. A concoction of false conclusions led Ley to the conviction that Mrs Brook was having an affair with John Mudie, a barman who had only spoken to her on one occasion, and then casually. Ley gathered together a band of hirelings, one of whom lured Mudie to a basement-flat in South Kensington, leaving him there with two other hirelings, John Smith and John Buckingham, and with Ley himself. Ley or Smith, or both, savagely attacked Mudie; then one of them strangled him; the body was carted to and dumped in a chalk pit in Surrey. Two days later, the body was found and identified; a fortnight after the discovery, John Buckingham went to Scotland Yard of his own accord, and there, having been assured that he would be allowed to turn King's Evidence, made a full statement. Ley and Smith were tried for the murder, convicted, and sentenced to death. Neither of the sentences was carried out. Following the trial, doctors who examined Ley decided that he was insane, and he was consigned to the Broadmoor Criminal Lunatic Asylum; since it was felt that 'it would be wrong to let the paymaster live and yet hang the foreman', Smith was reprieved. After only a month in Broadmoor, Ley suffered a seizure from which he died. See *Trial of Ley and Smith*, edited by F. Tennyson Jesse, Edinburgh, 1947, or *The Trial of Ley and Smith*, edited by C.E. Bechhofer Roberts, London, 1947; and *The Chalk Pit Murder* by Edgar Lustgarten, London, 1974.

SURVIVORS
AND LEGACIES

◆————————◆

Selma Lewisohn was blessed with a pleasing lyric-soprano singing voice. In the early years of her marriage to Walter, he encouraged her to refine and strengthen her voice, which she did, aided by famous teachers in America and Europe; and then she sang with paid singers, at first at a festival at Baden-Baden, playing Zerlina in a production of Mozart's *Don Giovanni* that must have been enhanced by the presence in the company of Giuseppe De Luca and John McCormack, and alone in concerts, including several in France as a soloist with Casadesus's Society for Ancient Instruments. Soon after Walter was confined in the Blythewood Sanitarium, she again sought singing engagements, using the stage-name of Maria Selma, and succeeded in obtaining some, most of which were in Europe. When Walter was certified insane, she moved from the mansion on East Sixty-Third Street to a suite at the Plaza. In 1927, having uncomplicatedly got a divorce from Walter, she married H. Bartow Farr, a lawyer of good family, and lived happily with him, latterly in the village of Bedford, in New York State, till her death, at the age of sixty-nine, in 1957; when Farr died in 1972, he was buried with Selma in the St Matthew's churchyard at Bedford.

Joseph Sanford Elwell suffered a stroke on the first day of October 1920, and died a week later. His funeral, at the Valleau cemetery in Ridgewood, was conducted by the local Methodist minister, the Reverend Archey Ball, who, just over four months before, had conducted the funeral of his elder son. The obituarist for the Ridgewood *Herald News* noted that 'the sensational death of Joseph Bowne Elwell . . . was a great shock to Mr Elwell', and stated that 'the ordeal which he was compelled to go through undoubtedly undermined his health'. His remaining son, Walter, moved, with his family, into the house on Liberty Street that Joseph Bowne Elwell had bought. Not long after becoming a widow, Jennie Elwell left Ridgewood and returned to Brooklyn, taking rooms in the mackerel-coloured St George Hotel,[1] close to the bridge. She died there on 17 February 1927.

Press reports of her death caught the eye of Helen Elwell — one report in particular, which mentioned that Jennie's entire estate would be shared equally among her three children and her lawyer Andrew MacCreary, and guessed the worth of the estate at $200,000. Helen entered that amount, perhaps with a question-mark next to it, on a bridge scoring card that she had been using since July 1920 in an attempt to keep count of what, to her way of thinking, Richard Derby was entitled to.

The card was already cluttered with notes of the following:

> *July 1920.* Algernon Dangerfield, an official of the Jockey Club, commented that several of the sixteen horses of the Beach Racing Stables had been winning lately: 'They have had much better luck since Mr Elwell's death than they had before it.' But still, in
> *September 1920* they were sold at auction for $37,160,[2] far less than their valuation before the luck of several of them improved.
>
> *October 1920.* A four-day sale of Elwell's household furnishings, jewellery and works of art was held in the auction rooms of Darling & Company, 242 Fifth Avenue. The sale seems to have attracted as many reporters and sightseers as it did buyers. According to the reporter for *The Thoroughbred Record,*
>
>> The most furious bidding of the sale took place when a painting, an authentic Rembrandt, representing in a great composition Jesus Christ carrying the crucifix, was offered. The first bid was $5,000. It was finally knocked down to a Fifth Avenue dealer for $22,000. This painting brought more money than any other article in the sale.
>> Most of the Chinese rugs and tapestries were bought by Capt. R.J. Foster, head of the Foster Detective Agency. In all Mr Foster bought more than $3,000 worth of articles.
>> F.A. Bridgman's life-size portrait of a semi-nude girl, which for several

---

1. The scene of a murder on Thursday, 30 December 1943. Paula Wolfe returned to the rooms she infrequently shared with her husband Lewis, and — not for the first time, it seems — boasted of scores of lovers; then, tempting providence, she screamed, 'You're not a man or you'd kill me for all this.' Exhausted by loquacity, she fell asleep — but was soon awoken, though only for a brief, painful while, by the hammering of her head with a shoe, wielded by her sorely-tried spouse. The shoe having proved to be a lethal weapon, Lewis gave himself up to the police, and was subsequently sentenced to life imprisonment.

2. The present-day purchasing power of the 1920 dollar is about five dollars. In 1920, there were 3.66 dollars to the British pound. The present-day purchasing power of the 1920 pound is about eleven pounds.

days had been a centre of interest for spectators and buyers, was sold for
$105. The buyer bought under initials and refused to reveal his name.
The slain turfman's jewellery, which consisted of about seventeen pieces,
was sold for nearly $3,000. The set which brought the most was composed
of a pair of cuff-links and two studs to match, containing genuine sapphires
and diamonds, which was auctioned for $420.

At the [last evening] session several friends of the late sportsman were in
attendance and bought up several of the pieces of rare porcelains, jades,
crystals, wood carvings and curios of the Yang Shi and Oshima collection.

Most of the articles offered were of great value, but considering this, the
buyers were slow in bidding even a small amount of money for the
goods. . . . Louis Van Brink, the auctioneer, announced that approximately
$100,000 had been realised through the sale.

(Helen, who had obtained a catalogue of the items, was mightily
suspicious, chiefly on two counts: first, she felt sure that Elwell had
owned far more than *seventeen* pieces of jewellery; second, during her
visit to the house, six days after the murder, her inventorial gaze had
alighted upon a collection of eighteenth-century French porcelain that
she herself had put together — yet that collection was not among the
lots at the sale.)

October 1921. Elwell's estate was appraised at $287,404 gross,
$243,955 net — of which $95,586 was in securities and $68,632 in
personalty.

(Helen found it hard to understand how the figure for securities had
been arrived at, considering that one block of shares alone — ten shares
of the Beach-Long Realty Company, which Elwell had set up as a cover
for his property dealings in Palm Beach — was valued at $79,265. That
meant, apparently, that the rest of his holdings were reckoned to be
worth only $16,321.)

December 1921. Sticking to his word that Richard Derby would be
'provided for', Walter Elwell, with his sisters' consent, gave Helen's
lawyer a cheque (the amount of which is not known), on the
understanding that the money, less the lawyer's fees, was to be used
solely for the benefit of Richard Derby.

As soon as Jennie Elwell died, Helen instructed her lawyer to fight, on
behalf of Richard Derby, for a share of the estate. Without much ado, but
with the usual law's delays, an agreement was reached out of court that a
trust-fund, its starting capital $100,000, was to be set up for Richard
Derby; the fund was to be administered by Jennie's lawyer, Andrew
MacCreary, who had recently been appointed a New York City magistrate.

Richard Derby Elwell recalls that MacCreary 'stole the $100,000,
admitted it, and promised restitution in small amounts if I did not
prosecute. He died one month after the first small payment.'

(MacCreary died suddenly. There were strong and seemingly well-supported rumours that he had been beaten so severely for welshing on a final instalment of an agreed price for his appointment to the bench that he had suffered a heart attack. The District Attorney of New York County, C.T. Crain, sought to have the body exhumed, but gave up because of objections by the MacCreary family.)

Helen never remarried. In the years of her widowhood, she seems to have devoted almost as much time to arranging moves from one apartment to another, and decorating them, as to her job as a teacher of bridge. (Several authors have stated that a series of textbooks on auction bridge by Florence Irwin, the last published in 1927, were in fact written by Helen. That is not true.) She died in a private hospital in Manhattan in 1937, at the age of sixty-one.

Leaving Phillips Academy, Andover, in 1922, when he was eighteen, Richard Derby entered the Sheffield Scientific School of Yale University to study for a degree in engineering. He was brilliant at mathematics, and showed signs of having inherited some of his father's cleverness at card-games. He was also a fine athlete: in his freshman year, he was made a member of the university's lawn-tennis and fencing teams, and in his senior year he captained the latter team, which won the intercollegiate championship.

His first job, from 1926 till 1928, was at the giant Macy's department store in Manhattan, where he studied the 'micro-motions' of sales assistants, with the aim of eradicating such of those motions that seemed inefficient, under the leadership of Dr Lillian Gilbreth (whose marriage to the also efficiency-obsessed Frank Gilbreth was itself a model of efficiency, particularly so far as their procreative motions were concerned: adapting the principles of the assembly line and of unit-costs to parentage, they produced twelve mini-Gilbreths — whose upbringing, or product-enhancement, was chronicled in the book *Cheaper by the Dozen*, which in 1950 was used as the basis of a funny film starring Clifton Webb and Myrna Loy as the husband-and-wife production partnership).

Richard Derby was invited to join the US fencing team at the 1928 Olympics in Amsterdam; but as the Olympics were then for amateur sportsmen, he could not afford to accept.

Between 1928 and 1943, he worked as an efficiency-improver, chiefly in the retail trade, either as a full-time employee or as a free-lance. He spent the last two years of the Second World War in the navy, and was honourably discharged as a lieutenant-commander. Then, till 1953, he was a management consultant with McKinsey & Company, engaged on assignments both in America and abroad; in the following years, till his

The Widow Elwell

retirement in 1975, when he was seventy-one, he was an independent consultant, much sought after by companies experiencing problems with the distribution of their goods.

In June 1929, in Montreal, he married a Canadian, Ethel Joseph. There were two sons of the marriage: Richard Derby Elwell, Junior, born in April 1932 (who qualified as a lawyer, and now, married, lives in England), and David Henry Elwell, born in March 1935 (who, like his father, attended the Buckley School, Phillips Academy at Andover, and Yale, but who continued his education, at the universities of Cambridge, in England, and Princeton; he, now married and living in New York City, teaches architecture). Following Richard Derby's divorce from Ethel, he married Ruth Hatch in New York City in August 1949; almost exactly four years later, his second wife bore him a son, Daniel Bowne Elwell (who qualified as a Master of Business Administration, and now, married, lives in Boston).

Though, to Richard Derby, the game of bridge was never more than a game, he often played in major tournaments; and, when retired, he wrote a book (as yet unpublished) in which he explained his ideas on how the 'laws' of probability and chance could be applied to bidding.

Prior to 1970, he played bridge once or twice with his father's favourite partner, Harold Vanderbilt — not auction bridge but *contract* bridge, a game of Vanderbilt's devising. Writing in 1957 of 'The Origin of Contract Bridge,'[1] Vanderbilt recalled:

> My experience as a player of games of the Whist family — first Bridge, then Auction Bridge, and finally Contract Bridge — dates from the turn of the century when my mother [sic] persuaded Joe Elwell to give us some Bridge lessons in Newport, Rhode Island. I played Bridge until Auction appeared in 1907. Elwell became a few years later my favourite Auction Bridge partner, and remained so until his still unsolved murder in June, 1920. . . .
>
> In the early Twenties . . . I began to think about devising a new game of the Whist family. I had seen Whist go, Bridge come and go, Auction come. Was it time for Auction to go? I thought so and christened my game Contract Bridge after its principal divergence from Auction Bridge: having to contract for a game in order to make one. . . .
>
> The first chance I had to test my new game was on a ten-day cruise on board the steamship *Finland* en route from California to Havana via the Panama Canal in November 1925. I was travelling in company with three friends who agreed to try the game. So I produced my scoring table, which we changed slightly during the voyage, but by the time we reached Havana it was very similar to the one in use today. . . .
>
> We were at a loss to describe a side that is subject to higher penalties. A young lady we met on the boat — none of us can recall her name — who had

1. In *The Fireside Book of Cards*, New York.

played some strange game in California that called for higher penalties under certain conditions, gave us the word used in that game, and 'vulnerable' — what a perfect description — it has been ever since.[1]

After we got back to our respective homes in New York and Boston we made no particular effort to popularize our newborn game. It never occurred to me that it was destined to sweep the world, or that its eventual promoters were to make millions. I explained the scoring to a number of my friends. I may even have supplied them with typewritten scoring tables. Without exception, they all instantly gave up Auction. Like the flu, the new game spread by itself, despite the attempts of the old Auction addicts — too old to change — to devise a vaccine to stop it.

From *The Official Encyclopaedia of Bridge*:[2]

The rapid spread of contract bridge from 1926 to 1929 is largely attributable to Vanderbilt's espousal of it; his social standing made the game fashionable.... [His] principles were presented in his books. . . .

Vanderbilt was a member of the Laws Committee of the Whist Club of New York that made the American laws of contract bridge (1927, 1931) and the first international code (1932). . . .

In 1928 Vanderbilt presented the Harold S. Vanderbilt Cup for a national team-of-four championship. This became and remained for many years the most coveted American team trophy, not least because of the replicas donated personally by Vanderbilt to the winners. In 1960 Vanderbilt supplied the permanent trophy for the World Bridge Federation's Olympiad team tournaments, and again adopted the policy of giving replicas to the winners. . . .

As a player, Vanderbilt always ranked high. In 1932 and 1940 he won his own Vanderbilt Cup. . . .

Many honours and distinctions [were] awarded Vanderbilt: Commander of the Order of the British Empire for services as Director of British War Relief . . . and others. In 1969 [a year before his death], the World Bridge Federation made him its first honorary member. When a bridge Hall of Fame was inaugurated in 1964, Vanderbilt was one of the first three persons elected.

Joseph Bowne Elwell has no niche in the bridge Hall of Fame. That omission should surely be remedied, not only because he was the Grand

---

1. On Sunday, 29 September 1929, in Kansas City, a Mr and Mrs Bennett played a Mr and Mrs Hoffman at bridge, for 'fun stakes', at the home of the former couple. Incited by what he considered an instance of over-bidding by his partner, Bennett called her 'a bum bridge-player' and slapped her at least once — whereupon she went to their bedroom to fetch a bedside revolver and, returning, fired four shots from it, two of which struck her husband, one terminally so. Alexander Woollcott concludes his article on the case, 'By the Rude Bridge' (which appears in a few anthologies, one being *The Pleasures of Murder*, edited by Jonathan Goodman, London, 1983), by saying that his friend Harpo Marx persuaded him to write it: 'He even professed to have thought of a title for it. I enquired what this might be and he answered: "Vulnerable".'

2. Edited by Frey et al, 3rd ed., London, 1977.

Panjandrum of both bridge-whist and auction bridge, but also because, by introducing Harold Vanderbilt to the first of those games and helping him to excel at both of them, he played an indirect but not inconsiderable part in the creation of contract bridge, the game that remains the most popular variation on whist.

The faded headstone in the cemetery at Ridgewood is his only memorial. The 'house of cards' no longer stands on West Seventieth Street. Soon after the murder, it was sold by Bernard Sandler to an apartment-contriver who doesn't seem to have been choosy of customers: in September 1927, a crowd of Puerto Ricans, tenants of part of the basement, did a moonlight flit after stealing property from an upstairs room rented by two young men. Three weeks later, the *Times* reported that 'Mrs Elizabeth O'Brien, 23 years old, committed suicide . . . in the grey stone dwelling . . . by inhaling gas after she had made a voluntary agreement to separate from her husband. Her reason for taking her own life was not quite clear, the police said.' In the late-1950s, the house was made to tumble down, as were many of the buildings on each side, to give space for Public School 199, named after Jesse Isidor Straus, a philanthropic member of the family that in 1896 had acquired Macy's department store from heirs of the store's founder, Rowland Hussey Macy.

The House of Cards,[1] a novel by Hannah Gartland, appeared, unobtrusively, in New York in 1922. Its opening scene was condensed as follows by a taste-whetter for the *Book Review Digest*: 'Patrolman Dooley found Gregory Barwood, wealthy clubman and one of the most skilful card players in New York, sitting in one of the carved chairs in his luxurious reception room, with a bullet hole in his forehead.'

I have written elsewhere[2] that Willard Huntington Wright was:

> an American aesthete and critic who, after writing a series of articles that picked holes in the eleventh edition of the *Encyclopaedia Britannica*, and soon afterwards publishing them as a book entitled *Misinforming a Nation*, which caused quite a stir, suffered a nervous breakdown. That was in 1923, when he was thirty-five. He remained poorly for two years, during which his doctor forbade him to read anything more stimulating than detective novels. Having got through a couple of thousand of them, he thought to himself: 'Why, if

---

1. Not to be confused with the novel of the same title (New York, 1967) by Stanley Ellin. For a reason that will soon be apparent, it is worth noting that his first short story, 'The Specialty of the House', was published, in 1948, in *Ellery Queen's Mystery Magazine*.

2. In *Who He? Goodman's Dictionary of the Unknown Famous*, London, 1984.

A recent photograph, taken from Sherman Square, of the 200-282 block of
West Seventieth Street

other writers, with far less experience and training than I have had, can achieve
success at this kind of fiction, can't I? I have studied the detective novel, and I
understand its rules and techniques. I know its needs, and have learned its
pitfalls.' So he wrote thirty-thousand-word synopses of three books and showed
them to Maxwell Perkins, the famous editor for Charles Scribner's Sons
[Elwell's publisher]. . . . Perkins's response was immediate. He told Wright:
'The books are just what we want — and I believe you can do them. We'll take
all three.'

The first edition of the first of the books, *The Benson Murder Case*, published
under the pseudonym of S.S. Van Dine in October 1926, sold out within a
week. The story was based on a real case, the murder of Joseph Bowne
Elwell. . . .

The second book, *The Canary Murder Case*, published the following year,
sold in greater numbers than any earlier book of its genre. Like the first,
though less obviously, it was based on fact: the murder of the good-time girl
Anna Marie Keenan, better known as Dot King, whose body was found in her
apartment on West Fifty-Seventh Street, Manhattan, on the morning of 15
March 1923.

The first two books are still readable; the seven and a half that followed (all
with titles ending 'Murder Case') are not. I should explain that the half-a-book
is *The Winter Murder Case*, a thirty-thousand-word synopsis that was published
after Wright's death in 1939.

The star of all of the books is a master-detective named Philo Vance: partly a representation of the author, partly a representation of the sort of person Wright would like to have been or actually believed himself to be. Vance — who, in the opinion of Ogden Nash, deserved 'a kick in the pance' — lived in an art-filled apartment with his Boswell, S.S. Van Dine, smoked Regie cigarettes, [and] rarely pronounced the g of words ending *ing*. . . .

Between 1929 and 1947, thirty-odd Philo Vance films were released; the least unwatchable of them are the four that starred William Powell — *Canary* and *Greene* (1929), *Benson*[1] (1930), and *Kennel* (1933). Among other spin-offs from the books, there was a Canary ice-cream sundae and a Philo Vance cocktail.

From 'Death of a Don Juan' by Ellery Queen, published in *The American Weekly*, 14 September 1952:

The question is often asked, 'What is the origin of Ellery Queen?' The answers are many, and all are true, but perhaps the truest of the lot is that 'Ellery' was conceived in the union of a playboy's murder and an aesthete's sickbed.

It all goes back to the way Joseph Bowne Elwell died and what Willard Huntington Wright did about it. . . .

Wright determined single-handedly to lift the American detective story out of the literary slums, give it a bath and a suit of modish clothes — and an education! — and send it forth into the respectable world.

So in 1926 there appeared . . . *The Benson Murder Case*.

The Benson Murder Case was the Elwell case, cut by Wright-Van Dine's imagination to the measure of fiction.

Now it happened that two young New York advertising men [Frederick Dannay and Manfred Bennington Lee] — who were later to join forces under the pen-name of Ellery Queen — heard the rising din, read *The Benson Murder Case*. In the manner of immortal Sherlock in *A Study in Scarlet* we saw the handwriting on the wall and found it a revelation. We had been under-the-blanket addicts of crime fiction since boyhood. We had once gone so far as partially to plot one (in which the detective's monicker — hold your hat — was to have been 'Wilbur See'). But a decent respect for the opinions of mankind had (happily in that case) quenched our fire.

The Van Dine novel kindled it again.

With the publication of *The Benson Murder Case*, the back-alley American detective story crossed the tracks to sign a long-term lease in the most reputable part of town.

Accordingly, in 1928, we wrote *The Roman Hat Mystery* and Ellery Queen was born.

---

1. The film was not the first visual fictionalization of the Elwell case. A play, *The Elton Case* by William Devereux, opened at the Playhouse, Manhattan, on 10 September 1921, and closed within a fortnight.

So the Elwell case, from which *The Benson Murder Case* sprang, has always occupied the warmest corner of our hearts.

I believe that Joseph Bowne Elwell left another bequest to literature. According to Matthew J. Bruccoli, one of the many biographers of F. Scott Fitzgerald,[1]

> Long Island provided material for Fitzgerald's third novel [*The Great Gatsby*, New York, 1925] as impressions from that 'riotous island' went into the writer's process of cerebration. Jay Gatsby was partly inspired by a local figure, Max Gerlach. Near the end of her life Zelda Fitzgerald said that Gatsby was based on 'a neighbour named Von Guerlach or something who was said to be General Pershing's nephew and was in trouble over bootlegging'. This identification is supported by a newspaper photo of the Fitzgeralds in their scrapbook, with a note dated 7/20/23: 'En route from the coast — Here for a few days on business — How are you and the family old Sport? Gerlach.' Here is Gatsby's characterizing expression, *old sport*, from the hand of Gerlach. Attempts to fill in the history of Max Gerlach have failed; the only clue is a 1930 newspaper reference to him as a 'wealthy yachtsman'. ('Yachtsman' was sometimes a euphemism for rum-runner.)

Though Gerlach's use of the ubiquitously-used expression *old sport* can hardly be said to provide 'support' to the notion that he unwittingly helped Fitzgerald to make Gatsby, and though the notion itself came (as 'Von Guerlach or something') from a woman who 'near the end of her life' was not the most reliable of recollectors (and though one wonders why Professor Bruccoli has not, it seems, bothered with the surely simple researching task of finding out whether or not General John J. Pershing had a nephew, or any other relative, named Gerlach, Von Guerlach, or something similar), I don't disagree with Professor Bruccoli.

But I would add my belief that bits and pieces of Gatsby were derived, not from Joseph Bowne Elwell himself, but from the impression of him as a fascinatingly shady egotist that was created by reporters of the Elwell case. For well over a month, startling revelations about the slain bridge-player's extra-professional activities — as, for instance, turfman, spy-catcher, bootlegger, indiscriminate masher — appeared on the front page of newspapers. The murder was committed eleven weeks after the publication by Charles Scribner's Sons of Fitzgerald's first novel, the extraordinarily successful *This Side of Paradise*; ten weeks after his marriage to Zelda Sayre at St. Patrick's Cathedral, Manhattan. In reading the papers, just about all of the papers, for items about himself and Zelda,

1. *Some Sort of Epic Grandeur*, London, 1981.

he must, many times, have been side-tracked into reading about the fabulous Elwell. At the end of *Through the Looking-Glass*, Alice says of the Red King of chess, one of the few table-games that Elwell never sought to master: 'He was part of my dream, of course.' To me, it seems probable that when Fitzgerald looked back on the heady spring and summer of 1920, Elwell was part of *his* dream.

Edward Swann retired from public life in 1921. John Joyce remained an assistant district attorney, never as noticeably as when he was an investigator of the Elwell case, till the start of 1934, when he reached an age at which he was entitled to a pension. In 1921, John Dooling left the District Attorney's office and went into private practice, working from premises close to the Century Club (a building designed by Stanford White) on West Forty-Third Street; every so often, over the next ten years, he managed to get some free advertising by chatting with reporters about the Elwell case — even by telling one of them that he had 'heard no new facts concerning the case'.

Arthur Carey was retired from the New York Police Department in December 1928; a deputy inspector by then, he had been a policeman for thirty-nine years and nine months. He was still convinced, from 'patterns in his mind', that 'the slayer of Elwell . . . was an invader, most likely a type of thief known as an unoccupied house-worker or possibly a letter thief'. Thomas Walsh, unpromoted from the rank of captain, took his pension in 1929.

In 1932, a department of forensic medicine, the first in America, was established at the New York University Medical School, and Charles Norris was appointed its professor and chairman; he continued to be Chief Medical Examiner of the City of New York. Two years later, the New York Academy of Medicine awarded him a gold medal for distinguished service in medicine, explaining that 'he has carried on in spite of political handicaps and has been a great factor in cleaning up the very undesirable conditions which in former times existed in the coroner's office'. He carried on until the day before his death in September 1935.

Between the winters of 1920 and 1924, Leonora Hughes, as the more decorative half of the dancing act, Maurice & Leonora, travelled far and wide: in America; in Europe. She was the toast of many towns. Apart from breaks on behalf of her tired feet, she appears to have had only one brief, unchoreographed spell away from Maurice, that being early in 1924, when she played the insignificant role of Lucille Van Tuyl in *The Rejected Woman*, an eight-reel film made by Distinctive Pictures, and starring Alma

Rubens, Bela Lugosi, Conrad Nagel and Aubrey Smith.[1]

Some time in 1924, Leonora was introduced to Carlos Ortiz Basualdo, an Argentino who was in his mid-twenties, a year or so younger than her. It would be interesting to know whether or not the introduction was effected by Octavio Figueroa, who was by then spending almost as much time in Manhattan as in his native city of Buenos Aires; but there is no information either way. Senor Ortiz Basualdo was wealthy: a 'Cattle Croesus', according to one headline-writer; a reporter's estimate that he had 'an income of $8,000 a week' seems as credible as another's that he owned 'half of Argentina'. He courted Leonora (who, according to yet another reporter, had, over the past few years, 'rejected the proposals of half a dozen noblemen'), and they were married in St Patrick's Cathedral, Manhattan, in February 1925. Leonora must have told Maurice Mouvet of her matrimonial intention, if only to give him time to find and rehearse with a new dancing-partner, but perhaps she was not explicit as to the date and venue of the unification. In any event, he arrived at the cathedral long before the ceremony, and, weeping, told reporters that he was an uninvited guest — that he had only just heard that he was to be 'irrevocably parted from Leonora'. His subsequent behaviour, and Leonora's response to it, may be seen as an explanation for his omission from the guest-list:

> He took a seat in a pew, well down in front, and was still sobbing as the ceremonies began. His sobs became louder and louder, until they actually punctuated the words of the ritual.
>
> Carlos dutifully, and hungrily, kissed his bride, and they started down the aisle.
>
> As they passed the sobbing Maurice, Leonora squeezed her new husband's arm, and then darted away and sat down beside Maurice. She whispered comforting words in his ear, and kissed him.

1. *Motion Picture News* of 26 April 1924 outlined the film as 'Society romance dealing with the adventures of a Canadian northwest beauty who is sent to New York where she enters into a compromising proposition with the enemy of the hero. . . . The picture offers a goodly quota of stirring episodes. The radio is introduced in the early reels when the news of the death of the hero's father is sent into the ether from a Gotham broadcasting station and received in the northland by a friend who communicates it to the son. A novel idea and thoroughly modern.' Suggested 'exploitation angles' included 'Tie up with the radio stores' and 'If you have an airplane field near your town engage one of the aviators to drop heralds'. The reviewer considered that Alma Rubens made 'an attractive heroine' and Conrad Nagel 'an acceptable hero', and ended by saying that 'the remainder of the cast is adequate'.

But even this gesture didn't dry Maurice's tears. The bridegroom patted him on the shoulder, and whispered friendly words, but still he sobbed. Carlos slowly moved down the aisle, and Leonora followed — arm in arm with Maurice. Outside, the three of them posed together for cameramen.

And then, of all things, some way or other, Maurice got into a car and drove away with Leonora, and her new husband had to follow in a taxi-cab.

After a few days the newlyweds sailed for South America, advancing their departure to escape the gossip and talk about the sensational episode at their wedding.[1]

Leonora bore Carlos Ortiz Basualdo two children: a son, named after his father, in 1926, and, five years later, a daughter, called Maria Mathilde.

In 1931, soon after Leonora's second confinement, the Ortiz Basualdos entertained the Prince of Wales and his brother, the Duke of Kent, who were touring South America, at one of their several homes — a mansion on the shore of Lake Nahuel Huapi, in the Southern Andes.

In December 1935, Carlos Ortiz Basualdo was drowned when his speedboat capsized on Lake Nahuel Huapi. One or two reports of the tragedy mentioned that his mechanic also perished.

Contrary to American gossip-columnists' unanimous undoubtednesses that Leonora would soon remarry, would soon return to her homeland — only the sequence of those events being uncertain — she remained both a widow and a resident of Argentina, spending each summer at Lake Nahuel Huapi, till February 1978, when, a grandmother seven times over, she died peacefully at her house in Buenos Aires.

By 1923, Viola Kraus was permanently domiciled in France; usually in Paris. Her decision to leave America, and the infrequency and brevity of

---

1. Salient parts of this account, which appeared in the New York *Sunday Mirror* of 19 January 1936, are corroborated by newspaper photographs of scenes inside and outside the cathedral.

Maurice's first post-Leonora partner was Barbara Bennett, a daughter of the matinee-idol Richard Bennett, whose other daughters, Joan and Constance, achieved stardom in films. The last of Maurice's subsequent partners, Eleanor Ambrose from Kansas City, also became his wife — and, soon afterwards, in 1927, he having died from consumption in a Swiss clinic, his widow.

her return-visits, may have been due to her desire to escape from or evade the impolite stares of people who recognized her, not as Viola Kraus, nor even as Viola von Schlegell, but as The Kimono Girl or Miss Wilson; the same desire may explain her insistence that her surname was *Cross*. But the desire is hard to reconcile with the work she did, at first as a mannequin, for fashion houses in Paris, including those of Lanvin and Chanel.

She remained in France while that country was occupied by the Nazis during the Second World War. Prior to the entry of America into the war, she did good deeds as a member of the American Friends Service Committee and of other organizations concerned with the fostering of orphans.

Her second marriage, to a Frenchman, ended, like the first, in divorce; she subsequently married an expatriate American, who is now dead. Both marriages were childless.

The last I heard of her, when she was well into her nineties, was that she was kept in an institution for the senile. She had few memories of happenings in her life, of people she had known, and all of those memories were frail and none came at her bidding. So far as anyone could tell, she had quite forgotten a once-special friend who was slain when she was young.

Acknowledgements

For diverse reasons, I am prevented from publicly expressing my gratitude
to certain persons who have helped me. They know that I am grateful.

I wish to thank American friends: Jacques and Marguerite Barzun,
Albert and Helen Borowitz, the late Stanley Ellin and his widow Jeannie,
Richard Derby Elwell, Mary Groff, Mrs Robert F. Hussey, the late James
Keddie, Jr., Thomas M. McDade, Fred Pemberton, Patterson Smith. Also,
William H. Anderson of The Jockey Club; Linda Bailey of Kenton County
Public Library, Kentucky; Merrie Blocker, Director of Centro Lincoln;
Frank C. Campbell, Chief of the Music Division, The New York Public
Library; Kenneth R. Cobb, Assistant Director, Municipal Archives, City of
New York; Kenneth Conboy, Deputy Commissioner, City of New York
Police Department; Eleanor Dana of The Ziegfeld Club, Inc.; Mary de
Bourbon, Director of Public Information, District Attorney of the County
of New York; Ellen Dickerson of Louisville Free Public Library, Kentucky;
Rosalyn Ebenholtz of the National Weather Service of the US Department
of Commerce; M. Finkelstein of the New Amsterdam Theatre, Manhat-
tan; Burton B. Fredericksen, Senior Curator for Research, The Getty Art
History Information Program; G.R. Frost, Town Manager, Palm Beach,
Florida; Olin Gentry; Dr Elliott M. Gross, Chief Medical Examiner, The
City of New York; Raymond G. Hardin, Archivist, Boston Symphony
Orchestra; Patricia Harpole of the Minnesota Historical Society; Professor
Julius S. Held; Alfred Hirsch and Richard Q. Hofacker, Jr., of AT&T Bell
Laboratories; Juliet R. Kellogg, Archivist, Phillips Academy, Andover;
Claire M. Lamers of The Long Island Historical Society; John R. McGhee,
Director, Greater Paterson General Hospital, New Jersey; Silvio J. Mollo,
First Assistant District Attorney, District Attorney of the County of New
York; W.R. Moran; Edward J. Murphy, Township Administrator, Cran-
ford, New Jersey; Carlos and Therese Ortiz Basualdo; Wesley H. Poling,
Director, Yale University; Jean F. Preston, Curator of Manuscripts,
Princeton University; Elizabeth Robb of the University of Minnesota;
Anne Schwartz, Senior Medical Correspondent, St. Joseph's Hospital, Far
Rockaway, NY; Edith Simon of the American Contract Bridge League;
Carolyn C. Smith of Ridgewood Library, New Jersey; Robert Tuggle,
Director of Archives, Metropolitan Opera Association; Marian Tonba of
The New-York Historical Society; Doris Vinton, National President, The
Ziegfeld Club, Inc.; William B. Walker, Chief Librarian, Thomas J.
Watson Library, The Metropolitan Museum of Art; Doris Jean Waren of
Keeneland Library, Lexington, Kentucky; Wendy Warnken of the
Museum of the City of New York; Gene F. Waters of The Association of

the Bar of the City of New York; Janet W. Wheeler of Cranford Public Library, New Jersey; Leonard Zeifman of the State of New York Unified Court System. The Academy of Motion Picture Arts and Sciences, G.P. Putnam's Sons, Smithsonian Institution Archives of American Art, US Department of Labor, US Department of the Treasury.

I wish to thank British friends: David Allen of the Bank of England, Dr. Donald Blair, Richard Boyd-Carpenter, Ivan Butler, Philip Chadwick, Peter Cotes, Henry Somake, Richard and Molly Whittington-Egan, Ian Will. Also, Guy Butchers of the International Racing Bureau; Elizabeth Cuthbert, Deputy Registrar, Royal Archives, Windsor Castle; Prince Abbas Helmi; Teresa Kane; Jimmy Lamb of the Norwich Union Insurance Group; E.C. Milnes of *Bridge Magazine*; Alf Richards of *The Sporting Life*; the Hon. Giles St. Aubyn; Desmond Shawe-Taylor; D.P. Stockwell, Director of Arthur H. Stockwell Ltd.; Linda Wood of the British Film Institute.

Lastly, I wish to thank my editor, Pamela Ruff.

Jonathan Goodman

The publishers are grateful to the following for permission to use illustrations in this book:
UPI Bettmann Newsphotos, New York (pages 41, 47 and 91).
Theatre Collection, Museum of the City of New York (pages 50, 194 and 199).

INDEX

(Throughout, the initials JBE stand for Joseph Bowne Elwell)